This book is to be returned on or before
the last date stamped below.

The L
POVE

The Long Debate on POVERTY

Eight essays on industrialisation and 'the condition of England'

R. M. HARTWELL
Professorial Fellow, Nuffield College, Oxford

G. E. MINGAY
Professor of Agrarian History, University of Kent

RHODES BOYSON
Headmaster, Highbury Grove School, London

NORMAN McCORD
Reader in Economic and Social History,
University of Newcastle upon Tyne

C. G. HANSON
Lecturer in Economics,
University of Newcastle upon Tyne

A. W. COATS
Professor of Economic and Social History,
University of Nottingham

W. H. CHALONER
Reader in Modern Economic History,
University of Manchester
and
W. O. HENDERSON
Reader in International Economic History,
University of Manchester

J. M. JEFFERSON

Published by
THE INSTITUTE OF ECONOMIC AFFAIRS
1972

First published in 1972 by

THE INSTITUTE OF ECONOMIC AFFAIRS

© 1972

SBN 255 36036–3

Printed in Great Britain
by Unwin Brothers Limited
The Gresham Press, Old Woking, Surrey, England
A member of the Staples Printing Group

Preface

This book is about poverty rather than about history. But since the nature and extent of poverty and the cures for it are the subject of prolonged debate among economists as well as sociologists, and since the origins of present-day poverty are commonly traced to the Industrial Revolution which is thought to have exacerbated it, economists must know what the historians have discovered.

For long, many historians and economists—G. R. Porter, T. B. Macaulay, J. S. Mill, J. E. Cairnes, Alfred Marshall—held that poverty and social distress were ameliorated in the late 18th and early 19th centuries by industrialisation. The almost opposite view, drawn from the works of Arnold Toynbee, and apparently confirmed by that of Sidney and Beatrice Webb, J. L. and Barbara Hammond, and later historians of social conditions like Professor E. J. Hobsbawm of Birkbeck College,[1] and Mr E. P. Thompson, formerly of the University of Warwick,[2] has contested this interpretation and argued that the poverty of 19th-century Britain was more acute than it had been in earlier periods. More recently their view has been challenged, *inter alia*, by historians trained in economics who considered there had been an improvement in living standards in the early and middle 19th century, or that, except for a few occupations like hand-loom weaving and tailoring, if there had been a decline for a time, or in some regions or occupations, it had been caused largely by the Napoleonic Wars rather than by industrialisation and early 'capitalism'.

The view that industrialisation raised living standards was re-asserted powerfully in modern form (with statistical evidence and economic argument) by Sir John Clapham in the 1920s. It was broadly supported in the more literary work of Dorothy George, Dorothy Marshall, and Dr Ivy Pinchbeck, and in several lesser-known works on aspects of social or working conditions, as in Professor W. H. Hutt's study of the Factory Acts and factory conditions.[3] It has been substantially confirmed by the recent research

---

[1] *Labouring Men, Studies in the History of Labour*, Weidenfeld and Nicolson, 1964; *Industry and Empire: An Economic History of Britain since 1750*, Weidenfeld and Nicolson 1968, and Penguin Books, 1969.

[2] *The Making of the English Working Class* (1963), Pelican Edition, Penguin Books, 1968.   [3] 'The Factory System of the 19th Century', *Economica*, March 1926.

of younger historians and economists interested in the history of poverty. Although widely known to historians and to students in the learned journals, it does not seem to have received as much attention by teachers and students of history, or by writers of works intended for general readers, as the view that industrialisation depressed living standards or exacerbated poverty. There is still a prevalent impression that the poverty of modern times originated in or was the consequence of early 19th-century developments. It continues in school and university text-books, and in some of the Open University, as the better authenticated interpretation of 19th-century social history. And many non-academics seem to believe that the famous novels of the early and mid-19th century were faithful descriptions of their times.

The significance of this historical debate for economists concerned with social policy in the 1970s is that contemporary thinking on the treatment of poverty often seems to be thrown back a century and a half and argued in terms of the economic and social changes accompanying the Industrial Revolution. It would seem that some protagonists, or their popularisers, have, perhaps unintentionally, used history to strengthen the case they make in diagnosing the causes of poverty and specifying remedies.

To clarify the contribution made to the debate on poverty by more recent researches, this volume has assembled new essays on the significant economic and social developments in the century and a half after 1760. Part 1 comprises an essay by Dr R. M. Hartwell of Oxford who, as an economist with a special interest in history, discusses the changing nature and extent of poverty down the centuries and its forms in the 19th century. Part 2 consists of five essays on more specialised studies, industries or regions. Professor G. E. Mingay of Kent discusses the transformation of agriculture. Dr Rhodes Boyson writes on the life of the Lancashire factory worker, and Dr Norman McCord of the University of Newcastle on the relief of poverty as exemplified in Newcastle and Durham. Dr C. G. Hanson, also of Newcastle, outlines the development of self-provision before the coming of the Welfare State. And Professor A. W. Coats analyses the views of the classical economists on industrialisation and poverty. Part 3 assesses contemporary writings. Dr W. O. Henderson and Dr W. H. Chaloner of the University of Manchester re-appraise the description by Friedrich Engels of the 'hungry forties'. Mr Michael Jefferson, an economist and a student of the early and mid-19th century social novel, writes an assessment

vi

of the degree to which it accurately portrayed the conditions of its times. His interpretation would seem broadly expressed by Lord David Cecil:

'... to read these books for information is not to read them with the purpose that their authors intended. Art is not like mathematics or philosophy. It is a subjective, sensual and highly personal activity in which facts and ideas are the servants of fancy and feeling; and the artist's first aim is not truth but delight.'[4]

The long debate on poverty and the effects of industrialisation will continue for decades. It may be that the debate is concerned with the wrong issue. Certainly there will be more contributions from outside the ranks of the historians offering different interpretations. The distinguished economist, Sir John Hicks, wrote recently:

'There is no doubt at all that industrialism, in the end, has been highly favourable to the real wage of labour. Real wages have risen enormously, in all industrialised countries, over the last century; and it is surely evident that without the increase in productive power that is due to industrialisation, the rise in real wages could not possibly have occurred. The important question is why it was so long delayed. There is no doubt at all that it was delayed; whether there was a small rise, or an actual fall, in the general level of real wages in England between (say) 1780 and 1840 leaves that issue untouched. It is the lag of wages behind industrialisation which . . . has to be explained.'[5]

Perhaps this is the debate to which the historians should address themselves: why economic growth did not raise living standards more quickly. Professor Hicks argues that the change from the casual employment of pre-industrialisation to the regular employment brought by the factory system enabled the workers in the new industries to 'combine' to strengthen their bargaining power. It would again appear to be not so much combination *per se* as industrialisation and its regularity of employment that indirectly and ultimately brought higher living standards and the prospect of increasing release from the poverty of the pre-industrial age.

This assembly of essays attempts to provide for economists, historians, students of social policy and the general reader a conspectus of the age of the Industrial Revolution to help them judge how far the poverty of the 20th century is a legacy of the 19th, or whether it was formalised, dramatised and publicised in the replacement of the 18th-century domestic system by the 19th-century

---

[4] 'The Art of Reading', in *English Critical Essays*, Oxford University Press, 1958, p. 182.
[5] *A Theory of Economic History*, Oxford University Press, 1969, p. 148.

industrial system financed by 'capitalism'. The authors write as individual scholars, with varying expertise, research and emphases to their essays, but the volume as a whole forms a corrective to the imbalance still widespread in historical teaching that modern poverty has its roots in the advent of industrialisation. As such it should be especially valuable to teachers of the economics of welfare policy in the present day as well as to students of social history.

September 1972   ARTHUR SELDON

Contents

PART II

3. INDUSTRIALISATION AND THE LIFE OF THE LANCASHIRE FACTORY WORKER

Rhodes Boyson

4. ASPECTS OF THE RELIEF OF POVERTY IN EARLY 19TH-CENTURY BRITAIN   89

Norman McCord

Part I

1. The Consequences of the Industrial Revolution in England for the Poor

R. M. HARTWELL
Professorial Fellow of Nuffield College,
University of Oxford

THE AUTHOR

RONALD MAX HARTWELL, M.A.(Syd.); M.A., D.Phil.(Oxon)., was born in 1921 and educated at the Universities of New England and Sydney (Australia) and Oxford. He has been Reader in Recent Social and Economic History, University of Oxford, since 1956 and Fellow Librarian of Nuffield College, Oxford, since 1958.

Before Oxford he was Professor of Economic History and Dean of the Faculty of Humanities and Social Sciences, University of New South Wales. He has been a Visiting Professor in the University of Ibadan, Nigeria, the Australian National University, Canberra, and the University of Virginia, Charlottesville.

Editor of *The Economic History Review*, 1957–72. Dr Hartwell's publications include: *The Economic Development of Van Diemens Land, 1820–1850* (1954); (ed.) *The Causes of the Industrial Revolution* (1967); (ed.) *The Industrial Revolution* (1970); *The Industrial Revolution and Economic Growth* (1971); (with R. W. Breach) *British Economy and Society, 1870–1970* (1972); and articles in learned journals.

He is married and has four daughters.

I. ECONOMICS, ECONOMIC HISTORY, AND THE HISTORY OF POVERTY

Economics is, in essence, the study of poverty; economic history, similarly, is largely the history of poverty. Economics is the study of the problems concerned with the scarcity of resources in relation to mankind's wants, and, consequently, with the problem of choice—between wants—and of allocation—of scarce resources to satisfy those wants. As Professor Robbins has written: economics is 'the science which studies human behaviour as a relationship between ends and scarce means which have alternative uses'.[1] Economic history is the study of the scarcity problem over time, and details the history of mankind's attempts to increase the available resources —through economic growth—and the history of the effects of the distribution and consumption of those resources between the members of society—economic welfare.

The supply of resources has been increased, either by bringing more factors of production into use (before the industrial revolution this meant, usually, more people tilling more land with the same primitive implements), or by increasing the productivity of existing resources (during the industrial revolution this meant changes in economic structure and organisation, by improving the quality of capital equipment through technical change and of human capital by better education and nutrition). The limits to poverty and welfare in any economy, at any time, have been set by its over-all productivity in relation to the size of its population, and economic growth has occurred during those rare intervals in history,[2] including the last two centuries, when average product per person was rising.

If the limits of welfare have been set by average productivity, the welfare of individuals or classes has been determined by the process of distribution, by the way in which the total product has been divided amongst its claimants. Generally, over the whole of history, there has been low productivity and, at best, very slow economic growth, along with a very unequal distribution of total product.

---

[1] L. Robbins, *An Essay on the Nature and Significance of Economic Science*, London, 1932; this book is a methodological discussion about 'the subject-matter of economics'. Implicitly the emphasis of the classical economists, and other social thinkers, on distribution as *the* problem of economics recognises the basic problems of scarcity and choice.

[2] R. M. Hartwell, 'Economic Growth in England before the Industrial Revolution', *Journal of Economic History*, March 1969, discusses earlier periods of growth.

Man's capacity to produce was, until the industrial revolution, at a very low level, and what was produced was divided up very unevenly, with a few getting large shares and the majority sharing the meagre residue. This has been the harsh reality of the economic history of world population; most men, at most times, and in most places, have lived short and miserable lives with little hope of betterment and no concept of progress. As J. M. Keynes pointed out:

'A belief in the material progress of man is not old. During the greater part of history such a belief was neither compatible with experience nor encouraged by religion. It is doubtful whether, taking one century with another, there was much variation in the lot of the unskilled labourer at the centres of civilisation in the two thousand years from the Greece of Solon to the England of Charles II or the France of Louis XIV. Paganism placed the Golden Age behind us; Christianity raised Heaven above us; and anyone, before the middle of the eighteenth century, who had expected a progressive improvement in material welfare here, as a result of the division of labour, the discoveries of science and the boundless fecundity of the species, would have been thought eccentric. In the eighteenth century, for obscure reasons which economic historians have not yet sufficiently explored, material progress commenced over wide areas in a decided and cumulative fashion not previously experienced.'[3]

Three epochs of economic growth

The history of economic growth divides into three distinct epochs, separated by the agricultural and industrial revolutions. The agricultural revolution began about the 8th millennium BC in the Middle East; the beginnings of the industrial revolution can be dated and placed more precisely in the England of the 18th century AD. The agricultural revolution consisted, essentially, of a change from food-gathering and hunting to farming with permanent settlements, and led to the growth of urban civilisation. The industrial revolution consisted, essentially, of a change from farming to industry and services, and led to a rapid growth of output, population and urbanisation. Both revolutions radically changed mankind's history by significantly enlarging his capacity to produce and by allowing the long-term growth of population, slowly after the agricultural revolution, explosively with the industrial revolution. These revolutions created, as Carlo Cipolla has argued,

'deep breaches in the continuity of the historical process. With each one of these two Revolutions, a "new story" begins: a new story dramatically and completely

---

3 J. M. Keynes, Preface to H. Wright, *Population*, Cambridge University Press, 1923, p. vii.

4

alien to the previous one. Continuity is broken between the cave-man and the builders of pyramids, just as all continuity is broken between the ancient plough-man and the modern operator of a power station'.[4]

But whereas the agricultural revolution produced very slow growth over nine millennia, the industrial revolution produced sustained and rapid economic growth over two centuries.

Ricardo argued that 'the principal problem in Political Economy' was 'to determine the laws which regulate . . . distribution', but economists have never been able to determine decisively the comparative impact of market and power forces in determining distributive shares.[5]

Thus the long-term history of distribution cannot be so neatly divided as that of production, but it can be demonstrated that the industrial revolution saw both the more efficient working of the market, so that distributive shares were related more directly to factor productivity (i.e. wages rose with increasing labour productivity), and also the more effective organisation of workmen into combinations to protect and raise wage-rates. The result of both developments was to increase the labour share of the national income. Before the industrial revolution, however, distributive shares were determined largely by command, by the arbitrary and authoritarian decision of rulers and a privileged few, according to power, status and other non-market criteria. But distributive shares since the beginnings of the industrial revolution have been modified increasingly by the power of the working classes to affect distribution, and by interference with the market mechanism by governments hoping (or professing) either to increase social justice or to improve economic efficiency.

With the onset of industrialisation the working classes were able, for the first time in history, to organise effectively as a pressure group in their own interest; at the same time governments, imbued with doctrines of justice, with belief in the social morality of equality of distributive shares, and with socialist hopes in macro-economic social engineering to improve productivity, have increasingly intervened directly in the management of economies and redistributed income through progressive taxation and the institutions of the

---

[4] Carlo Cipolla, *The Economic History of World Population*, Penguin Books, 1962, pp. 29–30. On the industrial revolution as 'The Great Discontinuity', cf. R. M. Hartwell, *The Industrial Revolution and Economic Growth*, London, 1971, Chapter 3.

[5] Clark Kerr, 'Wage-Relationships. The Comparative Impact of Market and Power Forces', in J. T. Dunlop (ed.), *The Theory of Wage Determination*, London, 1957.

5

Welfare State. Even before the industrial revolution the Old Poor Law had been a public agency for the redistribution of income, but the origins of the Welfare State are to be found unambiguously in the great social inquiries, and the consequent legislation, of the Victorian era.[6]

Growth, not redistribution, the key

The result has been, as long-term studies of distribution show, a clear trend, since the beginnings of industrialisation, towards more equality of incomes.[7] The same studies have shown that, whatever the causes and effects of redistribution, the major component of increasing *per capita* income, of increasing welfare, has been economic growth. Any redistribution, because of trade union pressure or government social policy, has been insignificant compared with the relentless growth of product per head achieved by industrialisation. Growth, not redistribution, has been the main cause of increasing welfare. As G. Slater has pointed out:

'The poverty of the past, from the earliest beginnings of human society up till very recently, was due to lack of power to produce adequately the necessaries of life.'[8]

The lesson of history, only too well understood by the under-developed economies of the world today, is that poverty can be cured only by economic growth, not by income redistribution. Whatever the short-term fluctuation in growth, because of the trade cycle, whatever the continuing reality of some poverty even in the richest economies, the effect of industrialisation and growth has been, unambiguously, to make both the rich and the poor better off, and to narrow the gap between the two. Only industrialisation saw the beginning of the end of that extreme, debilitating and demoralising poverty which had been the lot of most of mankind over most of history, and which still characterises so much of the world today. The essential difference between the high-income and low-income economies of the world, between the rich and the poor, is that the former have experienced industrial revolutions which profoundly altered their economic structures and which raised living standards. It is for this reason that every under-developed country wants and

---

6 D. Roberts, *Victorian Origins of the British Welfare State*, Yale, 1960.

7 S. Kuznets, 'Economic Growth and Income Inequality', *Economic Growth and Structure. Selected Essays*, London, 1966, For Great Britain see A. L. Bowley, *The Change in the Distribution of the National Income, 1880–1913*, Oxford, 1920.

8 G. Slater, *Poverty and the State*, London, 1930, p. 1.

plans to industrialise and grow. 'Industrialisation', C. P. Snow argued dramatically in *The Two Cultures and the Scientific Revolution*, 'is the only hope of the poor'. Or, as the late Professor T. S. Ashton wrote in 1948:

'There are today on the plains of India and China men and women, plague-ridden and hungry, living lives little better, to outward appearance, than those of the cattle that toil with them by day and share their places of sleep at night. Such Asiatic standards, and such unmechanised horrors, are the lot of those who increase their numbers without passing through an industrial revolution.'[9]

The lesson of history is obvious, and the aspiration to industrialise is now universal.[10]

II. THE INDUSTRIAL REVOLUTION IN ENGLAND AND ECONOMIC PROGRESS

Here we are concerned with industrialisation and poverty, with the effect of the industrial revolution on the poor and under-privileged. But what was the industrial revolution? Although one of the great discontinuities of history—'the great transformation', as K. Polanyi called it[1]—marking the divide in history between a world of slow and one of sustained and substantial growth, historians generally have not defined it carefully. For long, indeed, the pre-occupation of historians of the industrial revolution was with distribution and the ills of industrialisation.[2] It is more relevant, however, to see the industrial revolution primarily as the first example of modern economic growth, and thus to shift the emphasis from distribution to production.

The industrial revolution was that economic growth which occurred in the century *c.* 1750 to *c.* 1850 as a result of industrialisation. During that century there was a revolution in the structure and performance of the economy which resulted in sustained economic

---

[9] T. S. Ashton, *The Industrial Revolution, 1760–1830*, London, 1948, p. 129.

[10] R. M. Hartwell, 'Lessons from History', in *The Industrial Revolution and Economic Growth*, London, 1971.

[1] K. Polyani, *The Great Transformation*, London, 1944.

[2] The large literature on social consequences began with the first great book on the industrial revolution by Arnold Toynbee (*Lectures on the Industrial Revolution of the Eighteenth Century in England*, London, 1884) and was reinforced by the writings of historians like the Webbs and the Hammonds, and, more recently, E. P. Thompson.

growth. Increasing productivity was the consequence of three inter-related changes:[3] *first*, structural change (transferring resources from lower-productivity agriculture to higher-productivity industry and services; *second*, increasing factor inputs (rapidly increasing population and capital accumulation, increased tillage and a massive increase in the extraction of raw materials, especially coal and iron); *third*, increasing efficiency (better economic organisation through the development of the factory to replace workshop or home, nucleated farming to replace open-field agriculture, better capital equipment because of technical change, better human capital because of better nutrition and education, economies of scale and the increasing division of labour permitting more specialisation).

These improvements were made possible, to a large extent, by the freeing of man's creative powers to innovate. This was the result of fundamental changes in social and political institutions, in particular, through the growth of political democracy and market economy. It was this powerful combination of democracy and a free market which produced the first industrial revolution. The Whig Revolution finally destroyed the centralising tendencies of the King-dominated national state, dispersed political initiative, and strengthened local government. It also reinforced the rule of law.

It was the development of market economy, however, which was the fundamental pre-requisite of English growth. This basically depended on increasingly explicit and legally-enforced views about property rights which enabled confident reliance on the market as an efficient mechanism for the allocation of resources and the distribution of goods and services. There had to be confidence in the ability to dispose freely of resources, and in gaining from market activity without arbitrary penalties.

'If one views the industrial revolution as the outcome, institutionally, of an increasingly efficient market (i.e., of a market in which economic behaviour, rational, maximising behaviour, could operate with expectations of reward and punishment according to the successful prediction of market needs and responses), then factors making for the efficiency of the market were of paramount importance for the industrial revolution. Those changes which enabled economic behaviour, whether by consumers or producers, to be satisfied and rewarded,

---

3 C. Clark has formulated 'the simple but important principle that economic progress in any country, in the sense of a rise of the average national income per head of the working population, may take place (a) as a result of improvement in real output per head in all or any of these three fields [of industry, agriculture and services], or (b) as a result of transference of labour from the less productive to the more productive fields'. (*The Conditions of Economic Progress*, London, 1940, pp. 6–7.)

and hence encouraged, gave the market system an ongoing impetus. As consumers maximised satisfaction and producers maximised profit, incentives to work and to produce were sustained and reinforced. As custom and command ceased to determine economic decision-making, and as the market increasingly determined such decisions, rationality permeated the whole of social life in a mutually reinforcing process of change.'[4]

Opposition to industrialisation

The industrial revolution was opposed in some circles and by some interests, just as it has been subsequently misinterpreted and attacked by some historians. Opposition stemmed mainly from those economically or socially threatened by industrialisation, for example, some landowners, or by those whose opposition was moral or aesthetic, for example, some poets and novelists. Undoubtedly, also, there were real victims of industrialisation, especially those handworkers who were displaced by machines, of whom the hand-loom weavers are the best known and the largest example. But, generally, the factories created more jobs than were lost by making some workers redundant and, such was the increasing demand for labour, there was no great 'reserve army of unemployed'.

Obviously the industrial revolution changed or modified social values just as it changed the environment;[5] it replaced status and custom by contract in much of human relations, for example in the fixing of wages; it created a new urban environment which in many ways was less attractive than the village green. But the persistent misinterpretation of the industrial revolution in England as a catastrophe for the working classes—

'a period as disastrous and as terrible as any through which a nation ever passed; disastrous and terrible, because side by side with a great increase of wealth was seen an enormous increase in pauperism; and production on a vast scale, the result of free competition, led to a rapid alienation of classes and the degradation of a large body of producers'[6]

—has been the consequence mainly of an increased and concerned awareness of the persistence of poverty and other social ills, and of Marxian doctrines about historical change. Much criticism of industrialism has been motivated by humane and moral indignation; much has been motivated by doctrinaire theories about inevitable

---

[4] R. M. Hartwell, *op. cit.*, p. 258.

[5] F. Klingender, *Art and the Industrial Revolution*, London, 1947, gives an interesting account of the artistic reaction to the environment of the industrial revolution.

[6] A. Toynbee, *op. cit.*, p. 84.

economic change. Marx misinterpreted poverty and social unrest as fundamental signs of disequilibrium in capitalist economy, heralding the immiseration of the working classes and the breakdown of society. As Engels wrote, prophetically but incorrectly in 1844: 'The Revolution must come; it is already too late to bring about a peaceful solution.'[7]

In spite of the critics, however, the industrial revolution was generally received sympathetically, mainly because most people, and the working classes in particular, saw in it the chances of greater individual opportunity for wealth and social advancement. The industrial revolution was a period of increasing social mobility. 'There is probably no period in English history', wrote Leslie Stephen, 'at which a greater number of poor men have risen to distinction'. The men who were 'the chief instruments' of industrialisation were 'self-made' and 'owed nothing to government or to the universities which passed for the organs of national culture'.[8]

'The century of progress'

It was because of obvious gains from industrialisation that the 19th century became the century of progress, and it took the problems of the 20th century to shake the complacent belief in inevitable progress. In the 19th century the main social motivation, by all classes, was to take advantage of progress, of economic growth. As J. A. Froude wrote:

'Amidst the varied reflections which the nineteenth century is in the habit of making on its condition and its prospects, there is one common opinion in which all parties coincide—that we live in an era of progress . . . in every department of life—in its business and in its pleasures, in its beliefs and in its theories, in its material developments and in its spiritual convictions—we thank God that we are not like our fathers. And while we admit their merits, making allowances for their disadvantages, we do not blind ourselves in mistaken modesty to our immeasurable superiority.'[9]

The widespread belief in progress and the universal desire to share its benefits were generalised into almost mystical beliefs in *laissez-faire*, the ethic of work, and, particularly for the working classes,

---

[7] F. Engels, *The Condition of the Working-Class in England in 1844*, English Ed., London, 1892, p. 297.

[8] L. Stephen, *The English Utilitarians*, London, 1900, Vol. I, pp. 61, 111–12.

[9] J. A. Froude, *Short Studies in Great Subjects*, London, 1907, Vol. III, pp. 149–50.

self-help.[10] That wealth could be earned by members of all classes was the obvious stimulus to effort; the attainment of wealth, once dependent on birth or patronage, was now available, if not to all, then certainly to enough of the working classes to justify ambition and work as social virtues. That economic freedom—the private pursuit of wealth in a *laissez-faire* competitive system—was a most efficient means of promoting economic progress, became a rarely challenged axiom of economic behaviour. *Laissez-faire*, an economic system of property-rights in all goods, with government and the rule of law protecting those rights, and a market system of exchange, with individuals freely exchanging property rights for consumer satisfaction or economic betterment, were the fundamental social bases of 19th-century progress. It was the pervasive and powerful stimulus of wealth in privately-owned property that produced, in the words of J. M. Keynes, 'the magnificent episode of the nineteenth century'.

III. POVERTY AND ITS CURE

'There is, perhaps, no better test of the progress of a nation than that which shows what proportion are in poverty'.[1] But what, exactly, is poverty? It is usually defined as 'an insufficiency of basic needs', but there is, unfortunately, no universally acceptable or unambiguous definition of poverty. Although three groups of scholars have concerned themselves with poverty—historians, economists and sociologists—they have not between them solved the problem of definition.[2] Historians, to be fair about their methodological innocence, have been more concerned with documentation than with

---

[10] For example, the works of Samuel Smiles, the apostle of self-help, who wrote books with titles like *Self Help*, *Thrift*, etc.

[1] A. L. Bowley, *The Nature and Purpose of the Measurement of Social Phenomena*, London, 1923, p. 214.

[2] The classic studies of poverty, partly historical and partly sociological, date back to the work of Arthur Young and Sir Frederick Eden in the 18th century, but the great 19th-century studies were by Henry Mayhew, Charles Booth and Seebohm Rowntree. Booth and Rowntree, in particular, set the pattern for future study with their detailed and comprehensive area studies. 'The condition of England question', a 19th-century political problem, meantime attracted the historians who, in the work of great humanists like R. H. Tawney, were as much concerned with contemporary social criticism as with determining the facts of history. (F. M. Eden, *The State of the Poor*, 4 vols., London, 1797; C. Booth, *Life and Labour of the People in London*, 17 vols., London, 1889–1897; and B. S. Rowntree, *Poverty: A Study of Town Life*, London, 1901.)

definition; to them poverty was an obvious phenomenon of history not needing the backing of definitional exactness, and they have chronicled the conditions of life and work of the bottom strata of society using common-sense criteria to determine at what level poverty began. Economists, with more operational tools of scholarship, have defined poverty usually in terms of real wages (i.e. the command of money wages over goods and services) below some accepted norm of 'a reasonable standard of living'. Sometimes, however, the term has been used to describe a level of real wages which provided only 'the bare necessities of life' (i.e. enough for subsistence). But what is 'reasonable' or 'subsistence' differs from time to time and from place to place: what is subsistence in India today is well below subsistence in present-day England; and what was reasonable in 18th-century England, before the industrial revolution, would be quite unreasonable in England today. Sociologists, who more recently have concerned themselves with poverty, have been responsible, in particular, for introducing the concept of relativity into the study of poverty; while agreeing about the difficulties of determining poverty by absolute standards, they have shown that it is perhaps more easily determined by relative standards, stressing inequality as its primary criterion.

'Thus, poverty, particularly in the advanced industrial democratic nations where the bare physical wants have been met, is a matter of deviation from social and economic norms.'[3]

Three concepts of poverty

There are, thus, three concepts which underline all ideas of poverty: first, *subsistence*, an empirical concept of the real wage necessary to maintain life and economic efficiency; second, *normative*, a value concept of what is reasonable in any given society; third, *relative*, a relative deprivation concept of poverty felt, and experienced, because of inequality. All three concepts have changed over time. Poverty of the subsistence kind, that of 18th- and 19th-century destitution and pauperism, has now been reduced to unimportant dimensions. At the same time the idea of what constitutes reasonable and normal has continually expanded. As A. L. Bowley argued:

'The idea of progress is largely psychological and certainly relative; people are apt to measure their progress not from a forgotten position in the past, but

---

[3] S. Mencher, 'The problem of measuring poverty', *British Journal of Sociology*, vol. 18, no. 1, 1967, p. 12.

towards an ideal, which, like an horizon, continually recedes. The present generation is not interested in the earlier needs and successes of its progenitors, but in its own distresses and frustration considered in the light of the presumed possibility of universal comfort or riches.'[4]

And, with the advance of living standards and education, it is possible that the sense of relative deprivation in advanced societies has increased.[5]

If poverty is difficult to define, it is easier to see its causes.[6] For the individual, poverty was, and still is, the result of a variety of factors of which the most important are:

> low money wage in relation to prices;
> irregularity of employment;
> a large number of dependants;
> old age, sickness and widowhood;
> the failure of self-help, charity or government to bridge the gap between income and basic needs.

Over history the importance of these various factors has changed, although general trends can be observed. First, money wages in relation to prices have been rising steadily, although with setbacks, since the beginnings of the industrial revolution.[7]

Second, unemployment and under-employment, though constant and varying features of industrial society, have not increased in scale

---

[4] A. L. Bowley, *Wages and Incomes in the United Kingdom since 1860*, Cambridge University Press, 1937, p. x.

[5] W. G. Runciman, *Relative Deprivation and Social Justice: A Study of Attitudes to Social Inequality in Twentieth Century England*, London, 1966.

[6] H. A. Silverman, *The Economics of Social Problems*, London, 1928, for an analysis of the causes of poverty, and a detailed examination of the work of Booth, Rowntree and Bowley. On modern poverty, J. L. and J. K. Roach (eds.), *Poverty. Selected Readings*, Penguin Books, 1972, especially Part 2. A large modern literature on economic under-development is also concerned with poverty, and, in particular, with 'the Malthusian Trap,' the situation in which population is growing faster than output, and the gap, possibly growing, between the rich and poor countries of the world: for example, Gunnar Myrdal's massive *Asian Drama: An Inquiry into the Poverty of Nations*, Penguin Books, 1968.

[7] For the industrial revolution period there is controversy—the standard of living controversy—about whether living standards declined, before rising at some time during the 19th century. (For example, B. Inglis, 'The Poor Who Were With Us', *Encounter*, September 1971.) Other historians who have debated this issue include J. H. Clapham, T. S. Ashton and R. M. Hartwell, who argue for improvement, and the Hammonds, E. J. Hobsbawm and E. P. Thompson, who argue for deterioration. The debate is summarised by R. M. Hartwell in Chapter 8 of *The Industrial Revolution*, Nuffield College Studies in Economic History, No. I, Oxford, 1970.

or intensity over the last two centuries; indeed, the only long period of sustained high unemployment was between the two world wars. For particular groups of workers, like those rendered redundant by technological change, and for particular individuals, unemployment has been the main cause of poverty, but it must be seen as a constant and not as an intensifying cause of poverty, and a cause whose effects have been partly remedied by the growth of the welfare state, and particularly by increasingly adequate provision of insurance.[8]

Third, the problem of dependants has been alleviated by the decreasing size of family and by the provision of family endowment. The birth rate was already declining by the mid-19th century, with a consequent downward trend in family size, and the gradual breakdown of the extended family removed from the individual much of the responsibility of caring for parents and other ageing or sick relatives.

Fourth, and following on from the last point, the importance of old age and sickness as causes of poverty declined as they were increasingly and effectively dealt with by pensions and a network of welfare services; throughout the 19th century, however, they were prime causes of poverty.

Long-run reduction of poverty

In the long run, therefore, rising real wages, insurance protection against unemployment, child allowances and other family subsidies, pensions (for the old, sick and widowed), and the massive growth of the welfare state (for example, the provision of medical care), have eroded the traditional bases of poverty, and have reduced the pool of poverty to a small but persistent residue. It is perhaps curious that neither economic growth nor government action have been able to eliminate poverty completely. It is complacent to argue that there will always be, at the fringe of society, individuals who cannot come to terms with its demands, and who will need institutional or semi-institutional care. It is realistic to argue that there will always be poverty in the sense that some people will feel relative deprivation and that resources will always be scarce in relation to the demands for them.

Ultimately poverty is a matter of real income, of goods and services, measured against some norm. Redistribution of income can,

---

[8] B. B. Gilbert, *The Evolution of National Insurance in Great Britain: The Origins of the Welfare State*, London, 1966.

and has, reduced such poverty, both in the relative and absolute senses, but in the future as in the past poverty will be reduced mainly by economic growth. But neither growth nor income distribution can completely eliminate that psychic poverty which is the result of relative deprivation. Increasing absolute wealth might even aggravate it, and the paradox of a wealthy society like England is that increasing redistribution by the state has persisted along with increasing individual wealth through the mechanism of the market in the context of persistent economic growth.

IV. ECONOMIC GROWTH AND CHANGING ATTITUDES TOWARDS POVERTY

Poverty, on any definition, was omnipresent in pre-industrial England, which offered little of material comfort and less of hope of improvement to the majority of its people. At a reasonable estimate more than a quarter of England's population (and more of the population of the Celtic Fringe) was in a state of chronic poverty, barely able to sustain life, and this figure could double in time of harvest failure. Food shortages and under-nourishment, lack of hygiene and medical ignorance, endemic and epidemic diseases, held population in a continuous Malthusian trap with the positive check of a persistently high death rate. With such a low average output of goods and services per person being produced, the decline of any individual to poverty was terrifyingly easy and commonplace.[1]

Material advance

But just how low was the average, and how quickly did it rise with industrialisation? Estimates of national income go back to the 17th-century political arithmeticians, the honour of the first calculation going to William Petty.[2] Between Petty's estimate of 1667 and the regular annual calculation of national income by government after 1941, there were more than 30 individual estimates of English

---

[1] Studies of the pre-industrial poor are, e.g. P. Laslett, *The World we have Lost*, London, 1965; E. S. Furniss, *The Position of the Labourer in a System of Nationalism*, New York, 1920; S. and B. Webb, *English Poor Law History: Part I. The Old Poor Law*, London, 1927; D. Marshall, *The English Poor in the Eighteenth Century*, London, 1926.

[2] P. Studenski, *The Income of Nations*, New York, 1958, gives a comparative history of national income estimates; for the long-term history of British income and output, see P. Deane and W. A. Cole, *British Economic Growth, 1688–1959*, Cambridge, 1962.

(and British) national income which between them give a precise enough measure of the results of industrialisation on the absolute and average output of goods and services. Measurements were made in money terms, and, allowing for price trends, real national income per person increased as follows: 50 per cent in the 18th century before 1780; 50 to 100 per cent between 1780 and 1850 (the period of 'the standard of living' debate, in which some historians claim actual deterioration); 80 to 100 per cent between 1850 and 1914; and another 50 per cent or more between 1914 and the 1950s. Between the end of the 17th century, well before the industrial revolution, and the outbreak of the First World War, when the first industrial revolution had ended, the goods and services available in England, on average per person, increased four- to six-fold at the same time as population was increasing six-fold; the absolute increase in goods and services was at least thirty-fold, and as high as fifty-fold.

Even at the lower figure there is a massive increase in production to be accounted for, and a massive increase to be distributed to improve living standards. Over the 19th century output per person was growing at the rate of 1·5 per cent per annum, at a rate which quadrupled productivity per person over the century. The Englishman before the industrial revolution, before 1750, was between a sixth and a seventh as well off in material wealth as the Englishman of 1950. On any criterion of well-being—food, clothing, shelter, health, life expectancy, infantile mortality, education, material possessions—the Englishman of the 20th century is immeasurably better off than his predecessor before industrialisation. At the time of Gregory King, life expectancy was less than 30 years, the infantile mortality rate was as high as 200 per 1,000 births, and income inequality was marked. By the mid-20th century, life expectancy had more than doubled, the infantile mortality rate was down to 33, and, as Lee Saltau has demonstrated, income inequality with a massively enlarged total income was much reduced.

'Statistical evidence indicates that income inequality, particularly in upper income groups, has decreased for several centuries. The trend has been accelerated in the twentieth century.'[3]

But if the long-term effects of industrialisation were obvious by 1900 they were less obvious in 1800 or even in 1850. At the same

---

3 L. Saltau, 'Long-Run Changes in British Income Inequality', *Economic History Review*, April 1968, p. 29.

time as the industrial revolution was resulting in sustained economic growth, the English economy in the early 19th century was faced by a series of formidable economic and social problems partly at least caused by the great war against France. To contemporaries the problems seemed more significant than the achievements. In a world of poverty and under-nourishment it is not surprising that the rise of population at the end of the 18th century was seen, not as a sign of the ability of the economy to support increasing numbers, but rather as a threat to already scarce resources of food. Malthus voiced the fears of his generation when he wrote:

'Throughout the animal and vegetable kingdoms nature has scattered the seeds of life abroad with the most profuse and liberal hand; but it has been comparatively sparing in the room and in the nourishment necessary to rear them.'

Because of the law of diminishing returns in agriculture, Malthus argued, more and more resources would have to be devoted to increasingly less fertile soil to feed a continually increasing population. In the context of man's history as a struggle for subsistence, it is not surprising that the classical economists were preoccupied with fears of over-population and the vision of the stationary state.[4] Exponential population growth in a finite world was, and still is, a terrifying prospect for mankind. Classical economics became, in consequence, 'the gloomy science', culminating in the pessimism of Mill and the savage prophecy of Marx.

Collapse of Malthusian fears

Equally understandable as this profound pessimism, however, was its disappearance after about 1840 in the face of the massive productivity of the new industry. Fears of over-population, along with associated fears of environmental pollution on a universal scale, did not reappear until the third quarter of the 20th century. As the 19th century progressed, however, it became obvious that the immiseration of the working classes, the nightmare of Malthus and the hope of Marx, was not taking place. Instead there was a slow but gradual improvement in the condition of the masses. Even by 1840 Malthusianism in its starkest form was no longer accepted.

Criticism was both on theoretical and empirical grounds, but the main argument against Malthus and Ricardo was in the obviousness

---

[4] The most formidable analysis came from the pen of David Ricardo whose *On the Principles of Political Economy and Taxation* (1817) pointed rigorously towards the end of economic progress and the emergence of the stationary state.

of economic growth.[5] By the end of the century it was widely believed that the law of diminishing returns had not set in, and would not set in. Improved organisation and technology had more than offset any tendencies towards diminishing returns. Optimism had replaced pessimism, and Marshall and the young Keynes looked confidently to the future. 'That happy age', as Keynes described the pre-1914 world, in which the only change was 'in the direction of furthei improvement'.[6]

Equally important as the material betterment that came with the fruits of industrialisation were new attitudes towards the social problems of poverty. Briefly it was that social ills like poverty that had always existed, and had always been accepted as inevitable, came to be regarded as new ills to be remedied rather than as old ills to be endured. The period of the industrial revolution produced a great debate about poverty and its remedies, and also about other social problems. Such problems were identified, publicised, examined and analysed, and remedied, or partly remedied, by voluntary or legislative action.

There was certainly no complacency in the 19th century about poverty; rather there was intensified concern as it was realised that economic growth did not automatically remedy all poverty. Thus, from the 1830s onwards there were a remarkable series of social inquiries, mainly initiated by government, which culminated at the end of the century in three important private investigations, the social surveys of Booth on London (1889–97) and Rowntree on York (1901), and the analysis of unemployment by Beveridge (1909).[7] Whether concern was the result of 'a remarkable flowering in the social conscience of the English middle classes',[8] or prudence motivated by a desire for harmony between social classes, or rational calculation of the social costs of poverty and unemployment, 'the social question' of urban poverty along with increasing average wealth motivated decisive action in the decade before the First World War.

'The condition of England question', which had worried those who governed Britain in the first half of the 19th century, had also

---

[5] M. Blaug, *Ricardian Economics: A Historical Study*, Yale, 1958; R. L. Meek *Economics and Ideology and Other Essays*, London, 1967.

[6] J. M. Keynes, *The Economic Consquences of the Peace*, London, 1924, p. 7.

[7] Booth and Rowntree, *op. cit.*; W. H. Beveridge, *Unemployment: A Problem of Industry*, London, 1909.

[8] D. Winch, *Economics and Policy*, London, 1969, p. 29.

resulted in extensive legislation, but to remedy particular social ills rather than to treat poverty as a general and continuous problem. The focus of the 19th-century debate on poverty centred in the Poor Law, 'a network of law and practice which in two hundred years had become entwined in the fabric of society and the economic system'. As J. R. Poynter points out:

'The Poor Law survived, but . . . in 1834 the system was subjected to drastic surgery in accordance with a new creed of poverty and its relief which had emerged in the debate and was to continue as social orthodoxy until well into the twentieth century, when both the Poor Law and the "principles of 1834" were smothered by the institutions and values of the Welfare State.'[9]

By the 20th century the two traditional ideas about poverty—that it was mainly the result of individual weakness and that it could be cured by casual charity—were disappearing, to be replaced by the view that poverty was a social evil largely beyond the control of the individual, an evil that could be alleviated or cured only by social, collective action.[10] Individual effort, in this view, even aided by 'voluntary co-operation and private benevolence', was an inadequate agency either for the alleviation or the prevention of poverty, and needed to be replaced by public effort through government agencies. Beveridge argued powerfully that this was particularly true of the greatest cause of poverty, unemployment, and he emphasised that while unemployment or under-employment was as old as civil society, the unemployment of industrial society was a general problem that needed a general solution. Hence the moves, before the First World War, to provide effective relief for the aged and the unemployed.

V. CONCLUSION

This essay has been concerned with the industrial revolution in England and its effects on poverty. The industrial revolution began and ended with great debates on poverty: the first, beginning in the 18th century and resulting in classic studies of poverty like that of Eden, ended with the passing of the New Poor Law in 1834; the

---

[9] J. R. Poynter, *Society and Pauperism. English Ideas on Poor Relief, 1795–1834*, London, 1969, p. xi.

[10] M. E. Rose, *The Relief of Poverty, 1834–1914*, London, 1972, gives an excellent brief account of the workings of the New Poor Law, and more generally of attitudes towards, and treatment of, poverty.

19

second, which accelerated towards the end of the 19th century, producing the new classics of Booth and Rowntree, ended with the *Royal Commission on the Poor Laws and the Relief of Distress* in 1909.[1] Both debates led to significant changes in the official treatment of poverty, a 'hard' treatment in 1834 and a 'soft' treatment in 1909, and 1834 saw the beginnings of one essential feature of the 20th-century Welfare State, the general treatment of social problems by centralised decision and authorities.

The industrial revolution undoubtedly made the problem of poverty more explicit; even if industrialisation did not aggravate, it enlarged the scale of poverty through the growth of population and urbanisation, and made it more obvious. The dispersed rural poverty of pre-industrial England was never as spectacular, even though its effects on the individual were more lethal, as the slums of the new industrial towns. But, more important, the idea of progress which so characterised the 19th century also had its effects on attitudes towards poverty: poverty was a problem to be solved. Middle-class reformers, who combined a belief in progress with humanitarianism, utilitarianism and 'a ferocious goodness', galvanised society and government into increasingly effective action against social ills. The origins of the Welfare State can be seen clearly in the actions of these men.[2]

But if the solution of the social problems of the poor has depended, to an important degree, on public services, on the better provision of medical care and the control of infectious diseases, on improvements of the environment through public health controls and the plentiful provision of clean water, on an effective system for the relief of poverty and destitution, it depended much more on economic growth. On social aids, the 19th century saw massive and lasting improvements, but the most fundamental contribution of the 19th century to the relief of poverty was industrialisation and economic growth. Economic growth, both by raising the productivity of the economy as a whole and by improving the quality of people through investment in human capital, made more goods available and more people capable of profiting from their distribution. This went along with a more sophisticated and humane understanding

---

[1] S. and B. Webb, *English Poor Law Policy*, London, 1910, give an account of the 19th-century controversy, and J. R. Poynter, *op. cit.*, of the industrial revolution debate.

[2] D. Roberts, *Victorian Origins of the British Welfare State*, Yale, 1960.

of the causes of poverty as a complex mix of social and personal misfortunes and weaknesses. Booth's list of causes, for example, included

'crime, vice, drink, laziness, pauper association, heredity, mental disease, incapacity, early marriage, large family, extravagance, lack of work, trade misfortune, restlessness, no relations, death of husband, desertion, death of father or mother, sickness, accident, ill-luck, old age.'[3]

If the solution to these persistent problems lay, in the long run, in economic growth and the institutions of the Welfare State, it is important to realise, also, that the solution was partly political. It was a beneficial combination in England of political democracy, which ensured the emergence of powerful political forces to protect and enlarge the interests of the working classes, and economic growth, which provided an ever-increasing stream of goods and services, which finally eroded the bases of the age-old structure of poverty. At the same time increasing understanding of social processes changed views about individual responsibility for being poor, while recognising that investment in human beings, especially in the form of education, enabled more of them to combat exogenous misfortune. Knowledge of poverty increased markedly with continuing and intensive investigation; attitudes towards poverty changed radically; treatment of poverty moved from the workhouse to the state; but, above all, an increasing proportion of the total population was lifted above any defined poverty line by economic growth and the more equal distribution of incomes.

A SELECT BIBLIOGRAPHY

I. CLASSIC STUDIES OF POVERTY

    Eden, F. M., *The State of the Poor: or an History of the Labouring Classes in England*, 4 vols., 1797.

    Porter, G. R., *The Progress of the Nation*, 1836–8, and subsequent editions.

    Engels, F., *The Condition of the Working-Class in England in 1844*, English edition, 1892.

    Mayhew, H., *London Labour and London Poor*, 4 vols., 1851–62.

---

[3] C. Booth, *Life and Labour of the People in London*, London, 1897, vol. IX, pp. 53, 70. Narrowed down Booth's main causes were 'lack of work, low pay, idleness, drunkenness, or thriftlessness, sickness or large families'.

Thorold Rogers, J. E., *Six Centuries of Work and Wages*, 1884.

Booth, C., *Life and Labour of the People in London*, 17 vols., 1889–1897.

Bowley, A. L., *Wages in the United Kingdom in the Nineteenth Century*, 1900.

Rowntree, B. S., *Poverty: A Study of Town Life*, 1901.

Giffen, R., *Economic Inquiries and Studies*, 2 vols., 1904.

Hammond, J. L. and B., *The Village Labourer*, 1911.

The Town Labourer, 1917.

The Skilled Labourer, 1919.

II. THE POOR LAW AND OTHER WELFARE SERVICES

Beveridge, W. H., *Unemployment: A Problem of Industry*, 1909.

Slater, G., *Poverty and the State*, 1930.

de Schweinitz, K., *England's Road to Social Security*, 1943.

Roberts, D., *Victorian Origins of the British Welfare State*, 1960.

Bruce, M., *The Coming of the Welfare State*, 1961.

Owen, D., *English Philanthropy, 1660–1960*, 1965.

Gilbert, B. B., *The Evolution of National Insurance in Great Britain: The Origins of the Welfare State*, 1966.

Marshall, J. D., *The Old Poor Law, 1795–1834*, 1968.

Poynter, J. R., *Society and Pauperism. English Ideas on Poor Relief, 1795–1834*, 1969.

Rose, M. E., *The Relief of Poverty, 1834–1914*, 1972.

III. WAGES AND THE STANDARD OF LIVING

Bowley, A. L., *Wages in the United Kingdom in the Nineteenth Century*, 1900.

George, D., *England in Transition*, 1931.

Gilboy, E. W., *Wages in Eighteenth Century England*, 1934.

Beveridge, W. H., *Full Employment in a Free Society*, 1944.

Hayek, F. A., *Capitalism and the Historians*, 1954.

Thompson, E. P., *The Making of the English Working Class*, 1963.

Hobsbawm, E. J., *Labouring Men*, 1964.

Phelps Brown, E. H., and Browne, M. H., *A Century of Pay*, 1968.

Hartwell, R. M., *The Industrial Revolution and Economic Growth*, 1971.

Stedman Jones, G., *Outcast London*, 1971.

Part II

2. The Transformation of Agriculture

G. E. MINGAY
Professor of Agrarian History, University of Kent

THE AUTHOR

G. E. MINGAY was educated at Sir Joseph Williamson's School, Rochester, and Nottingham University. He served for five years with the Royal Navy in the Second World War and took his Ph.D. in 1958. After teaching appointments at Woolwich Polytechnic, the London School of Economics and a number of American universities, he became Reader in Economic and Social History in the new University of Kent. In 1968 he was elected to the Chair of Agrarian History, the only one of its kind in Britain. His books include *English Landed Society in the Eighteenth Century* (1963), *The Agricultural Revolution, 1750–1880* (with J. D. Chambers, 1966), and *Britain and America* (with Philip S. Bagwell, 1970).

I. INTRODUCTION: THE DECLINE OF AGRICULTURE

The recent history of advanced countries reveals a common tendency for industrialisation to be accompanied by two developments: the apparently inevitable long-term decline of the agricultural sector and the growth of pressure on agricultural incomes. Accompanying these developments have been shifts in the methods and patterns of agricultural production, changes in the farm structure, and a large and sometimes precipitous fall in the numbers employed on the land.

Complex process

The process of agricultural decline is complex, the details varying from one country to another, and even between regions, while the extent and chronology of the changes are affected by a wide variety of influences. In Europe the growth of the non-agricultural population in the 18th and 19th centuries enormously expanded the markets for both foodstuffs and domestically-produced raw materials such as wool, flax, hides, tallow, malting barley, and timber. In response, agricultural output increased, partly by improved techniques but also by extending the area of cultivation to formerly unused or lightly cultivated land. More profitable markets in big industrial cities and the growth of agricultural science involving new crops and chemical fertilisers encouraged the development of more advanced farming systems. Larger crops of grain resulted from the inclusion in field rotations of roots, legumes, and grasses, while the increased availability of fodder in such rotations made for heavier stocking of farms, more ample supplies of animal manures, and hence more fertile cropland. Experiments in selective breeding, associated with such names as Bakewell, Colling, Culley and Ellman, led to improved varieties of livestock which fattened earlier and yielded a higher proportion of valuable product per animal. Higher fertility and easier working of the soil resulted from the application of more effective means of pipe and tile drainage and the powerful effects of guano and superphosphates. Better-designed implements, such as the Rotherham plough and powered machinery which included threshers, reapers and hay tedders speeded up farm work and reduced losses from bad weather. The reorganisation of scattered holdings into more compact blocks, the more soundly constructed and enlarged farm buildings, and the gradual consolidation of small farms into larger units made for more efficiency and provided the

25

basic framework within which improved techniques could be exploited more successfully.

In the early stages of industrialisation the demand for larger output generally led to a rise in the total numbers employed on the land. Improvements in farming methods and in the layout of farms raised the productivity of both land and labour, but were usually aimed more at obtaining a higher yield per acre. The advanced farming systems of the period up to the middle 19th century were to a large extent labour-intensive rather than labour-saving, and machinery that economised drastically in labour was not widely adopted before about 1850. In England and Wales the agricultural labour force continued to expand up to the 1850s, although as a proportion of the total working population it fell gradually from probably something over two-fifths in the mid-18th century to a third in 1811, and to a little over a fifth in 1851.

On the Continent these trends appeared later. In absolute numbers the French farm labour force hardly declined at all between the mid-19th century and the First World War, and as a proportion of the total it fell only a little, from over a half to still over 40 per cent in 1914. In Germany farm workers increased between 1882 and 1907, and as a proportion of the total labour force fell only from 43 to 38 per cent. In the United States the westward movement rapidly increased the farm population as ranchers and homesteaders moved into the vast areas of free or cheap land roamed only by the Indian and the buffalo. The expansion of farming was encouraged, too, by the demands of the growing city population and overseas markets. As a result the farm work-force more than doubled between 1850 and the end of the century, and only began to fall after 1910. As a proportion of total labour, however, American farming employed only 38 per cent in 1900 as compared with 64 per cent fifty years earlier. Today Britain and America have the smallest proportion of agricultural labour in the world, well under 5 per cent in each case. The figures have been falling rapidly also in western Europe since the First World War, and particularly since 1945: France has now only some 15 per cent of its labour force on the land, and Germany less than 10 per cent, a trend which has been reinforced by EEC farm policies.

Effects of rising incomes and transport revolution

Two principal developments led to the major shifts in the patterns of agricultural production in industrialising countries. One was the marked rise of real incomes among consumers from about the middle 19th century and a consequent move away from basic foodstuffs such as bread and potatoes towards meat, poultry, bacon, eggs, cheese, fruit, and vegetables. As James Caird, the English agriculturist, remarked in 1851:

'In the manufacturing districts where wages are good, the use of butcher's meat and cheese is enormously on the increase; and even in the agricultural districts the labourer does now occasionally indulge himself in a meat dinner or seasons his dry bread with a morsel of cheese.'[1]

Consequently it paid English farmers to shift away from grain towards fattening, dairying, and market gardening, and in the second half of the 19th century they increasingly did so. Subsequent improvements in living standards reinforced the trend, which has been marked also in other countries. A long-term effect of rising real incomes and improved living standards has been that although consumers have moved gradually towards the more expensive foods, the proportion of income spent on food has tended to decline. With a smaller proportion of consumers' total expenditure on food, incomes in the agricultural sector have tended to lag behind those elsewhere, one of the major causes of government intervention on behalf of farmers over the past 50 years.

The second development was the increased international trade in foodstuffs following the transport revolution of the 19th century. Such trade indirectly encouraged the trend towards livestock and dairy products by lowering the prices of bread grains and feeding stuffs more than it did those of refrigerated meat and dairy produce and imported fruit and vegetables. More directly, the sharp falls in the prices of grain and feeding stuffs forced free-trade countries like Britain and Denmark to reform farming patterns radically. In England and Wales the acreage under wheat fell by a half in the 30 years after 1870 while the area under permanent grass rose by 4 million acres or over a third. Only pastoral districts and areas of specialised production remained reasonably profitable in the 'Great Depression' of the last quarter of the 19th century, and liquid milk, a commodity in which farmers enjoyed high natural protection, became the major product of English farming. The shifts in production tended to favour the smaller farmers, while the larger producers economised in labour. By 1911 the proportion of hired workers to

---

[1] James Caird, *English Agriculture in 1850–51*, New Edn., 1968, p. 484.

farmers was only a little over three to one. In Denmark the imports of cheap grain were transformed into an advantage rather than a threat as the farmers turned to them to supplement home supplies for feeding cows and pigs. High-quality production of butter, cheese, and bacon, largely geared to the demands of the British market, proved to be the salvation of the Danish family farmer.

Elsewhere on the Continent tariffs kept out most of the cheap food and helped to limit the run-down of the farm population. In free-trade Britain, however, the shift towards pasture and to specialised forms of production suitable for small farms combined with other factors to reduce the labour force. Pasture required less labour than arable, while the increasing use of machinery after 1850 and the attractions of higher wages, more varied employment, and better amenities in the towns caused a large outward flow of hands from farming. In the 20 years after 1851 the number of agricultural labourers fell by 22 per cent. Railways, and a better-educated and better-informed labour force—by this time some farm labourers were regular readers of newspapers—sped the outflow. As Professor Cairncross's figures show,[2] by the 1870s heavy migration from rural areas had spread from the south and east to the south-western counties and to Wales, and in the 1880s the movement from Wales rose to a peak. The decade of the 'eighties was also a period of heavy emigration which temporarily checked the drift from the country to the towns; and after the turn of the century too emigration was heavy, leading many towns to show a net loss by migration.

Between the 1850s and the 1890s the average outflow of rural population (including industrial as well as agricultural workers) was over 75,000 a year, but by the end of the century the movement was in decline, mainly because of falling fertility in country districts: the parents of potential migrants had themselves migrated. Only occasionally, however, did the rural areas show a net fall in total population: in general it was the natural increase in numbers which was removed by migration, leaving behind a stable population. In all, the balance of population swung strongly in favour of the towns: in the 70 years between 1841 and 1911 the population of the rural districts fell from 39 per cent of the country to no more than 19 per cent.[3]

---

2 A. K. Cairncross, *Home and Foreign Investment 1870–1939*, 1953, pp. 68–79.
3 Cairncross, *ibid.*

28

Slower change in Europe

In western Europe the farm workers were generally slow to feel the call of new opportunities in the cities or overseas. The small scale of much of the farming made for family units and also limited the use of machinery; tariffs softened the impact of foreign competition; and industrialisation itself started later and in some cases proceeded more slowly. The First World War, however, widened the horizons of the younger farm workers, and in some areas of France the appearance of rural radicalism led by leaders such as Renaud Jean and Henri Dorgères was a powerful agent in changing traditional attitudes.[4] After the Second World War rapid industrial recovery and government policies of farm reorganisation caused large inroads into the still massive labour force in farming.

In America urbanisation made rapid headway in the later 19th century, and the numbers of people living in towns of over 8,000 inhabitants rose eight times as fast as the farm population. The rise of the city, it has been argued by Shannon, provided 'a safety-valve for rural discontent'—the reverse of the old supposition that free western land offered a safety-valve for disgruntled city workers.[5] A revival of prosperity in farming reduced the urban drift from the 1890s, and by the 1930s depression conditions in the cities brought it to a standstill, with no net shift of population. From the Second World War, however, parallel influences to those operating in Europe—the pressures on rural incomes, mechanisation, amalgamation of holdings, government support policies which operated in favour of the large producers, inferior social conditions, and a general sense of rural isolation—combined to revive the townwards movement.

Growth of farm protection

So large a shift of agricultural populations inevitably gave rise to comment, and indeed not a little alarm. Migration of cheap rural labour threatened jobs and living standards among urban workers and added to the pressures on urban housing, educational facilities, and public health. From the 1880s there was in England a significant number of private inquiries by writers, journalists and land reformers into the causes of the rural outflow—particularly wages, housing,

---

[4] Gordon Wright, *Rural Revolution in France*, 1964, Ch. 3.
[5] F. A. Shannon, *The Farmer's Last Frontier*, New York, 1961, p. 359.

and landlessness.[6] Remedial measures, however, were slow in appearing and were only partially effective. To some extent, the continued fall in the agricultural labour force brought about its own remedy, by obliging farmers to raise wages and improve conditions. On the Continent the backward conditions of the countryside attracted little attention before the 1920s, but subsequently the adoption of farm support policies was influenced by the growth of radicalism among the farmers as well as by the depression of the 1930s. More recently some countries' farm policies have been consciously directed towards the deliberate running down of small farms judged incapable of providing their occupiers with an adequate income. In America the growth of farmers' organisations after the Civil War resulted mainly in local and minor concessions. It was not until the farm depression of the inter-war years that the Federal Government entered the arena and began to develop the policies of crop restriction and purchase and disposal of surpluses that have continued in varying forms to the present.

II. THE TRANSFORMATION OF AGRICULTURE IN ENGLAND

In England the effects of the agricultural changes on farmers and labourers were generally slow in appearing. Valid generalisations are peculiarly difficult since agriculture is really a complex of separate but inter-connected industries with varying histories. For example, the prices of farm commodities did not always move in the same direction or at the same pace, while marked regional variations arose from differences in soils, climate, situation, communications and proximity to markets. Therefore changes in prices, markets, techniques, and farm structure were often limited in scope and affected some sectors of the industry more and earlier than others. Agricultural change did mean sweeping changes in farms in some areas, although usually over a lengthy period, but left other areas untouched or even served to reinforce the existing farm structure.

Early rise of large-scale farming

Differences in local situation and specialisation were elements in the limited and gradual effects of agricultural adaptation. But there were

---

6 See my Introduction to E. C. K. Gonner, *Common Land and Inclosure* (2nd edn., 1966), pp. xxxiii–xxxviii.

others. Many features of a modern agricultural system were present in the early 18th century. Long before that time large commercial units of two or three hundred acres or more had become well established. Necessarily these were occupied by men who deployed a substantial capital in the form of stock and equipment, and who produced on a considerable scale for distant markets. By the 18th century farms of this sort were found in many common-field villages as well as in enclosed ones. The majority of even the smaller farms were not so small as to be concerned only with subsistence production. On the contrary, they sent quantities of grain and cattle to market, and frequently specialised in dairying, poultry, and market gardening.

There was, apparently, a slow, long-term decline in the numbers of small farms, a trend noticeable towards the end of the 17th century. After the middle 18th century it continued but does not seem to have been much affected by the enclosure movement of the later 18th and early 19th centuries, partly because of the practical difficulties of replacing small farmers by large on a considerable scale. Further, the market trends associated with the growth of the urban population encouraged many forms of specialised farming in which small units were more appropriate.

There are no reliable figures for the numbers of small farms until the 19th century: in the 1890s there were 129,000 holdings of between 20 and 100 acres in England and Wales, and the occupiers represented nearly 60 per cent of the total number of farmers. It is reasonable to assume that two hundred years earlier the small farmers were more numerous, but clearly the decline in their numbers was small, and very far from catastrophic. Owner-occupying farmers, however, appear to have declined more dramatically. They may have occupied as much as a third of the cultivated area at the end of the 17th century. Estimates for the end of the 18th century agree in giving them a much smaller share, probably about 15 per cent, of a considerably larger cultivated acreage. In the late 19th century owner-occupiers, including some owners who had their main occupation outside farming, occupied about 16 per cent of a further enlarged area. The figures suggest, therefore, that the main period of decline for owner-occupiers was in the 18th century, and other evidence indicates that most of their decline, and perhaps all of it, occurred before about 1750.[1]

---

[1] G. E. Mingay, *Enclosure and the Small Farmer in the Age of the Industrial Revolution*, 1968, pp. 12–25.

Decline of small farm owners

It appears, then, that owner-occupiers declined much more sharply than small farmers as a whole. The survival of small tenant-farmers was associated, first, with the generally conservative and paternalistic policies in estate management of the large landowners, and, second, with the expanding markets for dairy produce and the specialised production in which the family farmer could do well. In the staple arable and mixed farming systems the small farmer was usually less efficient and less progressive than the larger, and it was probably here that his decline was more pronounced.

In England there were relatively few peasant-type producers, small producers making a living from varied forms of cultivation on a small acreage, still very common on the Continent in the 19th century. The causes of this contrast were numerous, no doubt, and included climate and natural conditions, the rule of primogeniture, the early decline of owner-occupiers, the gradual long-term tendency towards engrossing or amalgamation of farms, the earlier industrialisation of the country and the consequent reduction in the availability of part-time industrial work in the countryside, and perhaps the early growth of large urban markets encouraging the development of production on a larger scale than the peasant-type smallholding. In consequence there soon appeared a marked social and economic gap between the farmers, the majority of whom were in a substantial way of business, and the agricultural labourers, most of whom had no access to land beyond a cottage garden or a vegetable patch.

The debate on enclosures

Indeed, the feature of the English agricultural labourers which most attracted attention in the late 19th century was their landlessness. Their lack of roots in the soil, it was held, was responsible in large part for their poverty and for the alarming scale of their migration to the towns. Historians searched various periods of the past for explanations of this phenomenon, but of many distinguished works to appear in this period the Hammonds' *Village Labourer* (1911) proved to be the most generally influential. The Hammonds directed attention to the parliamentary enclosure movement of the 18th and early 19th centuries. These enclosures, they argued, removed from the labourers the basic prop of their way of life—access to the commons and waste lands. In meeting the demands for food and raw materials of a rapidly swelling non-agricultural population the landlords used enclosure to reorganise existing farms and bring new land into cultivation, and in the process the labourer lost his rights.

'The effect on the cottager can best be described by saying that before enclosure the cottager was a labourer with land, after enclosure he was a labourer without land. The economic basis of his independence was destroyed.'[2]

The Hammonds' argument rested on two assumptions: first, that the large majority of cottagers enjoyed common rights in the 18th century; second, that such rights—to pasture animals on the common, cut turf, and gather fuel—were universally valuable. But by concentrating on 18th-century enclosure the Hammonds obscured the fact that even at the beginning of the 18th century much of the ancient common and waste land had disappeared over large areas of the country. Further, the analyses of other scholars showed that, even in the central midland plain where the bulk of the remaining common fields and common pastures had survived, there were substantial numbers of labourers with no right of access to the common. Indeed, this had been the situation long before the 18th century. There is also much evidence that in the midlands the surviving commons had become inadequate, a point neglected by the Hammonds. Quite often the farmers were obliged to 'stint' or ration the use of the common so as to prevent the surface from being eaten bare by excessive pasturing. An Act of 1773 allowed a majority of the occupiers to regulate stinted commons and proceed with schemes for drainage and other improvements, an indication of the seriousness of the problem. And the inadequacy of existing commons was itself an important reason for bringing forward a parliamentary enclosure.

In practice the right to use the common was confined to village inhabitants with holdings in the common fields or certain ancient homesteads. When the common was enclosed compensation was paid to the owners of common rights in the form of land, but of course cottagers who enjoyed access to the common merely by virtue of a tenancy received no compensation. It may be true, as the Hammonds argued, that the quantity of land given in compensation to cottagers owning common rights was too small to be of much practical use. A parcel of an acre or so, which had to be fenced at the owner's expense, was clearly not equivalent to the right to share in

---

[2] J. L. and B. Hammond, *The Village Labourer 1760–1832* (1911; Guild Books edn., 1948), I, p. 95.

using a much larger area of land. Many cottagers, probably, sold their new allotments to neighbouring farmers. In some instances, however, substantial acreage of former common were allotted by the enclosure commissioners for the poor. In others, as in parts of the eastern counties, large areas of common and waste were left open, presumably because the land was too poor to be worth the cost of bringing into cultivation, or because the lord of the manor would not consent to its enclosure. Here the cottagers, and the squatters who had built their hovels on the waste, eked out a living much as before, sometimes prospering and sometimes not.[3]

Value of common land related to wage levels

How valuable were the commons to the labourers? Contemporaries disagreed on this issue, and indeed it is very likely that much depended on local circumstances: the extent of the area available and the numbers wishing to use it; the quality of the herbage and the availability of woodland; the efficiency with which the common was stinted or regulated; and whether drainage or other necessary improvements had been carried out. It is doubtful how many cottagers, in practice, were able to keep cows on the common and to what extent this advantage was nullified by the frequent outbreaks of cattle disease rampant on open pastures. Possibly the lack of the necessary small capital prevented some cottagers from keeping cows, as it prevented them from becoming smallholders even when the common fields offered them a 'ladder of opportunity' by which they could rent a few acres and so transform their status to that of farmer.

It seems very likely that the commons were most important where the labourers' wages were low and there was a lack of alternative work outside farming. Low wages, labourers' poverty, and shortage of alternative occupations were closely associated. By the late 18th century, if not earlier, there had developed a marked differential between the average level of labourers' wages in the southern half of the country and the level prevailing in the north, a differential which persisted into the present century.

Sir James Caird, writing in 1851, found the average wages in 20 southern counties to be 8s 5d compared with 11s 6d for 12 northern counties. This differential, he noted, arose from 'the proximity of manufacturing and mining enterprise', and his line dividing the

---

[3] Arthur Young, *Annals of Agriculture*, XLII, 1804, p. 488; XLIII, 1805, p. 57; XLIV, 1806.

high-wage and low-wage areas ran westwards from the Wash through Leicestershire, skirted the southern end of Staffordshire, and turned northwards through Shropshire to end on the estuary of the Dee. Comparing northern wages with Young's figures of 1770 Caird found an increase of 66 per cent; in the southern counties the rise was under 14 per cent, while in some parts of Berkshire and Wiltshire the wages were no higher than 80 years before, and in Suffolk actually lower. Owing to the growth of industry and stronger competition for labour in the north, farm workers' reliance on the Poor Law was much less, the relief expenditure per head being nearly twice as high in the southern counties as in the north.[4] It might be supposed that migration to the north would soon have closed the wages gap. Up to the middle 19th century, however, as Redford's work showed, the movement of English labour was mainly short distance.[5] Farm labour in southern England was notoriously immobile, all but the most enterprising kept at home by a combination of apathy, ignorance, the restraints of the Settlement Law, and lack of the means of moving. The stagnant pool of labour stirred only gradually in the second half of the century and wage-rates continued to vary widely even in a few miles, reflecting supply and demand in the local labour market.

It remains true even at the present that the wages paid to agricultural labourers are strongly influenced by the rates paid in locally-available alternative occupations. In the 18th and 19th centuries the labourer's poverty was related not to enclosure (except in some limited instances) but to the nature of the local economy and its labour market. Even the farming system and the character of the countryside itself had a powerful influence. Cobbett noted that in arable areas where woodland was scarce the labourers were worse off than in wooded or pastoral districts. Passing through Thanet in 1823 he found the labourers' houses

'beggarly in the extreme. The people dirty, poor-looking; ragged but particularly *dirty*. The men and boys with dirty faces, and dirty smock-frocks, and dirty shirts; and, good God! what a difference between the wife of a labouring man here, and wife of a labouring man in the forests and woodlands of Hampshire and Sussex! Invariably have I observed that the richer the soil, and the more destitute of woods; that is to say, the more purely a corn country, the more miserable the labourers.'[6]

---

4 Caird, *op. cit.*, pp. 511–14.

5 A. Redford, *Labour Migration in England 1800–1850*, 2nd edn., Manchester, 1964.

6 W. Cobbett, *Rural Rides*, Everyman edn., 1912, I, pp. 248, 290, 304, 429; A. Young, *General View of Norfolk*, 1804, pp. 86, 89, 90, 97, 136, 152.

Neither Thanet nor the woodland areas of Hampshire and Sussex, of course, were prominent areas of enclosure in this period. The more severe rural poverty arose basically from the increase of numbers through population growth in conditions of stable or declining employment opportunities.

When Cobbett was writing the highest expenditure on poor relief was to be found in southern counties of low wages, often in areas completely unaffected by the enclosures of the past 50 years. Such areas tended to be entirely agricultural with few alternative labour outlets, and the situation was sometimes made worse by the recent decay of local industries such as clothmaking and the wealden iron industry. On balance, indeed, areas affected by enclosure were *less* likely to see extreme poverty because of the additional employment created by the introduction of more intensive farming, the cultivation of former waste land, and the work of fencing, road-building, and drainage commonly associated with enclosure.[7]

Of course it could be countered that if enclosure usually improved material conditions it may still have caused deterioration in the quality of life, turning a poor but semi-independent cottager into a subservient full-time labourer solely dependent on his wages and the goodwill of the employer. This argument again turns on the question of the availability of commons and their role in the labourer's way of life. It is significant that the worst of the rural unrest in the 15 years following Waterloo was in the southern and eastern counties rather than in the heavily-enclosed midlands. Even the recent revision by Hobsbawm and Rudé of the Hammonds' work on the 1830 riots has failed to show any clear connection between enclosure and the machine-breaking and rick-burning that erupted in Kent and ran through much of the south and East Anglia.[8]

The influence of local factors may be further adduced by reference to the distribution of allotments. The provision of vegetable allotments for renting by labourers was a popular avenue for social reform and the relief of poverty in the early 19th century. The demand for allotments was influenced, of course, by the fertility and location of the plots and the rents demanded, and often the land available was too far from the cottages and too expensive. Generally allotments were popular where low wages made the

---

[7] For the modern view, J. D. Chambers and G. E. Mingay, *The Agricultural Revolution 1750–1880*, 1966, Ch. 4.

[8] E. J. Hobsbawm and G. Rudé, *Captain Swing*, 1969, pp. 141–2, 178–80, 195. See my review in *The English Historical Review*, LXXXV, October 1970, pp. 810–14.

growing of vegetables or keeping a pig an attractive proposition. The demand therefore proved to be much stronger among the low-paid labourers of southern England than among the better-paid ones of the north. In 1833 allotment schemes were most common in Wiltshire, Bedfordshire, Northamptonshire, and Hampshire, and least common around London: only 18 per cent of northern parishes had schemes as compared with almost half of the parishes in the south and midlands.[9]

In addition to the plots made available by benevolent landowners, village parsons, and allotment societies, farmers sometimes allowed their labourers a potato patch. Farmers, however, were often opposed to the whole idea of allotments, arguing that they gave labourers too much independence and absorbed too much of the energy that should be expended in their fields. In southern England and the midlands, fortunately, many cottages had gardens attached to them and sometimes quite large pieces of ground. Cobbett, who firmly believed that nothing could add more to a labourer's well-being than a cow and a pig, stated that many cottages had 40 rods or more of ground; and 40 rods, he held, could be made quite adequate for keeping a cow. John Boys, who reported on Kent for the Board of Agriculture, stated that there were very few cottages in that county without vegetable ground, and 'a great many' had sufficient land for a cow.[10] The investigation of 1833 showed that gardens were held by all or most of the poor in 57 per cent of the parishes examined in southern England; only in 11 per cent of the parishes did few or none of the poor have them. The position was similar in the midlands, but in only a third of northern parishes did all or most of the poor have gardens.[11]

Encouragement of smallholdings

Probably the majority of labourers who wanted them possessed cottage gardens or rented allotments in the 19th century. In this sense they were not landless. But such land as they had merely served as a supplement to meagre wages and could not form the basis of an independent livelihood. Access to larger units of land,

---

[9] D. C. Barnett, 'Allotments and the Problem of Rural Poverty, 1780–1840,' in E. L. Jones and G. E. Mingay (eds.), *Land, Labour and Population in the Industrial Revolution*, 1967, pp. 171–2.

[10] W. Cobbett, *Cottage Economy*, 1912 edn., p. 81; J. Boys, *General View of Kent*, 1805, p. 33.

[11] Barnett, *loc. cit.*, p. 171.

smallholdings of between four and a score of acres, was needed if an independent peasantry was to be re-established. In the late 19th century, when the flight from the land was at its height, reformers saw smallholdings as the answer to the labourers' discontent and the over-crowding of the towns. Smallholding Acts were passed in 1892, 1907, and 1908, but little progress was made until after 1907 when the Board of Agriculture appointed special commissioners to encourage applications and stimulate the county councils into making use of their powers of compulsory purchase. The difficulty was not merely one of obtaining suitable land: experience showed that labourers often lacked the capital and specialised skills, and sometimes too the managerial ability and initiative essential for success; again not all smallholdings were on sufficiently good soils, of appropriate size, or well served by communications to adequate markets.[12] In the event it turned out that only 30 per cent of the applications for smallholdings under the Act of 1908 came from agricultural labourers, most of the remainder coming from small farmers and village tradesmen seeking additional land to rent. Co-operative credit societies, popular among continental peasants, failed to attract much support among English smallholders despite their obvious advantages to small men lacking capital. Nevertheless there was some progress: by the end of 1914 some 205,103 acres had been acquired by county councils for smallholdings and 14,045 smallholders had been settled. In 1926, following the further legislation of 1919, the acreage had risen to 438,522 occupied by 29,532 smallholders.[13] But in 1926 there were still 795,000 agricultural labourers in England and Wales.

Industrial depression, low prices, and the inadequate resources of many smallholders made their business a more risky one between the wars. The markets for their milk, vegetables, fruit, eggs, and poultry were expanding, but not sufficiently for all smallholders to make a good living, especially when the depressed prices of the main staples drove ordinary farmers into competition with them. Furthermore, a marked tendency appeared for the optimum acreage in most lines of production to rise. In the 1930s units of less than 20 acres did not give scope for profitable results, except in market gardening and poultry. Between 1913 and 1933 holdings of 1 to 5 acres fell from 21 to 18 per cent of all holdings, while those of 5 to 20 acres fell from

---

12 A. W. Ashby, *Allotments and Smallholdings in Oxfordshire*, Oxford, 1917, pp. 169–91.
13 C. S. Orwin and W. F. Darke, *Back to the Land*, 1935, pp. 23, 26, 28, 33.

28 to 26 per cent. In the 1930s even the holdings in the 20 to 50 acres category were beginning to decline in number, and after the Second World War the decline spread to all holdings under 300 acres. With this development, and with the rising costs of equipment, the possibility of smallholdings providing anything more than a very occasional ladder for the small man's advance has diminished. Even where very small acreages are still feasible, as in market gardening and poultry, market fluctuations and devastating outbreaks of disease create a high element of risk. For the majority of smallholders high risk is too often combined with an arduous and meagre livelihood. The attempt to create a landholding peasantry out of the English labourers has very largely failed, and the future appears to hold out no better prospects of success.

III. THE COURSE OF AGRICULTURAL LABOURERS' EARNINGS

The difficulty of generalising about the earnings of agricultural labourers in the 19th century arises only in part from regional differences (pp. 41–43). Wages were generally lower in southern England than in the north. Even within counties, however, there were notable differences, as between East and West Kent, for example, or 'corn' and 'cheese' Wiltshire. The problem is further complicated by the existence of three fairly distinct classes of labourers.

Labourers' class structure

Labourers residing with the farmer in the farmhouse, known as 'farm servants', were hired and paid by the year; beginning as 'farm apprentices', they sometimes lived with the same farmer all their lives. Some farm servants changed their employers annually. This practice was very common, for example, in Dorset where, as Hardy noted, on the day of the changeover one could hear from early in the morning the rumble of the carts moving the labourers' belongings. Usually the farm servants were skilled men and dairymaids whose care of the plough teams and the dairy called for constant attendance every day of the year. Farm servants were able to save from their wages; they married late and sometimes used their accumulated funds to start a small farm or other business of their own. In the

39

later 18th century male farm servants were paid between £5 and £12 a year (on average over £10), in addition to their board and lodging; dairymaids living-in received between £3 and £5 and their keep. As time went by the numbers of farm servants diminished, partly because the cost of boarding them rose with the rising prices of food, but mainly, perhaps, because farmers' habits changed and with rising social pretensions they came to want the farmhouse to themselves. Living-in survived to the early years of the 20th century, but mainly in the more remote parts of northern England.

The day labourers were generally hired, as their name indicates, by the day. Their livelihood was consequently more precarious than that of the farm servant, but in practice they were often employed regularly by one farmer, sometimes for years on end. They were not entitled to board, though sometimes they had their mid-day meal in the farmhouse. They lived in their own or rented cottages, and in some areas might have access to commons or waste land as well as their cottage garden. Their wages were low, usually about a shilling a day in the later 18th century, with higher rates at hay-time and harvest. Frequently a part of their wages was paid in kind, in the form, perhaps, of a free or low-rented cottage, a potato patch ploughed and manured by the farmer, free fuel supplied to the cottage, a daily ration of free milk and beer or cider, and the occasional sack of flour, bag of potatoes, or flitch of bacon. The value of payments in kind varied widely, and was often diminished by the wretched character of the cottage and the poor quality of the drink and provisions given by the farmer.

In his *Northern Tour* (1770) Young recorded the wages paid to male labourers at 82 places between Hertfordshire and Northumberland. The weekly average throughout the year ranged from as low as 4s 11d to as high as 9s 9d. The figures did not vary much with distance from London: it was only in areas over 300 miles from the capital that the average figure fell from about 7s to 5s 8d. Food, however, was much cheaper in the north, and Young's figures did not take account of additional payments for work performed at piece-rates or for supplements in kind. Young appreciated that total family earnings were more meaningful than the wages of the man alone. The full or part-time earnings of the wife and older children made a considerable difference to family incomes, and in some areas the farmers would not hire a man unless his wife and grown children were prepared to work on the farm also. In some calculations based on part-time work by the wife and the earnings of five children—a too favourable basis, no doubt—Young found total family cash earnings to average about £1 a week throughout the year.[1]

We know less about the earnings of the third class of labourers, men with specialist skills such as hedgers, thatchers, drainers, and mole-catchers, called in by the farmers when required. They worked on piece-rates and travelled over a wide area, and with their better earnings and more independence they formed a kind of 'labour aristocracy' in the rural community. Sometimes they did a little buying and selling on their own, and they helped farmers out with routine farm work when their regular men were sick. Quite different were the other irregularly employed labourers, the largely unskilled hands who turned out to help at harvest time or for fruit- and hop-picking. By the 19th century, as local resources became inadequate, much of this labour was supplied by itinerant harvest gangs of Irish, Scots or Welsh. In arable areas, particularly in areas newly reclaimed from waste, potato growing and weed control demanded large numbers of unskilled hands throughout most of the year. Such labour was provided by gangs, often consisting of women and children, employed under gang-masters at very low rates and chiefly used for labour-intensive tasks such as planting and lifting potatoes, spreading manure, weeding, and collecting large stones and couch-grass roots on freshly-ploughed land. The conditions of employment in these gangs, especially the arduous work expected of young children, led eventually to control under the Gangs Act of 1868, and the use of child labour in farming generally was subsequently restricted by compulsory education.

Varying pressures on labourers' wages

In the 19th century the wages of day labourers were affected by a number of contrasting influences. The growth of towns and the spread of industrial occupations into the villages of the northern midlands and the north raised farm wages through competition for labour. In Nottinghamshire, for example, the influence of coal-mining and framework knitting was to encourage weekly farm wages to rise from 9s in 1795 to 12s 6d by 1833. Living standards improved and labourers were able to save money and join friendly societies.[2]

However, wages remained low in areas which remained essentially

---

[1] A. Young, *Northern Tour*, 1770, IV, pp. 441–6, 450–4.
[2] J. D. Marshall, 'Nottinghamshire Labourers in the Early Nineteenth Century,' *Trans. Thoroton Soc.*, LXIV, 1960, pp. 60–4.

agricultural, particularly as old industrial by-employments were driven out by factory competition and the supply of labour was augmented by population growth. Supplementing wages from the poor rates under the Speenhamland 'system' of 1795–6 and the Settlement Laws reinforced the barriers of distance and ignorance to make outward migration insufficient to relieve the pressure of numbers.

It has been argued by Dr Collins that in the 19th century there were significant improvements in the efficiency of hand tools used for harvesting, and this development may have tended to reduce the effect of migration on wage-rates in the corn-producing areas. Further, recent discussions by economic historians have pointed to differences in labour productivity as a cause of regional wage differences, but whether the lower levels of productivity in low-wage areas were due to an unfavourable ratio of capital to labour or to a vicious circle of low wages giving rise to poor nutrition and hence low labour efficiency is a matter of dispute.[3] In the areas of extreme low wages, as in southern Wiltshire, the winter rate was not generally much above 7s a week in the long period between 1817 and 1844, hardly any improvement on the rate in the 1790s.[4] In some low-wage areas real wages probably fell seriously during the high food prices of the war years after 1793. With falling food prices after 1813 real wages recovered but apparently did not advance much beyond the pre-war level until the 1820s.

The unrest which revealed itself in rick-burning and attacks on machinery in the eastern and southern counties in the early 19th century was closely associated with low wages and poverty, under-employment, and concern over the spread of the threshing machine with its threat to winter work. The labourer felt alienated and isolated by his economic weakness and social inferiority, his humiliating dependence on the poor rates, and his subjection to the harsh restrictions of the Game Laws.

Down to 1850 the margin between the wages in agricultural and industrialised areas tended to widen, the lowest averaging less than two-thirds of the highest. From the middle of the century the gap

---

[3] E. J. T. Collins, 'Harvest Technology and Labour Supply in Britain, 1790–1870', *Econ. Hist. Rev.*, 2nd ser., XXII, 3 (1969), pp. 453–73; E. H. Hunt, 'Labour Productivity in English Agriculture, 1850–1914', *ibid.*, 2nd ser. XX, 2 (1967), pp. 280–92; Paul A. David, 'Labour Productivity in English Agriculture, 1850–1914: Some Quantitative Evidence on Regional Differences', *ibid.*, 2nd ser., XXXIII, 3 (1970), pp. 504–14.

[4] R. Molland, *Victoria County History Wiltshire*, IV (ed. E. Crittall), 1959, pp. 80–1.

tended to close somewhat as intensified migration, the employment created by railways and land drainage works, the growth of manufacturing in country towns, and, not least, the general expansion of the economy and improved prosperity of the mid-Victorian boom, combined to reduce the agricultural surplus. The exception to this trend was found in East Anglia: here wages rose only marginally after 1850, and indeed fell a little in the 1890s.

Table I refers to cash wages.[5] The value of additional payments in kind varied from area to area and probably declined relatively to cash earnings as time went by. The analysis made by Wilson-Fox in his official inquiries at the end of the century showed that payments in kind were higher in the low-wage areas, where they were estimated at about 3s per week, as compared with 2s 3d elsewhere, but the difference was not enough to even up the wages between districts. Between 1879–81 and 1892–3 depression conditions caused a fall of cash wages in some areas, but in northern areas the trend was steadily upwards from mid-century. In real terms, the 16 per cent increase in average cash wages obtained by farmworkers in the last 30 years of the century represented a much larger improvement. In this period falling prices of food, drink, and tobacco resulted in an advance of some 25 or 30 per cent in purchasing power. As this was a period of heavily depressed rents and farm profits over much of the country, it appears that the labourers' position relatively to the landlords' and farmers' was significantly improved.[6] Between 1900 and 1913 farm wages lagged behind the rise in food prices, but wages came back into line with the sharp increase of 1913–14, so restoring the substantial gain in real incomes that had been achieved in the later 19th century.[7]

From rioting to education . . .

The farm unrest of the early 19th century was the result of a variety of forces, not least, perhaps, the revolutionary atmosphere of the period and the beginnings of political consciousness among the labourers. After the 'last labourers' revolt' of 1830 unrest died down as migration reduced local pressure on employment and wages eventually rose. Rioting was the traditional form of protest against

[5] C. S. Orwin and B. I. Felton, 'A Century of Wages and Earnings in Agriculture', *Journal of the Royal Agricultural Society of England*, 92 (1931), pp. 3, 17.

[6] *Ibid.*, p. 16; J. H. Clapham, *Economic History of Modern Britain*, Vol. II, Cambridge, 1932, pp. 285, 296.

[7] Clapham, *op. cit.*, Vol. III, 1938, pp. 98–100.

TABLE I. WEEKLY CASH WAGES OF ENGLISH AGRICULTURAL LABOURERS, 1824–1907

	1 Cumberland Westmorland Northumberland Durham Yorks. Lancs. Cheshire		2 Derbys. Notts. Lincs. Rutland Leics.		3 Warwicks. Worcs. Staffs. Shrops. Herefords. Gloucs.		4 Somerset Cornwall Devon Dorset Wilts.		5 Cambs. Beds. Hunts. Northants. Herts. Bucks. Oxfords.		6 Hants. Sussex Kent Surrey Middx. Berks.		7 Essex Suffolk Norfolk		Average	
	s.	d.	s.	d.	s.	d.	s.	d.	s.	d.	s.	d.	s.	d.	s.	d.
1824	11	6	10	3	8	10	7	8	8	4	10	1	8	11	9	6
1833	11	1	12	3	9	8	8	9	10	4	11	10	10	4	10	8
1837	12	2	11	6	9	7	8	1	9	3	10	8	10	4	10	3
1850–51	12	2	10	1	8	4	7	9	8	8	9	1	7	10	9	7
1860–61	12	3	12	6	10	4	9	7	10	7	11	10	11	7	11	7
1867–71	15	1	13	4	11	4	10	6	11	7	11	8	11	0	12	5
1879–81	16	2	14	5	13	4	12	4	13	0	13	10	12	6	13	9
1892–93	16	5	15	2	12	6	11	8	12	4	12	10	11	10	13	4
1898	16	10	16	2	13	10	12	7	13	0	14	10	11	11	14	5
1907	17	3	16	3	14	8	13	8	13	11	15	9	12	10	14	11

Source: Orwin & Felton, *op. cit.*

grievances, but after 1830 violence gave way to self-help as the labourers turned towards friendly societies and unions.

For many years progress was slow and uncertain: the first flush of enthusiasm for unionism was disastrously blighted by the infamous episode of the Tolpuddle martyrs; but in time the gradual growth of friendly society membership and of savings banks gave evidence of improvement in the labourers' situation. Village schools provided by the churches, landowners and charities made inroads into illiteracy and gave young minds an opportunity of following the progress of the wider world. By the 1860s many more labourers were found to be reading newspapers and interesting themselves in politics. Undeniably, enlightenment added to the rural outflow but among those who stayed behind it encouraged support of unionism and the development of a more independent attitude towards the employers.

. . . and trade unionism

Just as the earlier unrest had been largely confined to the areas of low wages in East Anglia and the southern counties, so it was in these same areas that the agricultural unions of the 1860s made the greatest headway. Both the old rioting and the new unionism were connected with large-scale arable farming, principally because of the larger number of day-labourers employed, the limited opportunities for additional family earnings and for self-advancement, and the low wages. Local circumstances were always influential; the first tender growth of organisation might be influenced, for example, by the development of a village school, a friendly society or reading room, a lack of allotments, a dispute between farmers and land-owners and, especially, by a radical craftsman, shopkeeper or teacher of exceptional intelligence and initiative. Many of the leaders of village unions were men of some degree of independence, and not a few, like Joseph Arch, were self-educated Methodist lay-preachers.[8] Disunity and local dissensions, 'lock-outs' and 'blacklegs', labour economies resorted to by depressed farmers—all led inevitably to the collapse of agricultural unions in the 1870s. The hopeful revival of the late 1880s again came to grief in the bad years of 1893 and 1894.

The early years of the 20th century saw detailed discussion of the conditions of agricultural labour, much influenced by contemporary concern with townward migration and revelations of urban poverty.

---

[8] J. P. D. Dunbabin, 'The "Revolt of the Field": the Agricultural Labourers' Movement in the 1870's,' *Past and Present*, No. 26, November 1963.

Among the many tributaries which flowed into this stream we may detect the influence of the investigations into the poor of London and York carried out by Charles Booth and Seebohm Rowntree, the consequent fear that urban poverty and overcrowding might be intensified by heavier influxes of labour from the countryside, the accumulating evidence of general poor health and physique among town dwellers, and the need to maintain a stable population of healthy farm workers in the interests of agricultural production and the security of the nation. All aspects of the farmworker's life, his social position and prospects as well as material standards, came under scrutiny.

'Cash and kind' earnings controversy

Considerable controversy centred round the interpretation of the Board of Trade's 1907 figures of farm earnings and payments in kind, the allotments and smallholdings question, and the problems of rural housing and cottage rents. The pattern of wages was indeed far more complicated than the bare statistics suggested. While it was possible to identify low-wage and high-wage counties, under the influence of the range of alternative occupations and the nature of the farming wages still varied widely within counties. Further, 'ordinary labourers' and farm servants together formed only about three-fifths of the total work-force: there were half as many again as the labourers of 'men in charge of animals' (at slightly higher wages but often longer hours), as well as substantial numbers of farm bailiffs, foremen, and woodmen. Probably the 'ordinary labourers' were rather more numerous in the low-wage areas since it was estimated that over 60 per cent of English labourers earned less than 18s a week in 1907, when average earnings (including payments in kind) were 17s 6d.[9]

Problems arose also over the value to be assigned to payments in kind. It was contended by the Land Agents' Society, for example, that the average cash value of £4 a year allowed for a free cottage and garden by the Board of Trade did not do justice to the true market rent. The Land Agents argued, too, that contrary to some assertions, many labourers preferred to receive part of their wages in kind as a protection against rising prices of food and fuel. Certainly the usual working hours were long in summer—between 9½ and 10½ after deducting 1½ hours for meals—but in winter they were as little

---

[9] *The Land: the Report of the Land Enquiry Committee*, 4th edn., 1913, p. 7.

as 8 to 8½ hours. It was not clear to what extent earnings were lost through wet or frosty weather. On the one hand, it was argued that in low-wage areas winter earnings could fall as low as 8s, while it was counter-argued that wet days were practically days off with pay since the indoor work the labourers were put to was often of a nominal character.[10]

Shortage of rural housing

Reformers like F. G. Heath, William Savage, and the members of the unofficial Liberal Land Enquiry Committee, attacked rural housing as not merely defective in quality but also deficient in quantity.[11] Further, the lowness of the men's wages made it unlikely that new cottages could be built for rents that the labourers could pay. The shortage of cottages, it was contended, by the Land Enquiry Committee, was a factor not only in overcrowding but also in immorality, long tramps to work, and the flight of labour from farming.[12] In reply the Land Agents' Society urged that such generalisations were unsound since in practice conditions varied so widely. The worst housing, it was true, exhibited such defects as lack of damp-courses, insufficient guttering, solid nine-inch walls in exposed places, internal damp, and bad water supplies. Such houses were generally built by speculators and were owned by small investors who could not keep up the property. On landed estates the cottages had been built mainly by the landowners and were well maintained; they were usually let at below-market rents to attract labour and tenants to the estate. The Duke of Manchester, for example, built cottages on his estate at Grafham, Huntingdonshire, with three good bedrooms and a living room 14 ft. by 12 ft.; and at North Stoke in Sussex, Lord Leconfield, in 1893, supplied a newly-built house with four bedrooms, a living room 12 ft. by 12 ft., kitchen, and large garden for 1s 6d a week. Many other examples could be cited, and an inquiry by the Land Agents' Society in 1914 showed that on landed estates nearly three-quarters of the cottages had gardens of over an eighth of an acre.

In many other areas, however, there were large numbers of one-

---

[10] *Ibid.*, pp. 20–22; Land Agents' Society, *Facts about Land: a reply to 'The Land'*, *the Report of the Unofficial Land Enquiry Committee*, 1916, pp. 25–9; B. Seebohm Rowntree and May Kendall, *How the Labourer Lives: a Study of the Rural Labour Problem*, 1913, p. 33.

[11] F. G. Heath, *British Rural Life and Labour*, 1911; W. G. Savage, *Rural Housing*, 1915; *The Land, op. cit.*   [12] *The Land, op. cit.*, pp. 85–105, 118–19.

bedroom cottages. In the Norfolk Union of Swaffham, for instance, nearly a quarter of the 2,096 cottages in 1867 had only one bedroom, and only 303 had the ideal of three bedrooms. There were cases of father, mother and seven children all sleeping in a single room, and of the mother producing an eighth child in the night; there were others where the children were put to bed in the loft while the mother slept on the brick floor of the 'downstairs' until the bottom board of the bed fell to pieces from the damp. Obviously there was a very wide variety of conditions, from roomy, well-built and cheap houses to relatively expensive, insanitary hovels in the last stages of dilapidation. In general, however, it could be hazarded that at the end of the 19th century the majority of rural cottages possessed four rooms, while many had rooms no smaller or fewer than houses of recent construction in the towns. By later standards the absence of indoor plumbing and of a pure water supply frequently remained the most serious deficiencies.[13]

The generally admitted shortage of cottages was due to a variety of factors: the setting of stringent bye-laws, the rising cost of building and repairs at a time when landlords were experiencing a fall in rents and, not least, the occupation of cottages by other kinds of workers, railway men, the staffs of local authorities, occupiers of county council allotments, and miners and other industrial workers seeking cheap accommodation. About a third of the cottages on landed estates were let direct to the labourers, but the rest were let to the farmers and hence were 'tied' cottages—many necessarily so since they were occupied by men in charge of animals who had to live near the farm. For ordinary labourers the increased dependence on the farmer which the tied cottage implied was offset by the security of employment and nearness to work (although the children might have further to go to school); and, so far from objecting, many labourers welcomed the offer of a job which carried a cheap or free house with it.[14] On the other hand, the tied cottage had the effect of increasing the labourer's dependence on the goodwill of the farmer and made him reluctant to ask for repairs and improvements.

'Poverty line' living standards?

Low agricultural wages meant low standards of living. When Seebohm Rowntree applied his concept of a 'poverty line' to farm

---

13 G. E. Fussell, *The English Rural Labourer*, 1949, pp. 109–12, 117.
14 *Facts about Land, op. cit.*, pp. 46–7, 97–8, 115–18, 144.

labourers for 1913 he found that the weekly minimum expenditure necessary to maintain 'physical efficiency' for a family of two adults and three children worked out at 20s 6d a week.

TABLE II. ESTIMATED MINIMUM WEEKLY EXPENDITURE REQUIRED FOR FARM LABOURERS AND FAMILY BASED ON ROWNTREE'S 'POVERTY LINE', 1913

	s	d
Food	13	9
Fuel	1	4
Rent	2	0
Clothing*	2	3
Insurance	0	4
Sundries	0	10
	20	6

* 6d per week for each adult and 5d per week for each child.

This expenditure allowed nothing for tobacco, beer, newspapers, amusements, railway fares, emergencies, or luxuries of any kind, and the food requirements were based on a standard of nutriment considered appropriate for 'moderate' work only and was more austere than that provided in the workhouses. Rowntree also noted that his figures did not allow for the higher cost of goods in village shops than in towns, nor for errors or carelessness in the wife's management of the home. He emphasised that his standard was concerned solely with 'physical efficiency' and could not be regarded as a minimum living wage which would have to include additional sums for emergencies and some few amenities of life. Yet, he stated, average earnings including payments in kind, in every county in England and Wales, with five exceptions (Northumberland, Durham, Westmorland, Lancashire and Derbyshire), fell below his poverty line.[15]

There were, however, some qualifications to be made: the husband's additional earnings at piece-work and the subsidiary earnings by other members of the household raised the total of family earnings; the number in the family was often less than five; and, in return for some additional hours of labour, many farm workers raised a substantial part of their food requirements on their

---

15 Rowntree and Kendall, *op. cit.*, pp. 28–33.

gardens or allotments. Moreover, even at this period, there were still numbers of farm servants living in, whose conditions of board and lodging might be superior to those of the majority of labourers living in cottages. It appears, too, that Rowntree exaggerated the problem by comparing the prices of 1913 with the earnings of 1907, neglecting the considerable rise in earnings which had occurred in the interim. Indeed, if the figures collected by the Central Land Association for 1912–13 were typical, the average earnings of ordinary labourers had risen from 17s 6d in 1907 to 19s 10d by 1912–13; and at the later date the average earnings exceeded Rowntree's poverty line of 20s 6d in not five but 21 English counties.[16]

Even when all the qualifications are made it remains true that owing to low wages a large number of agricultural labourers were living in poverty. This undeniable conclusion was the natural extension of Rowntree's work on urban conditions which had revealed the low wages of unskilled workers rather than unemployment as the main cause of 'primary' poverty among the inhabitants of York. Since even the Central Land Association's figures showed that the ordinary labourers of 17 English counties had average earnings of less than 20s 6d in 1912–13, it seems probable that rural poverty was even more extensive than in the towns. However, as the wide gap between farm and non-farm earnings was a long-recognised feature of the labour market, persisting despite heavy migration from the countryside, this finding was not perhaps very remarkable. What was remarkable was that despite low wages, the prevalence of lower standards of living, a meagre diet, and often bad housing, the countryman enjoyed a markedly better state of health than did the townsman. In 1911 the death rate per thousand in rural districts was 11·4 compared with 16·6 in county boroughs and 14·0 in urban districts, and the rural districts had the advantage also in infant mortality and in major causes of death except influenza. The inhabitants of rural districts included many people besides agricultural labourers, but the evidence indicates that the farm workers' health and physique were superior even to those of many other better-off inhabitants, even running the farmers themselves very close. It was perhaps significant, too, that two-thirds of the London police force was recruited from farm workers, and indeed they had always supplied a large proportion of the manpower in occupations where good health and physique were essential requisites.[17]

---

16 *Facts about Land*, *op. cit.*, pp. 14–15.　　　17 *Ibid.*, pp. 35–45.

The Boer War recruiting figures, showing nearly half of army volunteers in industrial towns to be undersized or suffering from physical defects or active disease, shocked the nation. For the future safety of the country it was obviously essential that health conditions in towns should be improved and measures taken to preserve the reservoir of our fit manhood on the land. Thus followed the official inquiry into 'physical deterioration', steps to improve the health of schoolchildren, and renewed attempts to stabilise agricultural employment. Rowntree himself went on to produce in 1914 a programme for government action on the land, advising minimum wages for farm labourers, regulation of farm rents and encouragement of allotments and smallholdings, statutory reduction of working hours, and establishment of farm institutes and farm schools.[18]

Rising productivity and unionism

The amelioration of the labourer's lot proved to lie with the statutory regulation of wages first introduced during the First World War; the further reduction in the numbers working on the land and the wider range of skills required as farm machinery increasingly replaced horse power and human muscle; the eventual adoption of policies of agricultural protection and subsidies; and, not least perhaps, the revival of agricultural unionism.

Unionism on permanent foundations finally developed in the environment of rising prices and wage-lag before 1914. The 7,000 members of 1911 more than quadrupled in the following three years, although of course the new growth still left the vast majority of labourers unorganised. The wartime expansion dwindled away again with the abolition of wage regulation in 1921. Then, from the low point reached about 1926, more stable growth was resumed, particularly in the old areas of activity in East Anglia and the south. By 1939 about 35,000 members were enrolled in the National Union of Agricultural Workers (NUAW) and some 15,000 in the agricultural section of the Transport and General Workers' Union. The total of some 50,000 still represented only a little over 8 per cent of full-time agricultural workers in Great Britain.

The difficulties of fostering agricultural unionism are fairly self-evident. Despite the modest level of contributions low farm wages were always an obstacle, while the close personal relationship with the employer made recruitment difficult: tied cottages considerably

---

[18] B. Seebohm Rowntree, *The Labourer and the Land*, 1914.

increased the risks in displeasing the farmer. Ignorance, too, remained an important influence. Even in the 1930s many labourers knew nothing of wages machinery, nor that they had union representation. Poor education and the isolated nature of the employment encouraged indifference and apathy. Among existing members there was a high turnover, reflecting the continuing flow from the land. Scattered membership led to reliance on local enthusiasm and made keeping in touch both costly and arduous. The war years, however, brought a big increase in union membership: in 1947 the NUAAW could boast of over 162,000 members, well over three times the 1938 figure.

Meanwhile war-time inflation, labour scarcity, and wage regulation raised the average minimum wage of male labourers in England and Wales from the 16s 9d of 1914 to 46s 10½d by 1921. The gain in real terms was of course much less than the improvement in money income, the Ministry of Labour Retail Prices Index showing a rise from 100 to 226 in the same period. When, after the repeal of wage regulation, the level settled down at some 31s 8d a week in 1926–30, the real advance over 1914 proved to be of the order of 30 per cent. By 1939 the average minimum wage was 34s 8d, representing a considerable further improvement in real terms over 1914. Hours, too, had fallen—from an average of 58 a week in 1914 to a little over 50. There were still wide differences between regions but the inter-war years saw an interesting new development. Contrary to the persistent pattern of a high-wage north and low-wage south established in the 19th century, the effects of wage regulation and of heavy industrial unemployment between the wars were to make the old highly-agricultural low-wage areas much better placed than before. In 1937, for example, the former low-wage counties of Norfolk, Suffolk, Dorset and Wiltshire had minimum rates of 32s 6d or more, while the old high-wage counties of Cumberland, Westmorland and Northumberland were only at the same level, Durham was slightly lower, and southern Lancashire, Staffordshire and Yorkshire only 2s or 3s higher.

In comparison with industrial earnings and hours, however, farm labour was still badly off. At the end of 1937 railway porters, one-horse carters employed in road transport, builders' labourers, and labourers working for local authorities all earned at least 9s a week more than the average farm worker, and some of them earned as much as 20s more. The farm worker's hours, averaging about 50 for the minimum wage, were also substantially higher than in many other occupations. It is not surprising, therefore, that despite the high levels of unemployment in industry, the flow from the land continued. The farm labourers' other grievances concerned social amenities, housing, and the lack of an annual holiday. Few, apparently, felt deprived by the limited opportunities for rising to the status of farmer or showed much enthusiasm for an allotment or smallholding. Social life was dull for village labourers: most activity centred round the church, the sports clubs, and the Women's Institute, and tended to be dominated by the farmers and other middle-class residents; the labourers rarely participated.

The tied cottage added to many labourers' feelings of inferiority and insecurity. They were afraid to ask for a rise or even for repairs to be made for fear of dismissal; and through similar, if exaggerated, fears some men felt it unwise to take part in elections or union work. Many cottages were not only small and antiquated, still lacking piped water and indoor sanitation, but suffered also from damp and disrepair. In 1937 some 200,000 labourers lived in tied cottages, 50,000 in more modern council houses, and 250,000 in ordinary private houses. Rents ranged from as little as 2s to as high as 10s, although in 1937 it was argued that the maximum a farm labourer could be expected to pay was 4s to 5s inclusive of rates.

Health, physique and the appeal of the land

The health and physique of farm workers, however, continued to be superior to those of town people—the consequence, no doubt, of plenty of exercise in the open air and a simple diet with plenty of fresh vegetables and milk. In 1930–32 male agricultural labourers had lower mortality rates than those of the majority of other labourers, and even than those of the farmers. They were inferior, indeed, only to building workers, draughtsmen, bank and insurance officials, workers in chemical processes, teachers, Anglican clergymen, and civil servants. On the other hand, there was evidence of under-nourishment and of the prevalence of rheumatism and pleurisy brought on by working in the wet and cold and by living in damp and draughty cottages.[19]

But by no means all farm workers wanted to leave for the towns. Many felt a love for the countryside and showed a pride in their distinctive work and its skills. Indeed, regardless of the low wages and longer hours, some urban workers took up farm work, attracted

---

[19] W. H. Pedley, *Labour on the Land*, 1942, pp. 73, 101–9.

by the prospect of living in the country and the opportunity of occupying a reasonably good house at a low rent.

Not all rural living was bad. Many farm workers lived in estate cottages, mainly built in the 19th century, but well built; and on some estates care had been taken to keep the houses in good repair and to provide modern amenities such as electricity, bathrooms, and indoor sanitation. That such houses belonged to the estate caused little concern because of low rents and the expectation that the worker could keep the house when he retired.[20]

Improvement in living standards since 1939

The years since 1939 have seen a steady improvement in farm workers' conditions under the influence of revived wage regulation and increased labour shortages. The average minimum wage in England and Wales rose from 39s 5½d in 1939–40 to 72s 2d in 1945–6. Twenty years later it had reached 207s 11¼d. Over the whole period basic hours fell from 50·2 to 44·3, while in real terms the purchasing power of the minimum wage increased by 67 per cent between 1945–6 and 1965–6. Average earnings, as distinct from minimum wages, showed even more improvement, rising from 88s 9d in 1945–6 to 285s 6d in 1965–6, an increase in real terms of over 100 per cent.

The reasons for this improvement are to be found in the progressive decline in the total numbers employed and the rise in labour productivity achieved by a smaller, more heavily mechanised, workforce. Between 1939 and 1966 the number of full-time agricultural workers in England and Wales fell from 511,000 to 295,000, resulting in a heavier relative dependence on part-time and seasonal workers than in the past. The numbers of such workers rose substantially during the Second World War and the post-war years, and the total in 1966, 135,000, was still 40 per cent higher than in 1939.

IV. CONCLUSION

In 1970 average earnings in agriculture were £18·61 for average weekly hours of 48·3. When compared with average earnings in industry of £28·05 for 45·7 hours, it is clear that, even allowing for cheap or free housing, the ancient gap between farm and industrial

---

[20] M. A. Havinden, *Estate Villages*, 1966, pp. 173–86.

54

earnings remains a prominent feature of the labour market, and this despite the scarcity of farm workers and the increased complexity and heavy physical demands of farm work. Indeed, it is remarkable that the traditional gap should still be so wide. The farm worker of today, after all, is a very different man from the ill-educated, slow-witted Hodge of the 19th century: of necessity, the present-day farm worker is a fully-fledged member of the machine society, a master of modern as well as of ancient skills. As a skilled man the continuing gap between his earnings and those of the rank and file of industrial workers is explicable only by reference to his preference for the individual and varied nature of farm work, his inability to apply the full sanctions of industrial action against some 76,000 separate employers, and the partial compensation he enjoys of cheap accommodation in a period of rising costs and scarcity in the housing market.

The farm worker remains essentially an employee: only rarely does he contemplate independent means of livelihood. The small-holdings movement, as was noted, did not make much headway among the labourers, and there are few other lines of business open to the farm worker of little capital. With the development of world markets and the enlarged scale of commercial farming, the difficulties of climbing up the farming ladder are probably more insurmountable now than they ever have been. Besides, the small marginal agricultural producer is no longer the darling of governments. On the contrary, he is under increasing pressure to acknowledge his inability to cope with modern technology and current market forces and to withdraw from production; and even on the Continent governments both within and outside the European Economic Community are forcing the peasant producer to face the realities of farming in an industrial environment.

In England the rise of commercial farming, decline of the peasantry, and appearance of a large force of landless labour long preceded the rise of modern industry. The growth of urban markets and of new means of transport in the 18th and 19th centuries only went to reinforce a long-established trend towards production for the market. Industrialisation modified and re-shaped the pattern and structure of farming but did not result in the dramatic conversion of a peasant agriculture to a commercial basis—that change had been in train since the Middle Ages. For the small cultivators and farm labourers, indeed, the growth of industry in the 19th century meant an expansion of the non-agricultural occupations that provided an alternative and more attractive means of obtaining a livelihood. The increased availability of alternative employment, however, was only partially successful in relieving the pressure of swelling numbers on the rural labour force, as the development of the high-wage and low-wage areas bears witness. Migration did not proceed so far as to make the comparative rewards of agricultural and non-agricultural employment equivalent everywhere. Even today farm wages are lower where alternative employment is less easily available.

Nevertheless, the outflow from farming has been a continuing if erratic process. Except for short periods of unusually high unemployment, the towns have maintained their superior attractions. The low wages in the eastern and southern counties during the 19th century are explicable primarily in terms of the relative immobility of the labourers—their ignorance, apathy, and lack of the means for moving—rather than the associated factors of the prevalence of arable farming and the low productivity of the labour force. For the immobile low-paid who remained on the land there was indeed a period in the first half of the century when conditions deteriorated, both in relation to pre-war days and, during the 1820s at least, to improving standards of employment generally. This deterioration was experienced not so much in material terms as in status, self-respect, and social relationships. Persistent under-employment, the harshness of the Poor Laws and the Game Laws, and the hostility or indifference of too many of the ruling class of landlords, farmers, clergymen, and magistrates, created a resentment which futilely expended itself in arson and machine-breaking. When the unrest died away acute poverty remained. There were labourers who subsisted on a diet of bread and cheese, a little bacon, milk stiffened with flour, and 'frog-water' of burnt crust tea, and there were young farm servants who on entering into service refused the butcher's meat they had never tasted. In the Dorset of 1867 the women worked in the fields and at the threshing machines for 6d or 8d a day, and their sons went to work from the age of six in order to supplement the husband's wage of 8s a week (or 9s without a cottage). Whole rows of cottages had only one privy between them, the fuel in the grates consisted only of gorse, and the farmers sometimes required Sunday work for nothing.[1]

By the end of the 19th century conditions in Dorset had improved,

---

[1] Fussell, *op. cit.*, p. 133; R. C. Employment of Children, Young Persons and Women in Agriculture, *P.P.*, 1868–9, XIII, pp. 4–6.

as Thomas Hardy noted. Now there were empty cottages and farmers seeking men, rather than the reverse. Money earnings had improved and real earnings even more: one might see cottages with stair-carpet, and pianos and bicycles, and dancing lessons for the children, and the women did not go out to work so much. The men belonged to the Foresters and Oddfellows, and joined coal and clothing clubs. Old men could recall the days when they could not afford wheaten flour and they ate only barley cakes, but wages were now up to 10 to 12s, together with a cottage, potato ground, and sometimes fuel, while the carters and shepherds earned a shilling more. In one sample family the total earnings of 17s 6d (man 11s, boy aged fourteen 5s, and boy aged eleven 1s 6d) kept two adults and five children; their expenditure included 6s 3d for bread, 1s 8d for bacon, 1s for cheese, 1s 3d for butter, 1s 9d for tea and sugar, $5\frac{1}{2}$d for flour, 9d for club subscriptions, 3d for tobacco, and 9d for lights and sundries—a total of 14s $1\frac{1}{2}$d.[2]

Labourers on estate farms were often better paid and better housed and could usually expect some maintenance in their old age; but they were more under the thumb of the farmer and landowner—the materially worse-off labourers in 'independent' villages scoffed at them for being afraid 'to blow their nose without permission'. Labourers generally associated themselves deeply with the land and resented under-farming and neglect: 'What was the land sent for, if it wasn't for the poor to live off?' But even so the land was less sought after as a livelihood. Vicars and village schoolmasters secured other jobs for promising lads, and the girls went off to service in the towns to escape the poverty and monotony of the old ways of life.[3]

Conditions continued to improve as migration reached areas formerly immune and as reformers campaigned for a better deal that would keep the labourer on the land. The introduction in 1917 of wage regulation and its return from 1924 marked an important turning point for the old low-wage era, although in more recent years it has perhaps rather limited than encouraged the general rise in farm wages. Eventually, revived prosperity in farming with the new protectionist policies of the 1930s and after made possible major advances in labour productivity and wages. Industrialisation certainly

[2] H. Rider Haggard, *Rural England* (new edn., 1906), p. 261; R.C. on Labour, *P.P.*, 1893–4, XXXV, pp. 31–2; *P.P.*, 1895, XVII, p. 29.
[3] Rowntree and Kendall, *op. cit.*, pp. 319–27.

influenced the character of agriculture and eventually transformed the character of farm work through its long-term influences on migration, wages and working conditions, and the nature and lightening of labour. Perhaps something of value in the old way of life has been lost—the more closely-linked community, the authoritarian but humane paternalism of the squire, the old country lore and traditions—but on balance industrialisation has been a force making for improvement. As Ashton pointed out over twenty years ago, one need only consider for a moment the conditions of the rural population in 19th-century Ireland or in the over-populated countrysides of under-developed countries today to appreciate its significance.[4] That the present farm worker in England still finds a large gap between his and other workers' wages suggests only that he values his healthy open-air life and cheap housing, and the process of improvement through industrialisation still has some distance to go.

SUGGESTIONS FOR READING

(arranged in order of period covered)

Chambers, J. D., and Mingay, G. E., *The Agricultural Revolution, 1750–1880* (1966).
> The most up-to-date and comprehensive survey of the agrarian changes of the classical period of the 'agricultural revolution', incorporating the findings of recent research.

Mingay, G. E., *Enclosure and the Small Farmer in the Age of the Industrial Revolution* (1968).
> This brief pamphlet presents the findings of modern investigations and argues that the small farmer declined in the period before the height of the enclosure movement in the later 18th century.

Fussell, G. E., *The English Rural Labourer* (1949).
> The only modern general discussion, amply illustrated from secondary sources but lacking in systematic analysis.

Hobsbawm, E. J., and Rudé, G., *Captain Swing* (1969).
> The first up-to-date and comprehensive treatment of the farm labourers' riots of 1830 since the Hammonds, leaning heavily

---

4 T. S. Ashton, *The Industrial Revolution* (1948), p. 161.

towards the 'pessimistic' interpretation of the period and rather doubtful in its treatment of the evidence.

Caird, J., *English Agriculture in 1850–51* (new edn., with introduction by G. E. Mingay, 1968).
    The best-known and most authoritative contemporary account of farming conditions at the middle of the 19th century: an indispensable source of reference.

Orwin, C. S., and Whetham, E. H., *History of British Agriculture, 1846–1914* (1964).
    The only substantial and comprehensive discussion of farming developments in the period of high farming and the great depression since Clapham's *Economic History of Modern Britain*, especially valuable for its treatment of changes in farming techniques.

Ashby, M. K., *Joseph Ashby of Tysoe, 1859–1919: a study of English Village Life* (1961).
    A detailed study of village life as seen in the history of one Warwickshire labourer spanning the period from the last days of high farming to the First World War.

Haggard, H. Rider, *Rural England* (1902).
    A revealing account of rural life at the beginning of this century by the famous novelist, who knew not a little about the country-side and its social classes, and who gained much of his material by personal discussion with landlords and farmers.

Rowntree, B. Seebohm, and Kendall, May, *How the Labourer Lives: a study of the Rural Labour Problem* (1913, revised edn., 1918).
    Here Seebohm Rowntree applied his analysis of poverty, first tried at York at the end of the 19th century, to farm labourers before the First World War. Samples of domestic budgets from 42 families are included.

The Land: the Report of the Land Enquiry Committee (1913).
    Volume I contains the rural findings of this unofficial investigation by prominent Liberals, whose methods were much influenced by Rowntree (a member of the committee). The subjects covered included labourers' conditions, housing, allotments and small-holdings, game, security of tenure of tenant-farmers, rates, co-operation, and education.

Land Agents' Society, *Facts About Land: a reply to 'The Land'*, *the Report of the Unofficial Land Enquiry Committee* (1916).

This substantial volume makes a detailed reply to the Land Enquiry Committee's findings, criticising the Committee's methods of collecting evidence, and providing a wide range of counter-arguments supplemented by statistics. *The Land* and *Facts About Land* need to be read together and their evidence compared.

Havinden, M. A., *Estate Villages* (1966).

A handsomely produced volume concerned in detail with the social development of the Berkshire villages of Ardington and Lockinge under the control of Lord Wantage. It brings out admirably the advantages and disadvantages of the labourers' life on a landed estate.

Pedley, W. H., *Labour on the Land* (1942).

An extremely useful source for farmworkers' wages and conditions in the inter-war period, the sources of their discontent, and their ambitions for improvement.

3. Industrialisation and the Life of the Lancashire Factory Worker

RHODES BOYSON
Headmaster, Highbury Grove School

THE AUTHOR

DR RHODES BOYSON studied history and economics at Manchester, the London School of Economics, and Cambridge University. He has written a history of a co-operative society, a pamphlet on the N. E. Lancashire Poor Law, 1833–1871, and the *Ashworth Cotton Enterprise* (Clarendon, Oxford, 1970), which covers the philosophy of the Lancashire cotton entrepreneurs and the 19th-century Manchester School of free enterprise. He has been head of grammar, secondary modern and comprehensive schools. He writes for daily and weekly papers and broadcasts and televises regularly.

I. THE TRANSFORMATION OF A RURAL ECONOMY

Are the advantages and disadvantages of historical change to be assessed by their effect upon the people who lived through them or by their effect upon succeeding generations? Apart from modern 'primitives', most people welcome the material affluence of the present age, basically an outcome of the change in methods of production which first occurred in the Industrial Revolution in Britain in the late 18th and early 19th centuries. But what of the effect upon the lives and standard of living of the first factory workers? The cotton industry, which created that first-ever industrial society in Lancashire, is the ideal subject for such a study.

The domestic system

Some historians have eulogised the life of the pre-Industrial Revolution domestic workers and of the contemporary hand-loom weavers and condemned the early factories as a form of enslavement in which long hours of labour under arduous conditions for little reward represented a decline from a Golden Age.

Karl Marx certainly did not believe in this Golden Age. He said that the Industrial Revolution brought an end 'to the idiocy of rural life'.[1] Certainly the rural environment was not intellectually or socially stimulating. Rural living conditions in Lancashire as elsewhere were often very poor. Cottage accommodation frequently consisted of a two- or three-roomed cottage which served as a home for six to eight persons and as a spinning and weaving workshop for all members of the family from the earliest childhood. Food was limited to oatmeal porridge, milk, bread, cheese and potatoes with meat a rare luxury. Cooking utensils were few and fuel limited while many houses had no ovens—indeed iron grates began to be supplied only at the end of the 18th century, after the expansion of the iron trade as part of the Industrial Revolution. Close confinement to the spinning wheel and loom must have been very unhealthy: dust, oil and offensive smells ruined the atmosphere. In towns conditions were often worse and many families lived and worked in a single room amidst insanitary conditions.[2]

---

[1] K. Marx, *Das Kapital*, Everyman's Edition, London, 1930.
[2] I. Pinchbeck, *Women Workers and the Industrial Revolution, 1750–1850*, London, 1930, pp. 181, 310.

William E. Hickson, a member of the 1837-1841 Royal Commission on Handloom Weavers, wrote in 1840:

'But domestic happiness is not promoted, but impaired, by all the members of a family muddling together and jostling each other constantly in the same room.'[3]

The Hammonds wrote:

'In many domestic industries the hours were long, the pay was poor, children worked from a tender age, there was overcrowding, and both home and workshop were rendered less desirable from the combination of the two under the same roof.'[4]

Yet the Hammonds felt that the father of such a family was freer than the factory operative in so far as he controlled his hours of labour, he worked alongside his family, and if he lived in a rural cottage he could intersperse his day with gardening or field work, particularly at harvest time. It is arguable how much this freedom was a myth, and his children might come to welcome the freedom from family tyranny that came with the factory. It is certain that the life of such a family varied from periods of semi-idleness to strenuous activity for 20 hours a day when pieces had to be woven quickly. The domestic worker aimed at performing just sufficient work to earn enough money to maintain a fairly low, but conventionally accepted, standard of living. But the demand for cloth was far from regular. Only when trade was brisk could he decide the number of days necessary to earn this money. And he would then spend the rest of the week in drinking and pleasure.[5] It was a stagnant way of life which probably deserves Marx's comment.

The hand-loom weaver

It was the hand-loom weaver who remained longest as a domestic worker. His numbers rose from some 50,000 in 1769 to 184,000 in 1806 and to 240,000 in 1820 (including 100,000 in Lancashire) when the numbers remained fairly static for 10 years till they fell away to 123,000 in 1840 and 23,000 in 1856.[6] That so-called 'independent' workers remained independent for so long caused the hand-loom

---

[3] *P.P.* 1840 [636] Vol. XXIV, p. 682.

[4] J. L. and B. Hammond, *The Town Labourer 1760–1820*, London, 1917, p. 18.

[5] Arthur Young, *A Six Months Tour Through the North of England*, London, 1770; D. Defoe, *A Tour Thro' the Whole Island of Great Britain*, London, 1762.

[6] N. J. Smelser, *Social Change in the Industrial Revolution*, London, 1960, pp. 136, 137, 206–7.

weaver to be romanticised as if he were the last contact with a Golden Age. Yet his temporary prosperity arose from the factory system, he was basically unskilled, he was depressed in his standard of living before the coming of the power-loom, and he was never as 'independent' as many of his contemporary and latter-day admirers imagined who saw him as the equivalent of the yeoman farmer.

The hand-loom weaver with the five-pound note in his hat[7] was, if he ever existed, a weaver whose prosperity was due to Arkwright's water-frame (1768): it transformed cotton spinning into a factory industry whose production had outrun the capacity of the then hand-loom weavers to complete the next stage in the production of cotton piece-goods. Between 1770 and 1819 retained raw cotton imports into the United Kingdom rose from 3,246,000 pounds weight to 133,117,000 pounds weight.[8] Wages of up to 25s a week could be earned easily by hand-loom weavers at the end of the 18th century, and for the short period after the Peace of Amiens (1802) these rose to 45-80s a week. Because of over-recruitment and trade depression, however, they fell to 14s in 1811 and 9s in 1817.[9]

Hand-loom weaving was basically unskilled work and little capital was required. A plain weaver could be trained in two or three weeks, and hand-loom weaving was used in the workhouses as a 'test' for all inmates. Wages fell down to 1820 because of the ease with which people could learn to weave. The widespread introduction of power looms into the cotton industry in the 1820s simply meant that the wages for hand-loom weavers never recovered and indeed fell below 8s a week. Their prosperity was created by the mechanisation of the spinning process, and the mechanisation of weaving would mean their permanent disappearance.

Yet the independence of the hand-loom weaver was limited before the Industrial Revolution. He was already a wage-earner paid by a capitalist employer for each piece woven. He could be dependent upon one 'putter-out'; or one master could bind him by letting him have a house on credit or by giving him a loan in advance. Unlike the framework-knitters of the Midlands, he owned his loom, but he did not own the raw material or the more expensive parts of the loom, particularly the reed of which the versatile weaver needed a

---

[7] G. C. French, *Life and Times of Samuel Crompton*, Manchester, 1859, p. 102.
[8] B. R.Mitchell, *Abstract of British Historical Statistics*, Cambridge,1962, pp. 177–178.
[9] H. Perkin, *The Origins of Modern English Society, 1780–1880*, London, 1969, p. 145.

variety. He was a member of a numerous, scattered and unskilled labour force and any individual action he could take was very limited. If the 'putter-out' wanted his piece woven by a certain date, the hand-loom weaver's 'freedom' was in reality the freedom to decide not how much leisure he and his family should have but simply when they should snatch the few hours of sleep permitted them.[10]

The hand-loom weaver was also often employed by large-scale capitalists. As early as 1736 two brothers employed 600 looms and 3,000 persons in the Blackburn district.[11] William Radcliffe claimed to employ over 1,000 hand-loom weavers in 1801 and 'a whole countryside of [hand-loom] weavers' was employed to the extent of 7,000 workers by Horrockses of Preston in 1816. John Fielden of Todmorden once employed 3,000 on hand-looms and James Masseys of Manchester put out to 1,200 weavers in N.E. Lancashire in the 1830s.[12]

II. FACTORY AND DOMESTIC WORKING CONDITIONS

Many people have quoted the reluctance of the hand-loom weaver to enter the factories in the 1820s as a sign of the general hatred of mill work. Richard Needham, a hand-loom weaver from Bolton, told the 1834 Select Committee:

'...no man would like to work in a power-loom [shed]...there is such a clattering and noise it would almost make some men mad; and next, he would have to be subject to a discipline that a hand-loom weaver can never submit to.'[1]

Children's preferences at first hand

There were, however, two points of view about the desirability of factory as against domestic work. Mrs Cooke Taylor visited the Ashworth Mills at Turton and talked during the dinner-hour with boys whose fathers were hand-loom weavers. She asked them whether they would not have preferred to work at home with their fathers. They replied that at the mill they knew what their hours were

---

10 D. Bythell, *The Handloom Weavers*, London, 1969, p. 38.

11 A. P. Wadsworth and J. de L. Mann, *The Cotton Trade and Industrial Lancashire, 1600–1760*, Manchester, 1831, p. 211.

12 Bythell, *op. cit.*, p. 30.

1 *P.P.* 1834 [556] Vol. X, p. 432.

whilst at home they had to work long hours for little return.² It is very likely that dislike of the factory system was largely confined to those who for years had been domestic workers and whose life pattern had been fixed by it.

Nor were instances of child cruelty confined to the factories as one would imagine if one simply read books attacking the factory system. The domestic weaver, like the factory overseer, desired maximum output and was sometimes exceptionally callous in his attempts to achieve it. In January 1830, a Royton hand-loom weaver was arrested for cruelty to two boys and two girls he employed. After getting up at five, six and at the latest seven o'clock, the children were compelled to work at their looms until midnight and sometimes until one and two o'clock the next morning. When the master was dissatisfied with their work, he beat them with a knotted rope. The children were never allowed to go out of their house and their only food was porridge and occasionally potatoes. They were reduced to one meal a day if their master considered they were not working enough.³

Such cases of cruelty would be more difficult to trace under a scattered domestic system where families often worked in their own homes than under a factory system where hundreds and thousands of operatives were gathered in huge mills and sheds open to inspection by factory inspectors and other visitors.

Working conditions under the factory system were better than under the domestic system. W. E. Hickson reported in 1840:

'The great majority of hand-loom cotton-weavers work in cellars, sufficiently light to enable them to throw the shuttle, but cheerless because seldom visited by the sun . . . I have seen them working in cellars dug out of an undrained swamp; the streets formed by their houses without sewers, and flooded with rain; the water therefore running down the bare walls of the cellars, and rendering them unfit for the abode of dogs or cats . . . The floor is but seldom boarded or paved. . . '

and

'With regard to health, having seen the domestic weaver in his miserable apartments, and the power-loom weaver in the factory, I do not hesitate to say that the advantages are all on the side of the latter. The one, if a steady workman, confines himself to a single room, in which he eats, drinks and sleeps, and breathes throughout the day an impure air. The other has not only the exercise of walking to and from the factory, but, when there, lives and breathes in a

² W. C. Taylor, *Factories and the Factory System*, London, 1844, p. 50.
³ C. Aspin, *Lancashire, The First Industrial Society*, Helmshore, 1969, pp. 54–55.

large roomy apartment, in which the air is constantly changed. Some of the factories I have visited are models of neatness, cleanliness and perfect ventilation; and there is no reason all should not be the same.'[4]

Benefits of factory work

Many of the new factories with large machinery were airy and clean. Few saw the long and terrible conditions of man, wife and children under the scattered domestic system. The factory was open to inspection by commissioners, inspectors and parliamentary visitors. Henry and Edmond Ashworths' factories at Turton, near Bolton, were visited by Benjamin Disraeli, Lord John Manners, Lord Ashley, the Bishop of Manchester and many other influential men. Even Lord Ashley noted that 'Ashworth's Mills are worth seeing' and that they were 'clean' and quite 'astonishing' with much discipline and order. Sickness rates were low and there were already sick clubs. In the 1830s the Ashworth factories closed for the equivalent of six full days and all the operatives were given permission to take individually or in small groups a further week or more as a summer holiday where operatives chose the date and the Ashworths undertook to provide replacements in the mills. Operatives journeyed to London, Ireland and Scotland. In 1851 parties of Ashworth employees visited London for 10 days to see the Great Exhibition. The Ashworths also allowed a month's consecutive holiday in summer to children aged 9 to 13 years.[5] Higher wages also promised a future when the factory operative could use his evening and weekend leisure-time in pursuits more sensible than drinking and brutal sports, which had frequently occupied the free time of his predecessors under the domestic system.

The Ashworth mills were not exceptional. In January 1837, Leonard Horner said he could draw up a long list of well-run mills 'where order, cleanliness, and an attention on the part of the master to the comfort and welfare of his workpeople are conspicuous', and he added:

'...I have often wished that those who so thoughtlessly believe and give currency to tales of the miseries of the factory-workers, and of the cruelty and hard-heartedness of their masters, would go to some of the mills to which I could send them, and judge for themselves.'[6]

Jacob Bright of Rochdale, the Whitehead brothers of Rawtenstall,

---

4 *P.P.* 1840 [636] Vol. XXIV, pp. 645, 681.
5 Rhodes Boyson, *The Ashworth Cotton Enterprise*, London, 1970, p. 42.
6 *P.P.* 1837 [73] Vol. XXXI, p. 93.

Hindes and Derham near Lancaster, Joseph Fenton of Bamford Hall and James Thomson of Clitheroe are a few employers who would have been on this list. It is clear that a contented, stable and increasingly prosperous labour force was less likely to be affected by militant unionism and was in the employers' interest. It is of interest that in August 1845 the operative spinners of Bolton gave a tea party for a number of their employers and some 900 spinners attended.[7]

The blackspots

The real blackspots of the Industrial Revolution period were to be found not in the factories but in the unskilled outworking trades where new methods and new machines were used least. The hand-loom weavers whose ill-condition in the 1830s and 1840s was frequently reported on and won much sympathy came within this category—new machines were slow to replace hand labour. When short of work for two or three weeks a hand-loom weaver's family would be starving; when there was work they would labour 14 to 20 hours a day on two meals of oatmeal and potatoes for an adult wage as low as 5s a week. No wonder some of his children preferred factory work!

The first spinning-mill masters, however, had initial difficulty in recruiting labour since the first effect of the technical inventions in spinning was to increase the prosperity of the hand-loom weavers so that there was no inducement for members of their families to come into the mills. The masters were at first dependent upon casual employment; this is why they took parish apprentices, although they preferred free labour and one-year contract labour because they were less expensive as the employers were not then responsible for feeding and housing. Yet parish apprentices rarely made up more than a quarter or a third of the labour in a cotton factory, and even before legislation their numbers rapidly declined as it became possible to recruit other labour.[8] Country masters were often prepared to build good houses to encourage the recruitment and retention of settled 'free' operatives.

Higher wages in Lancashire factories

It was higher wages and regular employment that brought most people into the cotton factories. Adult male operatives in the period

---

[7] Aspin, *op. cit.*, pp. 136–137.
[8] A. Redford, *Labour Migration in England, 1800–1850*, Manchester, 1964.

1806 to 1846 could earn 15s to 18s in the blowing and carding rooms and up to 33s–42s for fine spinning on long mules. These wages compared with the 13s 6d of agricultural labourers in Lancashire.[9] Women and children earned lower wages in the factories since they were usually employed on different tasks. Friedrich Engels wrote that the 'rapid expansion of industry led to the demand for more labour' and this 'caused wages to rise and consequently hordes of workers migrated from the countryside to the towns'.[10]

This process of accepting higher wages with a rise in the standard of living as the price of the factory routine is paralleled amongst modern car workers who prefer the higher wages on routine production lines to the lower wages and less supervision and pressure of small shop, park, or bus work. Unwelcome as this observation might be to the romantic poets, these men realise that high wages give more choice of leisure activities and an improvement in their home conditions: for these advantages they are prepared to accept work-hour regulations.

The growing desire of the sons of hand-loom weavers and agricultural labourers to increase their purchasing power not only brought them into factories but also widened the market for the sale of the products of the Industrial Revolution. It represented a complete change of attitude from that of the earlier domestic workers and their relatively stagnant economy and standard of living. Nor was it a retreat from craftsmanship: the domestic worker was generally an unskilled producer of patterns and types determined by a middleman.

The Industrial Revolution brought a distinct rise in the standard of living of the factory operative. According to G. D. H. Cole's calculation on G. H. Wood's figures, real wages in the cotton industry more than doubled between the bad year of 1800 and 1830 and had almost trebled by 1850.[11] A larger proportionate share of the increased wealth went to the investing classes but it was essential to encourage further investment—in contrast with post-Second World War Britain where a switch of the gross national product to the working classes has been linked with economic stagnation and decline and, compared with other countries, a fall in the purchasing

---

9 Perkin, *op. cit.*, pp. 128–129.

10 F. Engels, *The Condition of the Working Class in England*, translated and edited by W. O. Henderson and W. H. Chaloner, Oxford, 1958, p. 24.

11 G. D. H. Cole, *A Short History of the British Working Class Movement, 1797–1937*, London, 1937, pp. 181–2.

power of workers' wages. Much of the increased home cotton consumption was bought by the working classes. Many cotton exports were exchanged for sugar, coffee, grain and tea and other goods bought by the cotton workers out of their increased wages. Meat and potatoes and wheat bread became part of the staple diet of the factory worker and much of the increased production of coal went to cheer domestic hearths and not to drive factory engines. Francis Collier comments that by the 1830s

'the majority of the factory operatives were in receipt of wages which brought within their reach a fairly abundant diet of plain food and, if careful and thrifty, tidy clothes and decent household goods.'[12]

Engels recognised this advantage of factory employment:

'the better-paid workers—particularly when the whole family works in the factories—enjoy good food as long as they are in employment. They have meat every day and bacon and cheese for the evening meal. The lower-paid workers have meat only two or three times a week, and sometimes only on Sundays.'[13]

Leonard Horner wrote in 1837 describing the Lancashire cotton and Yorkshire woollen factory workers:

'I am satisfied by what may then be seen would lead any unprejudiced observer to the conclusion that in no other occupation could there possibly exist among the working people a larger proportion of well-fed, well-clothed, healthy and cheerful looking people.'[14]

It is also likely that the factory work itself was lighter than domestic work for both men and women—the engine drove the machinery and it became more a case of attending rather than working it. Something like one minute in three was spent simply watching the machines.

III. EMPLOYMENT AND WAGES

Agricultural wages in Lancashire

It was not only the factory operative who owed his improved standard of living to the cotton factories. The Lancashire agricultural labourer's wage advanced very much faster than did that of his

---

[12] F. Collier, *The Family Economy in the Cotton Industry*, M.A. thesis, Manchester, 1921, p. 49.

[13] Engels, *op. cit.*, p. 85.

[14] *P.P.* 1837 [73] Vol. XXXI.

counterpart in the rural counties of the south. In about 1770, before the Industrial Revolution, an agricultural labourer's wage in the north of England averaged 10 per cent less than in the south, 6s 9d against 7s 6d a week. By 1837 it was 37 per cent higher—11s 6d against 8s 5d. In Lancashire it had more than doubled from 6s 6d to 13s 6d. Lancashire labourers began to afford meat, although it was still a rarity among the agricultural classes who lived largely on bread and potatoes. Labourers' wages near Lancashire towns were even higher. There is no doubt that it was the cotton factories that acted as a magnet to lift them higher.[1]

Regular employment in the factories

A standard of living depends as much upon regularity of employment as upon the wages received and the factory system is often unjustly accused of introducing a casual relationship between masters and men. The cotton factory operative was in fact much more secure in his employment than the hand-loom weaver since a factory master carried so many overheads that it paid him to make considerable losses before he closed his mills or even dismissed his less efficient operatives. Henry Ashworth calculated that a 52,000-spindle mill could afford a yearly loss of £6,334 before it was a financial advantage to its owner to close it.[2] The Commissioners on the Hand-Loom Weavers in 1840 quoted the evidence collected by Dr J. Mitchell from Samuel Courtauld in reference to the crape weavers:

'At present, the crape manufacturer does a great portion of his work in power-loom factories; but he also gives out his work to hand-loom weavers. Wherever there is a slackness of trade, he discontinues his hand-loom weavers; a part of them at any rate, or perhaps the whole of them. The weavers being dismissed, put him to no expense. But he continues on his power-looms, because in them he has capital embarked, the interest of which he cannot afford to lose. When trade becomes brisk, he again employs his hand-loom weavers.'[3]

Thus because of the amount of capital invested the factory operative was more secure than the pre-Industrial Revolution domestic worker. Workers with steam-driven machines were also more secure than workers under water-power, since the steam engine was not affected by drought and frost.

The lack of an established labour force meant that there was a

---

[1] Perkin, *op. cit.*, pp. 128, 144.
[2] Boyson, *op. cit.*, p. 81.
[3] *P.P.* 1840 [43–1] Vol. XXIII, pp. 226–227. Also see *P.P.* 1841 [296] Vol. X, pp. 305–306.

fast turnover of workers in the first factories, but it was in the interests of employers to build up a stable and contented labour force and they provided regular employment for all who desired it. A widely publicised advertisement by the Ashworths for spinners in 1830 asserted that no spinner had left their employment in the previous year except one discharged by them.[4] In 1841, out of the 52 spinners employed at their Egerton Mill, 18 had worked there since the mill was opened in 1830; 42 averaged seven years' service and of the remaining 10, five had been there for an average of two and a half years.[5] In 1833 one of the Ashworth spinners gave signed evidence to the Factory Commissioners that he knew of spinners dismissed from the Ashworth mills only because of defective sight and never for age or any other infirmity. This operative stated that most Ashworth spinners were discharged at the age of about 50, by which time they had frequently saved £100 and some had £600 or £700 with which they took a little shop or a public house.[6] Writing under a nom-de-plume in 1836, the Ashworth brothers claimed:

'There is scarcely an out-door labourer of 50 years of age who is free from rheumatism and other chronic affectations. Not so with the spinner who at the age of 50 years is hale and hearty, and if governed by frugality in his younger days may have saved a sum of money which would enable him by frugality, having earned twice or three times as much as the common labourer, to launch into some respectable business and thereby make a provision for himself and family through life.'[7]

Ten years later Henry Ashworth informed the Lords' Commission on Special Burdens that he never dismissed men from the mills because of age but found them work in packing, sweeping and cleaning and repairing the roads as long as 'they have bodily strength left for it'.[8] Henry Ashworth always boasted that he found employment for all the children of his operatives. In 1859 it was stated that he employed children, their parents and their grandparents.[9] In his answers to the Paris Universal Exhibition questionnaire in 1867, he claimed that many old people worked at New Eagley and instanced one workman who had died the previous year after 58 years' service there.[10]

---

[4] *Manchester Guardian*, 20 March, 1830.
[5] *Bolton Free Press*, 6 November, 1841, letter signed H. and E. Ashworth.
[6] *P.P.* 1833 [450] Vol. XX, p. 884.
[7] *Bolton Free Press*, 7th May, 1836, letter signed 'Veritas' [Henry and Edmund Ashworth].
[8] *P.P.* 1846 [411] Vol. VIi, pp. 359–60.   [9] *Manchester Guardian*, 22 April, 1859.
[10] Paris Universal Exhibition 1867, *Report 1868*, Vol. VI, p. 73.

Lord John Manners intended to be complimentary when he paid tribute in the House of Commons to Mr Ashworth's 'deep sense of the responsibility that devolves upon him as one of the great cotton barons'.[11] Lord John Manners was concerned, however, about what he considered was the uncertainty of the new industrial feudalism. He believed that an agricultural aristocracy maintained its dependants continuously, while the new trading aristocracy, represented by the cotton manufacturers, saw in the intense competition of their trade no place for pity, and as soon as a man was less economically useful than his potential substitute, he was discharged with no further responsibility resting upon the employer.[12] Yet by the 19th century the agricultural counties had moved a long way from feudalism. It is very doubtful whether the agricultural labourer had any more security in his old age than the discharged factory worker who would seem to have had far more opportunity to save to enter some other trade or to enjoy retirement cheerfully. The enclosures had marked the end of the agricultural workers' medieval security.

The vast numbers of the under-employed, pauperised agricultural labourers had been the chief argument for the New Poor Law. Some high Tories and members of the Factory Reform Party held up to the public an image of ruthless factory masters as if the alternative to the factory was a secure medieval feudal economy and not the destitution of the agricultural labourer and the hand-loom weaver.

The prosperity and regularity of employment of the more highly-paid operatives can be seen from an analysis prepared in 1844 of 197 men over the age of 40 who had left the spinning mills of Ashton-under-Lyne.[13] Fourteen of them had become master spinners or manufacturers, 61 shopkeepers, 42 publicans and beersellers, 11 grocers and tea dealers. Spinning employed more men than any other branch of factory work. They certainly did not seem members of a depressed or neglected class.

IV. IMMIGRATION AND HOUSING

Irish immigration

Undiscerning critics of the Industrial Revolution are given to citing the poor condition of the hand-loom weaver in the first half of the

---

11 *Hansard*, 3rd Series, Vol. LXXXIV, 27 February, 1846, pp. 246–247.
12 Lord John Manners to Granby, 31 October, 1841 (Belvoir Castle).
13 *Report of the Central Committee of the Association of Mill Owners and Manufacturers*, Manchester, 1845, p. 11.

19th century—few of whom were employed in factories—and of the dreadful housing conditions in the poorest quarters of the old towns. The former was a remnant of the domestic system and the latter was a problem of an urban way of life. Both these conditions were worsened by large-scale Irish immigration. The majority of the cellar dwellers of the 1840s were of Irish origin and many became hand-loom weavers. Manchester cellars were rented by the Irish in 1835 at 1s 6d a week, compared with 3s for the best Manchester two-roomed cottages.[1] New towns like Bury and Ashton-under-Lyne had few cellar-dwellings and few Irish. The Manchester cellar-dwellings would have been emptied and demolished much more quickly and hand-loom weaving would have declined more rapidly if there had been no Irish immigration.

The Irish immigrant came from a country where an agricultural labourer received only 1s 6d a day, where rates of wages for linen weavers were below the lowest rates paid in England, where by 1830 the Irish cotton, woollen and silk trades were moribund and there was no poor relief. They came to England for work and higher wages on a passage money which could drop from 2s 6d to as low as 4d. Dr J. P. Kay wrote that the Irish had discovered 'what is the minimum of the means of life, upon which existence may be prolonged . . .'[2] William Cobbett said in 1834 that England had 'meat and bread and knives and forks' while Ireland 'had only potatoes and paws'.[3] Friedrich Engels wrote that at home in Ireland the Irish labourer 'lived in a mud cabin where a single room suffered for all purposes'. He added: 'The Irish are not used to furniture: a heap of straw and a few rags too tattered to wear in the daytime suffice for bedding' and 'They are competitors whose standard of living is the lowest conceivable in a civilised country . . .' They introduced the keeping of pigs into Lancashire houses and even the habit of going barefoot.[4]

The 1841 census recorded 105,916 Irish in Lancashire of whom 34,300 were in Manchester. They were a very important cause of the poor conditions in large towns which was commented upon by subsequent commissions and investigations. It was their presence and continued immigration which not only seriously worsened the

---

[1] Collier, *op. cit.*, p. 98.
[2] *The Moral and Physical Condition of the Working Classes employed in the Cotton Manufacture in England*, London, 1832, 2nd edn., p. 21. Dr Kay became Sir James P. Kay-Shuttleworth.
[3] Redford, *op. cit.*, p. 159.
[4] Engels, *op. cit.*, pp. 80, 106–107.

sanitary conditions of the Lancashire towns but depressed the standards of the native unskilled operatives. Yet the Industrial Revolution could not be blamed for their conditions: without it they would have emigrated to America or starved to death in Ireland in the 1840s. In the long term the Irish immigrant, through the opportunities afforded by the Industrial Revolution in Lancashire, greatly improved his conditions of life.

Factory housing

But cellar-dwellings were only part of the old towns and many factories, even after the coming of steam, were still in small towns and villages. Lancashire is still covered with semi-rural factory villages built at the time of water-power around the first spinning mills. By the 1840s and 1850s many superior rows of cottages were erected near the factories to meet the rising tastes of the operatives. A table in the Poor Law Commissioners' 1842 *Report on the Sanitary Condition of the Labouring Population* shows that the average net rent return on cottage property in 24 poor-law unions in Cheshire, Stafford, Derby and Lancashire ranged from 8 to 9¾ per cent according to the size of cottage, so that by that date no-one was exploiting the new town and village workers.[5] This invalidates Peter Gaskell's allegation in 1833 that factory masters who built homes for their workers could reap an annual return of 13½ per cent.[6] Presumably it was only at the beginning of the Industrial Revolution that huge profits were made on cottage building—John Holt asserted in 1795 that many cottages were erected by 'building speculators' who hoped to gain an annual return of 10–20 per cent.[7] As more money was invested in cottage property the return dropped to a figure below that obtained in industrial investment which was more risky.

Country mill-owners like the Ashworths erected substantial two-bedroomed and later three- and four-bedroomed cottages for their workpeople. Charlotte Ashworth commented that when they first erected the larger cottages for their workmen a local prejudice existed against them and 'many droll remarks were made' of the 'lonely and unsocial character' of homes with more than two bedrooms.[8] This was certainly a commentary on the lack of space in the

---

5 *Lords Sessional Papers*, 1842, XXVII, p. 246.

6 P. Gaskell, *The Manufacturing Population of England*, London, 1833, p. 252.

7 John Holt, *General View of the Agriculture of Lancashire*, London, 1795, p. 19.

8 Charlotte Ashworth to Edwin Chadwick, 14 September, 1864: *Lords Sessional Papers*, 1842, Vol. XXVII, pp. 338–9.

pre-Industrial Revolution housing of the lower classes. Each of the Ashworth cottages had a living room and kitchen downstairs and the larger houses also had a pantry. There was a separate lavatory for each house in a walled and private backyard, and the kitchen had a water boiler and an oven by the fire-place. From 1835 piped water was provided to the 'slop-stone' (sink) and gas would soon be fitted piped from the mill gasometers. Such cottages must have seemed very luxurious in contrast with rural hovels. Lord Ashley visited these cottages in 1844 on a Monday, Lancashire's traditional washday, and he expressed astonishment at 'their household accommodation' and the '*good coal fires* which they possessed'. Each bed had a full complement of blankets, sheets, and quilts, and many of the bedrooms had bed- and window-curtains and strips of carpet at the bedside. There were mahogany chests of drawers full of good male and female clothing and some 10 to 30 books in each house. The net return on the Ashworth cottage property was only 5.2 per cent, less than the average return they received on their factories.[9]

Little, however, could be done even by factory owners like the Ashworths to stop the pollution of the rivers, streams and air which came in with the Industrial Revolution. G. J. French wrote in 1859 to describe Samuel Crompton's Hall i' th' Wood, near the Ashworth mills and cottages and the homes of the Ashworth brothers:

'The very success which has attended his [Samuel Crompton's] invention has covered the landscape with an almost perpetual veil of coal-smoke and polluted the clear river with dark stains of dye-woods. Thus one of the most lovely scenes in Lancashire is now rarely to be seen except through a dense and murky atmosphere.'[10]

If such environmental pollution occurred in rural Lancashire, where there were regular high winds, it must have been worse in the towns. Yet much of this air pollution came from house and not factory chimneys. The Lancashire workman probably preferred his big coal fires and hot water with air pollution to the scenic views with few coal fires, few hot meals and rare hot water under the domestic system.

The position of women

It was the better housing and the separation of work in factories away from the home which improved the lot of women and children.

---

[9] Boyson, *op. cit.*, pp. 118, 120, 124–5. (Italics by Henry Ashworth.)
[10] G. J. French, *op. cit.*, p. 48.

Despite Eyre Crowe's painting of 'The Dinner Hour, Wigan', exhibited at the 1874 Royal Academy, which depicts obviously healthy and neat mill women nourishing their babies, the proportion of married women employed in the factories was low, and the proportion with children employed there was lower still. Dr Mitchell, one of the Factory Commissioners, wrote in 1834: 'It is known by the returns, as well as from the evidence given by the District Commissioners, that very few women work in the factories after marriage'.[11] Certainly the ratio of agricultural labourers' wives who left their homes to work in the fields was very much higher.[12] Henry Ashworth told the Factory Commissioners in 1833:

'I am happy to say that there is no married female employed by us . . . nor do I know that we have any married workman who finds it necessary or is desirous that his wife should follow any employ but that of her domestic duties.'[13]

The Industrial Revolution brought a real advance for wives and families because it introduced the idea that men's wages should be sufficient to maintain a wife and family and that women should make their contribution by looking after the home. For the first time the wives of the industrial classes could concentrate on the business of home-making and the care of their children, who stood to benefit by the changed home conditions.

There was a similar advance in the emancipation of single women. Where they were employed in the factories to perform the same tasks at the same speed, they received the same wages as men. Men continued to monopolise the higher-paid trades like spinning, but in preparatory trades and weaving women enjoyed equal pay. In agricultural employment in Lancashire women received only half the wages of men doing the same work. W. E. Hickson considered that factory work aided the status of women and added that

'A young woman, prudent and careful, and living with her parents, from the age of 16 to 25, may, in that time, by factory employment, save £100 as a wedding portion.'[14]

This was no mean sum. Nineteenth-century factory women were in the van of all women—legislation safeguarded their conditions in an industry which itself, as explained above, helped their emancipation. The 1841 census returns show that women were largely employed

---

11 *P.P.* 1834, Vol. XIX [261], p. 38.
12 Pinchbeck, *op. cit.*, p. 199.
13 *P.P.* 1833, Vol. XX [450], p. 1,105.
14 *P.P.* 1840 [636] Vol. XXIV, p. 682.

under five headings: domestic servants, factory operatives, needle-women, agricultural labourers and in domestic industry; factory women earned most for the shortest hours.[15]

Visitors who expressed shock at the employment of women in factories should have remembered the drudgery of domestic service and the sweated labour of needlewomen. It was among lacemakers, straw plaiters, glovemakers, frame-work knitters, nailmakers and other domestic workers that women spent long hours labouring in overcrowded insanitary cottages for less than subsistence wages. They were also most open to payment in truck and other abuses. The London dressmakers and milliners often worked up to 18 or 20 hours a day for several months, sometimes through the night, and their working life was estimated at only 3 to 4 years, after which they would be replaced by women fresh from the country.[16]

Some observers were even alarmed at the growing independence of factory women. The Rev G. S. Bull, the great supporter of factory legislation, adversely commented that they bought smart clothes.[17] Others noted that some girls left home at 16 or simply lodged there, made independent by the wages they earned. Friedrich Engels, Lord Ashley, Richard Oastler, Peter Gaskell and Dr J. P. Kay were all concerned that the splitting up of the family in the daytime would break the family unit. Yet a man working as a spinner would often continue to employ his own children as piecers and scavengers in the mill.

Higher wages for women and more independence did tend to an increase in intemperance. There is just no evidence, however, that the morality of factory women was any lower than women employed or not employed elsewhere. W. E. Hickson considered that both men and women working in factories lived more moral lives than did those working on piece-work in their homes since they had to develop regularity of habits and were, whilst at work, under constant superintendence.[18] Marx wrote that 'large-scale industry . . . is building the new economic foundation for a higher form of the family and of the relations between the sexes'.[19] Certainly by the 1850s there is evidence that the textile workers, appreciating their rising standard of living, were limiting the size of their families.

---

[15] Pinchbeck, *op. cit.*, p. 315.
[16] *P.P.* 1843 [431] Vol. XIV, pp. 555–6.
[17] *P.P.* 1831–2 [706], Vol. XV, p. 423.
[18] *P.P.* 1840 [636], Vol. XXIV, pp. 681–2.
[19] Marx, *op. cit.*, 1.529.

Movement of southern labourers to Lancashire

Between 1835 and 1837 the poor law authorities encouraged the migration of 1,785 southern rural families into Lancashire to work on three-year contracts in the cotton factories which were then short of labour. The reports on this movement allow a comparison to be made between the standard of living of the southern agricultural labourer and the Lancashire factory operative. The scheme grew out of a suggestion made in 1834 by the Ashworth brothers and R. H. Greg. Henry and Edmund Ashworth and the Gregs then sponsored the pilot movements upon which the whole migration operation was developed.

Henry and Edmund Ashworth took 11 families with 54 persons of full-time or part-time working age from Great Bledlow in Buckinghamshire. They soon had new clothing, 'even some articles of finery', 'Butchers meat almost daily' and a 'good coal fire *all the day*' which compared very favourably with their life in Buckinghamshire where they could not afford the fuel to bake bread or even cook a hot meal more than once or twice a week. Dr Kay soon visited them at Egerton and noted the comfortable cottages they lived in with 'fabulous abundance', their high wages and the varied possessions of their neighbours. The older children were attending school on two evenings a week and on Sundays. In 1835 they were also visited by two gentry and two labourers from Blything Union in Suffolk who were surprised at their high standard of living. Certainly their family wages were twice what their wages and poor relief were in Buckinghamshire. By 1837 and 1838 families were earning three and four times their income in Great Bledlow, albeit that there were more at work in most families because of their growing children.[20]

Henry Ashworth contrasted the conditions of these Bledlow labourers working at his mills with those of the tenants on the Ashley estates in Dorset at that time, where average adult wages were not more than 7s 6d a week, they lived in hovels without chimneys, and their clothing was poor. No wonder Henry Ashworth considered the landowners would have been better employed improving the conditions of their tenants rather than legislating for the cotton industry![21] He related in a speech at Covent Garden Theatre how a friend of the Duke of Buckingham visited the Ashworth workers living in three-bedroomed cottages, not as in the agricultural counties

---

20 Boyson, *op. cit.*, pp. 189–194.
21 *Bolton Chronicle*, 4 September, 1841.

in 'a hut placed on the side of a hill, and covered with mud and thatch'. One of his Bledlow labourers said to the visitor, 'O, no sir, I got away at last, and all the horses of the Duke of Buckingham shan't draw me back again'.[22] Professor Redford concluded that the original contracted wage of the southern labourers on taking up employment in the cotton mills was 50 per cent higher than their rural wages.[23] Like the hand-loom weavers' families, however, it was the children of the rural migrants who adapted themselves best to factory life. There was difficulty in settling the migrant fathers into the mills which is not surprising since Dr Kay noted they were 'grievously round-shouldered and crippled with rheumatism'. Henry Ashworth employed them on farming and general repair work.

V. THE ENCOURAGEMENT OF EDUCATION

The Industrial Revolution increased the pollution of air and stream but it also widened the educational opportunities for the cotton operatives and their children. No-one ever heard of a hand-loom weaving master opening a school for his workmen. The cotton masters desired their operatives to be able to read and write. They were not hereditary landowners who wished, with the help of the Church, to keep the labourer in his place. They wanted to recruit foremen, book-keepers, salesmen, managers and even partners from their operatives. Twenty of the Ashworth spinners became mill managers and owners between 1818 and 1841; many of them had saved up their initial capital with the firm. As late as the early 20th century the majority of weaving employers had risen from operatives.[1]

Education and understanding

The more enlightened employers also accepted that education was necessary, so that a man would be able to identify his self-interest and allow the *laissez-faire* economy to function efficiently. Henry Ashworth opened mill and village schools and libraries in the 1820s

---

22 *The Struggle*, No. 116.
23 Redford, *op. cit.*, p. 116.

1 Professor S. J. Chapman and F. J. Marquis, 'The Recruiting of the Employing Classes from the Ranks of the Wage-Earners in the Cotton Industry', *Journal of the Royal Statistical Society*, Vol. LXXV, February 1912, pp. 293–313.

and 1830s and knocked from door to door to encourage his operatives to send their children to school. His mill libraries even provided
books for his spinners which they could read when the mules were
running well with few breaks.

The attitude of Henry Ashworth and that of the Bright/Cobden
school of factory-owners to education contrasted strongly with that
of Lord Ashley, Lord John Manners and others from the older
landowning class. In 1860 Henry Ashworth defined his aims in
education:

' . . . to enlarge their views, if possible, and to teach them not to be satisfied with
the conditions in which they were born, but to induce them to be uneasy about
it, and to make them feel uncomfortable if they do not improve upon the
example that their parents have set before them.'[2]

As with the provision of housing, Henry Ashworth saw his responsibility simply as the requirement to launch his workers on the path
to full independence.

How different was the attitude of Lord John Manners, MP, who
noted in his diary after visiting the Ashworth schools: 'I confess I'm
rather alarmed by this hot bed of intellect'.[3] C. P. Henderson, a
Manchester merchant who had accompanied Lord John Manners,
Hon. G. S. Smythe, MP, and H. H. Lindsay, MP, on this 1841 visit,
told Henry Ashworth that when the party came out of the school
'. . . One of the Gentn. remarked to another, that they had seen
there . . . what would occasion some trouble to deal with at a future
day!'[4] Lord Ashley's reaction when he visited the Ashworth schools
three years later was very similar:

'On leaving the school Lord Ashley observed to me in passing down the road
upon the intelligence and quickness of a boy named Lightbound whom he had
noticed as the first in giving the answers altho' he was only *nine* yrs. of age and
remarked "how providential it was, that there was no great number of those who
possessed such superior intellects or there would be a *difficulty in keeping them
in their stations*".'[5]

The Industrial Revolution and the first factory masters encouraged
men to rise above their station; this was one of the reasons why it
and they were disliked by the landowning classes. The factory-

---

2 *P.P.* 1860 [455], Vol. XII, p. 457.
3 Lord John Manners' diary, 28 October, 1841.
4 Henry Ashworth's manuscript on the visit of Lord John Manners, 1841.
5 Henry Ashworth's manuscript on the visit of Lord Ashley, 30 September, 1844
(underlining by Henry Ashworth).

owners and their middle-class allies were confident of the virtues of their new form of society and they considered education could only advance it further.

It was the concentration of operatives in the large factories that made obvious the defects of the provision for education and built up a public opinion in favour of widespread improvements. Henry Ashworth's claim that 98 per cent of his operatives could read and 45 per cent could write—a claim not disputed by Leonard Horner or Lord Ashley—was exceptional.[6] R. K. Webb estimates that between two-thirds and three-quarters of the British working-class could read in the 1830s and over a third could write and that the largest literate proportion came from the northern counties.[7] As the Industrial Revolution progressed the impetus to education gained momentum. The numbers receiving elementary education grew from 675,000 in 1818 (1 in 17 of the population) to 2,144,000 (1 in 8 of the population) in 1851.[8] The numbers attending Sunday schools also increased rapidly. A large demand for periodicals and cheap books was created.

Local involvement of employers

It was not only 'model' employers like the Ashworths and the Gregs who lived close to their spinning mills and weaving sheds. Statistics prepared and published in 1849 showed that only 29 out of 904 proprietors owning 550 Lancashire and Cheshire spinning mills did not live in the same town as their mills, and 17 of the 29 lived in Manchester to supervise their warehouses and sales. In Bolton only two of the 55 proprietors of the town's 42 mills lived outside it.[9] Since the masters lived close to their men they were generally aware of local feeling and local needs. They supported the Mechanics Institutes, which increased in number from 55 in 1831 with 7,000 members to 1,200 in 1860 with 200,000 members,[10] gave to charity and, often for their own protection as well as that of their operatives, advocated sanitary improvements.

The cotton masters, unlike the country guardians and the central poor law authority, also understood the cyclical unemployment which occasionally struck the cotton industry. Generally as Liberal

---

6 Boyson, *op. cit.*, pp. 132–3.

7 R. K. Webb, *The British Working-Class Reader, 1790–1848*, London, 1955, p. 22.

8 Perkin, *op. cit.*, p. 295; also E. G. West, *Education and the State*, IEA, London, 2nd edn., 1970.

9 F. Baker, *The Moral Tone of the Factory System Defended*, London, 1850, pp. 22, 30.

10 Perkin, *op. cit.*, p. 305.

members of the Boards of Guardians they advocated generous help to the temporarily unemployed at periods of trade recession. This brought them into conflict with Tory country guardians and the poor law commissioners.[11] In 1840 and 1841, when some 5,000 out of 8,000 of the factory workers in Bolton were unemployed, the town's mill-owners not only advocated generous relief with no workhouse or outdoor test but also raised £3,000 to £4,000 to ease local distress. An observer could comment that it was in the employers' interest to keep their labour force intact and healthy; of course that is true, but it is another illustration of the general identity of interest between the employers and their operatives. The poor rates were, however, generally very much lower in Lancashire than in the rural counties— in 1831 the average Lancashire poor rate at 4s 4¾d was the lowest in England and contrasted sharply with a rate of 18s 8¾d in Buckinghamshire and of 19s 4½d in Sussex, which were the highest.[12] Certainly the rise of the cotton industry lessened poverty.

VI. CONCLUSIONS

It was the Industrial Revolution, the growth of towns and the improvement of communications which made many defects in the life of the working classes obvious so that legislation to remedy them was introduced. The regulation of the hours of labour of factory women and children was the first breach in the so-called *laissez-faire* philosophy. The 1833 Factories Regulation Act prohibited the employment of children below the age of nine, limited the hours of labour for those between nine and twelve to 9 a day and between thirteen and seventeen years to 12 a day. Children between the ages of nine and twelve had also to receive two hours schooling daily at the expense of their employers, thus reinforcing a trend that we have seen was already being actively encouraged by the more enlightened mill-owners. The 1847 Act, as amended in 1851, brought in the 10-hour day for all. Certainly the hours then worked were far less than had been common under the domestic system.

The Manchester Statistical Society's report of 1837 which showed that an operative's expectancy of life in Manchester was less than

---

11 Boyson, *op. cit.*, p. 188; also my *The History of the Poor Law Administration in North East Lancashire, 1834–1871*, M.A. thesis, Manchester, 1960.

12 H. Ashworth [A Lancashire Cotton Spinner], *Letter to Lord Ashley*, Manchester, 1833, p. 15.

half that of a labourer in Rutland meant something would have to be done to improve the slums and sanitation. The cause of the higher death rate in Manchester was obviously urban conditions since tradesmen and their families in Manchester also had less than half and even professional persons and gentry just over two-thirds the expectancy of life of the same groups in Rutland. W. E. Hickson commented in 1840:

'The evils of close alleys, narrow streets, impure air, unhealthful employments and a demoralised population, are far from being inseparable from manufacturing industry. The causes of these evils are easily traced, and, if proper steps were taken, easily removed.'[1]

The Health of Towns Commission of 1843 and the first Public Health Act of 1848 quickly followed. Professor T. S. Ashton thus commented on the long series of Royal Commissions and Committees of Inquiry beginning in the 18th century but reaching full fruition in the 1830s, 1840s and 1850s:

'These reports are one of the glories of the Victorian age. They signalised a quickening of social conscience, a sensitiveness to distress, that had not been evident in any other period or in any other country.'[2]

An important aid to better sanitation was the mass production of the iron pipe, one of the fruits of the Industrial Revolution.

Impetus to growth of 'self-help'

It was the same improvement in the standard of living, large factories, growing urbanisation and the improvement of coach and rail travel, which enabled the new working classes to improve their conditions by trade unions, co-operative societies and self-help. The damage the hand-loom weavers could do their masters by striking was limited because little capital was involved, but the factory master with £40–£100 invested for each operative had to take the threats of the trade unions very seriously. The Combination Acts delayed the growth of trade unions and it was the 1870s before there was a big upsurge in union membership; the larger factories, however, made unionism almost inevitable by bringing hundreds and thousands of men with shared interests together almost every day.

Meanwhile, by 1849 there were 3 million members of friendly

---

[1] *P.P.* 1840 [636], Vol. XXIV, p. 680.
[2] T. S. Ashton, 'Workers' Living Standards: A Modern Revision', in P. A. M. Taylor (ed.), *The Industrial Revolution in Britain. Triumph or Disaster?*, Boston, USA, 1952, p. 46.

societies and by 1872 there were 927 retail co-operative societies with over 3 million members and annual sales approaching £10 million. These co-operative societies also organised reading rooms, libraries and lectures for their members. Savings banks, lending libraries and cheap factory canteens were spreading by the 1840s. By 1867 the working man had the vote and by 1869 the Labour Representation League was formed. The working man was becoming both more independent and more able to influence the course of events without recourse to demonstrations and violent action. In 1747 and 1748 John Wesley had preached in Rossendale, in the first year to 'a large congregation of wild men' and in the second to 'a mob savage as wild beasts, who, undeterred by the authorities, proceed to every extremity of persecution, short of murder'.[3] With this background it was no exaggeration for W. E. Gladstone, when opening a public park in Farnworth in 1864, to comment: 'It is not too much to say a moral transformation has passed over the district'.[4]

Rising standards of living

W. B. Ferrand, MP, and other opponents of the factory system, did not believe that the standard of living would be improved by machines, but between 1801 and 1901 the average annual income per head in England rose from £12.9 to £52.5 over a period when the purchasing power of money actually increased. The Industrial Revolution, in which the cotton industry played a decisive part, helped England to find work for her increasing population and to keep them alive at a rising standard of living. The population of Lancashire, which had increased in the 18th century, grew from 672,000 to 1,052,000 between 1801 and 1821 and to 1,701,000 by 1841. Manchester grew from 94,000 to 160,000 and Bolton from 29,000 to 50,000 in those first 20 years of the 19th century. It was no wonder these towns had to face new problems. The population of Great Britain practically doubled between 1800 and 1850. If England had remained rural and unindustrial she would not have been able to feed this increasing population. Ireland remained rural: in the 1840s during a period of bad harvests she lost one-fifth of her population by emigration and starvation. England not only fed her own population in those years but helped to solve Ireland's problems— 750,000 native-born Irish lived in England in 1851.

---

3 *Wesley's Journals*, May, June 1747 and August 1748.
4 Aspin, *op. cit.*, pp. 34–5.

If the Industrial Revolution is commended by most scholars because it vastly improved the standards of life of all classes, some will still claim that with state planning most of its black spots could have been prevented. The reply is that if there had been state planning the Industrial Revolution as the great force for the release of the energies and production of men would not have happened. The lack of real Industrial Revolution growth in the under-developed territories is not explained by a lack of planning!

Nor can one 'plan' for something one does not know will happen. No-one in 1760 or 1780 could see what England would look like in 1820, let alone 1860 or 1880. The Industrial Revolution was like an unexpectedly successful chemical experiment in a laboratory—the chain reactions had to be allowed to run on to see what would emerge. No-one had seen its like before. The delicate mechanism which calls forth vast increases of productivity is still beyond the control of governments. The Industrial Revolution happened. We are still living on its capital. Like most of the 19th century cotton factory workers, we should be grateful.

FURTHER READING

Boyson, R., *The Ashworth Cotton Enterprise*, Oxford University Press, London, 1970.

Bythell, D., *The Handloom Weavers*, London, 1969.

French, G. J., *The Life and Times of Samuel Crompton*, London, 1859.

Pinchbeck, I., *Women Workers in the Industrial Revolution, 1750–1850*, London, 1930.

Taylor, W. C., *Factories and the Factory System*, London, 1844.
Notes of a Tour in the Manufacturing Districts of Lancashire, London, 1842.

4. Aspects of the Relief of Poverty in Early 19th-Century Britain

NORMAN McCORD

Reader in Economic and Social History,
University of Newcastle upon Tyne

THE AUTHOR

NORMAN MCCORD was educated at Tynemouth High School, King's College, Newcastle upon Tyne (now Newcastle University), and Trinity College, Cambridge. After two years at University College, Cardiff, he returned to Newcastle in 1960, and is now Reader in Economic and Social History there. His publications include work on aerial photography as applied to history and archaeology, as well as books and articles on various aspects of 19th-century British history, especially the history of North-East England.

I. THE APPROACH TO HISTORICAL UNDERSTANDING

Few aspects of modern British history have aroused so much discussion and disagreement as the record of British society in alleviating poverty during the 19th century. The problems involved are complicated, and there is need for more research on both official and unofficial attitudes to poverty and its alleviation. One of the difficulties of these topics is their apparent close relevance to current political problems and questions of social policy. It is an area of historical scholarship in which anachronistic judgements are all too easy to make, and in which it is peculiarly difficult to avoid the snare of using 'history' as ammunition in our contemporary political and ideological battles. The snare exists for historians of the right and the left; in this area of historical scholarship it is difficult to achieve even a reasonable degree of objectivity.

Avoiding preconceptions

It is crucially important not to judge previous and very different societies with preconceptions and attitudes only recently accepted after a long period of accelerating social, economic and political change. To suppose, for example, that problems associated with poverty in the early 19th century should have been approached in any egalitarian or democratic spirit is an historical approach of very limited value.[1]

The purpose of this essay is to consider only one or two aspects of the alleviation of poverty, mainly outside the official poor law machinery, in the light of the realities of British society in the early 19th century.

Consider, for example, the claims made on behalf of his own society by Macaulay, a man of considerable ability, eminence and humanity, in this well-known passage from the celebrated third chapter of the first volume of his *History of England*.[2]

'The more carefully we examine the history of the past, the more reason shall we find to dissent from those who imagine that our age has been fruitful of new

---

[1] The point may be illustrated by the account of Chartism given in a popular history book of the later 19th century, Mrs Markham's *History of England*. I quote from the 1873 edition: 'Hardly any person of knowledge or observation can imagine that the extreme changes thus proposed could be productive of real benefit to any rank or order of men.' Even more scathingly, one supposes, the writer goes on to remark that the People's Charter 'resembles also the constitution of the United States of America'.

[2] Macaulay began to write the *History* in the spring of 1839; the first two volumes were published in 1848.

social evils. The truth is that the evils are, with scarcely an exception, old. That which is new is the intelligence which discerns and the humanity which remedies them . . . the more we study the annals of the past the more shall we rejoice that we live in a merciful age, in an age in which cruelty is abhorred, and in which pain, even when deserved, is inflicted reluctantly and from a sense of duty. Every class doubtless has gained largely by this great moral change: but the class which has gained most is the poorest, the most dependent, and the most defenceless.'

This could easily be dismissed as a striking example of Whig smugness, yet if these high claims are examined in relation to the full realities of early Victorian Britain it is hard to dismiss them as baseless, especially if, like Macaulay, the reader is prepared to make the two-way comparison with earlier as well as later periods.

In a whole variety of ways British society in the early 19th century was very different from ours, and it is not surprising that there were marked differences in the attitudes and the methods employed in alleviating poverty. The population was much smaller and predominantly grouped in smaller though usually more integrated local communities. For most of the population life was far more bounded by local horizons than it is today, and it was in local and private activity that most of the dynamism of that society existed, in the treatment of poverty as in other matters. The society was dominated by small privileged minorities, as it always had been. These groups controlled the machinery of central and local government, but in practice derived most of their power from other unofficial sources, such as their command of property, employment, education. The point can be simply illustrated by the magistracy, the key office in local government. In early 19th-century Britain a man did not acquire local influence simply because he was a Justice of the Peace; more accurately, a man who already for other reasons possessed local influence was likely to find himself clothed in addition with the functions and the authority of the magistracy.

II. THE ROLE OF THE STATE

The part played in national life by the formal agencies of government was in any case very small by our standards. Government possessed only rudimentary resources for administration and social analysis, and the prospect of the extension of government power, interference and expenditure was viewed with a natural suspicion by propertied classes accustomed over many generations to official patronage being deployed for partisan political purposes. While the developing 'science' of political economy was making large and often exaggerated claims for its capacity to solve at least some of society's problems, these claims were not generally accepted, and in any event the prevailing theoretical conceptions contained a large element of doubt about the wisdom of extending government's sphere of action.

Lack of administrative expertise

The creation of a reliable and tolerably efficient civil service was still in its early stages at the beginning of the Victorian era, although Macaulay's lifetime had seen important stages in that process. To understand comtemporary approaches to poverty, it must be remembered that large numbers of trained officials equipped to administer well-designed and widespread ameliorative activities did not exist. In the official poor law machinery, before and after 1834, one of the biggest practical difficulties, and the source of much of the distress caused by the system's shortcomings, was that of building up a sufficient staff which was efficient, industrious and honest.

Agent of last resort

It is scarcely surprising in these circumstances that the role of the state in the alleviation of poverty was very different from that today. In the second half of the 20th century we are increasingly accustomed to agencies of the state as the first line of defence in tackling the social problems of poverty. Early 19th-century conceptions were very different. Then the official agencies of relief were seen as a last resort, after other more natural and proper expedients had failed. Responsibility rested initially on the individual himself. This was not simply a callous attitude, shrugging off possible social responsibilities. It derived in part from a fear that the extension of state aid might erode individual self-reliance and self-respect.

Recognition of this danger posed considerable difficulties even for fundamentally benevolent men in their approaches to the problem of poverty. In 1844 a Manchester man wrote an introduction to Leon Faucher's description of his town; part of it went as follows:[1]

'If habits of self-respect, and an honest pride of independence, are the safeguard of the working classes, and a barrier against the inroads of pauperism, it will follow that any public institutions which lead them, directly or indirectly, to

---

[1] Leon Faucher, *Manchester in 1844* (English translation, with additional notes, by 'A Member of the Manchester Athenaeum'), London and Manchester, 1844.

depend upon the bounty of others in times of poverty or sickness, and which tend to encourage idleness and improvidence, are not really and truly (as their supporters desire them to be) public charities, but public evils ... Let no one cavil at these remarks, and say that they are dictated by an uncharitable feeling against the poor. We expressly exclude from them, cases such as sudden accidents, which no foresight can guard against, and we would be the last to refuse solace and relief to those who are already suffering ... There is no charity more profound than that which habituates the working man to rely upon his own resources, and which enables him to be independent of the charity of others.'

If our own society has largely rejected this kind of social conception, it does not mean that the ideals were ignoble, or the supporting arguments devoid of all validity, though it is true that this kind of argument could appeal very successfully to men whose constructive vision was confined to keeping down rates and taxes. Many contemporaries of this Manchester writer saw much further, and the arguments adduced here are among those that underlay the 1834 Poor Law Amendment Act.

It is not my purpose to discuss the New Poor Law at any length, but it is worth mentioning that the 1834 Act, accepted by an overwhelming majority of the influential groups in that society, aimed at removing any disincentive to independence and individual effort, while at the same time providing relief in cases of genuine need. Cutting down outdoor relief for the able-bodied was intended to coerce able-bodied workers into looking to their own resources; while from the beginning the use of this sanction was hedged about with a list of exemptions providing for relief in cases of sickness, accident or other urgent necessity. The creation of the new poor law medical facilities after 1834 was another attempt to protect where protection was necessary and justified, and where intervention might on the whole aid rather than discourage the individual's self-reliance.

III. THE EXTENT OF PRIVATE CHARITY

Before 1834, as after, it was accepted that some individuals would be unable to maintain themselves, and would have to rely on the help of others. In that period, however, public relief agencies were not regarded as the individual's first line of defence. The first recourse of an individual unable to support himself should be to his family, which the 19th century saw as under a clear obligation to help its members in need whenever possible. It was seen not merely as a moral obligation but was frequently enforced as a legal duty. Poor law authorities often successfully prosecuted children who, when financially able to do so, failed to support poor aged parents.

Network of charitable activity

Where the individual and the family group failed, the unofficial charitable activity of the local community was regarded as preferable to recourse to the poor law. Early 19th-century community life in Britain was very much bounded by local considerations, and widespread religious and humanitarian conceptions—though often differing from our own—made relief activities a commonplace in every community. Concentration by some 20th-century scholars on the poor laws has obscured the fact that more poor relief was done in the early 19th century by unofficial agencies than by the poor laws, new or old. Private charity, individual or organised institutionally, stretched, however patchily and imperfectly, over wide ranges of activities and engaged resources and energies much larger than those of the official agencies of relief. This was, of course, a natural reflection of a society in which government took a comparatively limited place, while private and local activity were, and were regarded as, more valuable and efficient.

The emphasis on individual responsibility and independence was firmly entrenched in the New Poor Law of 1834. When the Assistant Commissioners set out to introduce the new system they saw themselves not merely as bringing in somewhat different administrative arrangements, but also as applying a 'scientific' device for improving the position and character of British workers. It was hoped, by imposing deterrents against fecklessness and improvidence, to induce the workers to make more use of such desirable social machinery as savings banks and friendly societies, and thereby escape the taint of pauperism and enjoy instead a life of virtuous independence.[1] One of the most attractive features in the evolution of British society in the 19th century was the pragmatism of those who governed, and the poor laws were no exception. In many instances the harsher aspects of the 1834 system were mitigated in practice by the exercise of flexibility either locally or at the centre. This pragmatism is even more apparent in the wider range of private charitable activity.

---

[1] Sir John Walsham, Bart., an early Assistant Poor Law Commissioner, presents a good example of such an enthusiastic agent. (N. McCord, 'The Implementation of the 1834 Poor Law Amendment Act on Tyneside', *International Review of Social History*, 1969.)

The approach to charity

It is probable that many of those active in the financing and management of hospitals, dispensaries and other unofficial charitable institutions would have recognised the possible social dangers of too
easy a recourse to charitable help; yet in practice, where a serious
need arose, humanitarian instincts for the most part prevailed, if in
ways that reflected the inherently unequal nature of early 19th-
century society.

To understand the usefulness to the poorer classes of private
charitable institutions, and the ways in which they operated, it may
be illuminating to consider them at work in one town, and to see
something of their history there in the first half of the 19th century.

IV. NEWCASTLE CHARITIES: A CASE STUDY

At the time the New Poor Law came into effect in North-East
England the regional centre of Newcastle upon Tyne was already
undergoing a modest degree of industrial expansion—although by
modern standards, at about 50,000 population, it represented a
comparatively small urban community. The charitable activities in
which its 'respectable' citizens engaged in these years were reasonably
representative of those in other towns of the region, and of other
parts of the country. Indeed it is notable how little 19th-century
industrialisation affected attitudes to poverty and its alleviation,
even though the detailed problems were often different.

The kinds of charitable activity in Newcastle discussed here go
back very clearly to a pre-industrial 18th century, and are on the
whole simply extended and elaborated in the ensuing century, almost
entirely at the cost of the propertied classes of the town and its
neighbourhood.[1]

The Infirmary

The Newcastle Infirmary, founded in 1751, was substantially reformed
and extended in the first years of the next century as a result of a
special appeal to which local peers and baronets contributed more
than £2,000, fulfilling what to contemporary opinion was a natural

---

[1] The account of Newcastle charities is based on the large collection of relevant
material in Newcastle Central Library, and on Eneas Mackenzie's *History of Newcastle*,
1827.

responsibility associated with their rank and wealth. A further appeal in 1817 added 'warm baths, on an approved plan'.

The Infirmary fulfilled two main functions: it provided a 24-hour casualty service, and other facilities, for the poorer classes of the town. The emergency casualty service was available free and without formality. But the Infirmary's other main function was on a patronage basis typical of many contemporary charitable activities. Anyone who subscribed two guineas to the Infirmary's funds could present one in-patient or two out-patients in that year; the higher the subscription the larger the presentation powers. Before attending for treatment the intending patient must have a letter of introduction from a subscriber, except in the case of the emergency casualty service. Not all presentation rights were exercised by subscribers themselves; those absent often gave proxies to the Infirmary staff or other agents. The Town Council and other local bodies, official and unofficial, including trade unions, made regular block subscriptions and obtained presentation rights. The Mayor, or any two aldermen, could present any poor citizen to the Infirmary through the town's subscription. This is an example of the frequent overlaps between official and unofficial activities, natural enough at the time, since the local poor law boards and charitable associations were likely to be administered by the same or similar people. In 1825–26 the Newcastle Infirmary spent just under £3,000, and declared that 1,447 patients were 'restored to their friends and the community wholly freed from their complaints'.

Some interesting points emerged from the revision of the statutes governing the Infirmary in 1801. The older rules, in deference to 'respectable' opinion, had denied treatment to sufferers from venereal disease. In practice, however, this provision had been frequently evaded, usually by entering a false description of the case in the Infirmary records. The 1801 statutes modified the prohibition in two ways: a person who had innocently contracted the disease from an infected consort or parent could be treated, while a patient admitted for another reason could also be treated for venereal disease if found after entry to be infected. In any event there was to be no more false entry of details, in order 'to provide accurate registers and annual returns'.

Other parts of the Infirmary statutes are illuminating. Here is part of the standard printed instructions for patients:

'You are to attend the Infirmary every—at eleven o'clock in the forenoon, during the continuance of your disorder and you are every time to bring back all the medicines which you have not taken, and all your bottles, phials, and gallypots, well cleaned and washed. You are not to presume to loiter about the Infirmary gate or places adjacent, but come directly into the place appointed to receive you, and as soon as your business is despatched you must return home. When you have had notice to be discharged you shall appear at the Infirmary on the Thursday following at eleven o'clock in the forenoon to return thanks to the gentlemen of the house committee, for the benefit you have received from the charity.'

Neglect of this last stipulation would be answered by permanent exclusion from the Infirmary's facilities.

These minatory instructions were typical of many, natural enough in a society in which subordination in a wide variety of forms was the normal lot of many of the poorer sections of the community. Charity regulations frequently included the explicit condition that the beneficiary must take the first practicable opportunity to thank the patron who had presented him to the charity, and also give thanks to God in church or chapel as soon as possible. Future exclusion was often cited in the rules as the penalty for neglect of such obvious duties of gratitude.

The Dispensary

In addition to the Infirmary, Newcastle also possessed a large Dispensary, founded in 1778 but, like the Infirmary, much enlarged early in the 19th century. This provided free medicines for the poor and a free service without formality for 'slight casualties'. The Dispensary also operated under a patronage system, a donation of a guinea entitling the subscriber to introduce five patients in the year. In the 1820s, serving a population of about 40,000, the Dispensary would expect some 5,000 cases each year. In addition 20,000 free vaccinations were provided in the first quarter of the century. Most of its work was with out-patients, but its medical officers also operated a system of house visits where necessary.

Before Gateshead founded its own Dispensary, a block annual subscription of 30 guineas from Gateshead subscribers allowed the poor of the sister town to use the Newcastle Dispensary. There was a similar arrangement with the Mendicity Institute, a privately-supported institution for vagrants. In the late 1830s both the Gateshead and Newcastle Poor Law Unions continued to buy access to the Mendicity Institute's facilities until their own arrangements were deemed adequate.

Maternity hospitals

Newcastle also possessed two long-established maternity charities. The Lying-in Hospital moved into very fine new premises in 1826, built with money from a variety of sources. The Newcastle Music Festival of October 1824 raised £160; two special sermons brought in £52 and £61; Newcastle Corporation gave £100, Newcastle Trinity House £30. Individual donations made up the rest. Before entering this maternity hospital pregnant women were expected to produce evidence of their marriage and of their husband's settlement in the town. The Charity for Poor Married Women, dating from 1760, provided midwifery services in the mother's own home.

Newcastle also possessed a Lock Hospital, or specialised institution for the reception of prostitutes, who were normally excluded from the more 'respectable' charities. This charity was founded in 1814, with donations from prominent local dignitaries including the Bishop of Durham and the Duke of Northumberland. Its activities were handicapped by contemporary 'false delicacy', as one radical observer (Eneas Màckenzie) put it, but the work continued. By the 1860s the Infirmary had a special ward—quite separate from other patients— for prostitutes, and also a Home for Penitent Women, intended as a centre for rehabilitation.

The town's privately-administered lunatic asylum, founded in 1767, was substantially improved and extended in the 1820s. Many of its patients were lunatic paupers, sent to the asylum by poor law authorities at the ratepayers' expense.

Help for the handicapped

Throughout the early 19th century new agencies for relief proliferated as needs were appreciated and tackled. Early in 1838 a group of leading citizens met to found a Newcastle asylum for the blind but split a few months later on sectarian lines over the appointment of a chaplain. As a result the Dissenting foundation remained a blind asylum while the Anglican equivalent concentrated on the care of the deaf and dumb, pioneering their specialised treatment in the region. It became increasingly common for local poor law authorities to send patients to these institutions at public expense, thus combining official and unofficial relief activity, and paving the way for the later extension of publicly-financed welfare institutions.

These by no means complete the list of unofficial charitable foundations in this relatively small town. Much energy went into the provision of religious instruction and consolation for the poor, welfare work of considerable importance at that time, if of less interest to the modern observer. Thousands of pounds and a large amount of voluntary effort were expended annually on these devout causes in Newcastle alone.

Charity schools

Among the other unofficial charitable activities one deserves more extended treatment here, both because of its importance and because it too illuminates some important aspects of early 19th-century society. The charity schools, proliferating like other welfare agencies in the late 18th and even more in the early 19th century, fulfilled more than merely educational functions. That of All Saints parish (40 boys, 40 girls) arranged apprenticeships for graduating pupils who on apprenticeship, were presented with gifts: boys £2, a Bible, a Prayer Book, and a copy of 'The Whole Duty of Man'; girls £1 and the same basic texts. The larger charity school of St Nicholas' parish (about 400 boys, 150 girls, taught on Bell's monitorial system)[2] gave parting gifts of £1 to pupils leaving to go to work. Here parents were charged 1d per week while additional revenue came from the propertied citizens in subscriptions and bequests.

King George III's jubilee in 1810, and the aged monarch's much publicised wish that every child in his dominions should be able to read its Bible, led to the foundation by local subscriptions of Jubilee schools in many parts of the country including Newcastle, where by the late 1820s the Jubilee schools were teaching nearly 500 boys and more than 200 girls without fees from parents. The Lancasterian monitorial system was used, not merely as an economy measure, but because it was widely believed to represent the best in contemporary educational techniques. Eneas Mackenzie waxed enthusiastic over these schools in the 1820s when he stood well on the 'left' of local society as a keenly radical reformer. He wrote with favour of the graded incentive payments offered to Monitor Generals, Monitors of Classes, and ordinary pupils, and entirely approved of singling out the best pupils into an 'Order of Merit', for whom a special library was created after an appeal for donations for this purpose.

Some of Mackenzie's phraseology might horrify even the authors

---

2 Bell and Lancaster were pioneers in monitorial systems, i.e. systems of indirect teaching in which the older pupils passed on to classes lessons taught them by the teachers.

of educational Black Papers. He felt very strongly that this efficient monitorial system

'must soon bring into disrepute the old stupefying practice of fixing the trembling pupil in his seat, where he dozes over his hated task . . . It is a curious and pleasing spectacle, to see above 400 boys, in one room, actively and cheerfully engaged in acquiring the elements of education, while their movements are conducted with the regularity and celerity of disciplined troops . . . Some of the boys in the upper classes display an acuteness and rapidity of thought almost incredible.'

When it is realised that this is a voice uncompromisingly of the then contemporary left, the dangers of applying current political concepts to the early 19th century become clear.

Mackenzie also disliked the notion of completely free schooling which he feared

'must tend to blunt the delicate pride of both parents and children, to familiarise the mind to dependence on charitable institutions, and to prepare it for the degradation of pauperism. The demanding of a small weekly sum from the parents is evidently gratifying to their feelings.'

The 'Ragged School' movement

A further educational development towards the end of the first half of the century shows how unofficial charitable enterprise pioneered new ideas and tried new experiments in accordance with a growing recognition of society's problems. Experience showed that the many charitable schools already founded were not reaching the very poorest children, who often had to make shift to feed themselves or to do work of some kind, honest or otherwise, making school attendance impossible. The 'Ragged School' movement at mid-century sought to cater for these children.[3]

The Newcastle Ragged School's aims were outlined as follows:

'The education of Reading, Writing and Arithmetic, and a knowledge of the Holy Scriptures, and Moral and Industrial training of children whose poverty precludes their attendance at a superior school; and their necessary support while thus withdrawn from those habits of mendicity, theft and precarious employment, by which many of them are accustomed to obtain a livelihood.'

The school depended entirely on donations in cash and kind to keep it going and to enable its committee to give very poor children a mixture of education, moral training, feeding and trade training. Its

---

[3] In the 1860s Parliament expressly legislated to relieve such schools from paying rates (Ragged Schools Act, 1869).

annual reports and appeals for help are couched in terms which might well strike a modern reader as appallingly patronising and superior; they dwell at length on the scandalous homes from which some of the children came and the remarkable moral reformations achieved by the school's religious training. A potential subscriber of about 1850, however, might not be much disturbed by such language. Certainly the school did obtain useful help. Here, for example, is a passage from its 1849 Report:

'The Committee take this opportunity to express their grateful sense of the kindness of the Worshipful the Mayor, and the other gentlemen, in providing the children with a handsome dinner of roast beef and plum pudding, on Easter Monday . . . and they are of opinion that the social mingling of the rich and poor on such occasions, and the personal interest thus exhibited in the enjoyments of the humbler classes, are well adapted to strengthen and consolidate the bonds of civil society.'

Other charities

This short discussion of unofficial relief operations in one reasonably representative town does not contain a complete list of such activities. In Newcastle, and more generally, there were many individual charitable endowments, often deriving from bequests and applied to a wide variety of purposes and groups. Older endowments had often in the course of time deteriorated or been misapplied. But one of the justifications for Macaulay's high claims for his own generation was the increasing pressure during the first half of the 19th century for the reform of older charities, and even before the creation of the Charity Commissioners in 1874 much useful reform had been achieved by local and piecemeal efforts.

It cannot be charged, therefore, that the propertied classes were peculiarly callous in that period. In Eneas Mackenzie's opinion:

'Maugre the attempts of Malthus and the Scottish Philosophers to discourage the breeding of the industrious classes, the old English feeling of kindness and benevolence to the poor has been pleasingly evinced in Newcastle.'

V. PRIVATE HELP AND SELF-HELP

One form of charitable activity which is extremely difficult to assess is the extent of private individual help; it cannot be measured for in the nature of things the evidence is defective. It is clear, however, that private individual charity was very widespread and was widely recognised as a normal responsibility accompanying the possession of property. This is not to say that it was universally practised, though it could be found in most unexpected quarters, as for example in that ogre of early Victorian Britain, the third Marquis of Londonderry. A Tyneside mining expert, asked by a House of Lords Committee about the treatment of workers injured in mining accidents and their dependents, replied:[1]

'There is no provision, excepting parochial relief, and what arises out of the humanity of their employers, and which is carried to a great extent in a way which is not generally known. When there is a catastrophe of this kind, there are not only a great many killed but a great many disabled for life: it always produces an immense number of cripples; they must be provided with some employment which they can manage; many of them go to boys' work, what is called trapping, furnace-keeping, and a great many jobs that might be done by boys, if it were not for the sake of employing these cripples and disabled persons. Again, there are a great number of widows produced; it is not within my knowledge that any coal-owner ever disturbed a widow after an accident of that sort or put her out of her house; they have their houses and fuel continued to them probably as long as they live; and it frequently happened that a widow is left (having lost not only her husband but three or four sons) with a single boy quite an infant almost, probably six or seven, or eight years of age, and that boy is generally indulged with some employment that he is put to, at advanced wages, in consideration of the loss of his family; so that the coal-owners, though their charity does not appear publicly, yet to a very great extent in the way of giving extra wages, or certain work to cripples, finding houses for widows, and so on, do charity to a much greater extent than they are even themselves aware of. Sometimes they [the sufferers] have been relieved by public subscription, but there are individuals such as the Marquis of Londonderry and Lord Durham, who do private charity besides; I mean in direct payments to orphans and widows.'

While none of this may measure up to what our modern society may think necessary, in the rougher society of the early 19th century these were important socially ameliorative activities.

Charity and 'self-help'

Benevolent activities by members of the privileged and propertied minorities were not limited to the management and support of charitable institutions or to their private charitable efforts. Many early 19th-century 'self-help' organisations leaned heavily on the support and countenance of the wealthier sectors of society. The Tyneside Loyal Standard Seamen's Association, combining for many

---

[1] John Buddle, quoted in Mackenzie and Ross, *An Historical, Topographical, and Descriptive View of the County Palatine of Durham*, Newcastle, 1834, Vol. I, pp.cxv-cxvi.

years friendly society and trade union activities, was notable for its skilful lobbying of influential and wealthy local figures.[2] The expanding chemical and glass factories along the south bank of the lower Tyne developed strong friendly societies which were heavily backed by the proprietors of these firms, a situation with many parallels. A much humbler example can be found in the rules of the Ford Insurance Club,[3] founded in a small Northumberland village to insure the village workers' cows; the rules prescribed the participation of local farming employers in the valuation of the cows, while the two identifiable members of its governing committee were not themselves agricultural labourers but middle-class men.

There was, then, much welfare and relief work based almost entirely on private donations and subscriptions from the propertied classes. It was rarely administered in an egalitarian spirit, but there is no reason why it should have been. It could wear a highly minatory front, as in the 1836 rules for the Ravensworth Almshouses, which specified that

'Persons admitted into the Ravensworth Almshouses are to consider themselves as Residents only upon sufferance, and that they may be dismissed by the Lady Ravensworth, or any person deputed by Her Ladyship for any offence, or reason, that Her Ladyship may deem sufficient: and it is to be understood that drunkenness, dishonesty, want of cleanliness, quarrelling, meddling with or slandering their neighbours will be considered sufficient reasons for dismissal.'

Charity could appear unutterably smug, as when a few years later the Shipwrecked Mariners' Society held its main meeting at Gateshead. After arranging for the raising and spending of considerable sums of money for the relief of one of the most regularly endangered sections of the contemporary working class, the Society then

'sat down to a sumptuous dinner at the George Inn, and spent an evening of the most gratifying kind—happily engrafting upon the social enjoyments of the passing hour, a determination to relieve the distresses and promote the comforts of their less fortunate fellow-creatures.'

The account is from a radical newspaper, the *Gateshead Observer*.

Despite these reservations unofficial action for the relief of poverty

---

2 This is clear from documents in the Kelly collection, South Shields Public Library, as well as from the association's policies in the industrial disputes of 1831–32. (N. McCord, 'The Government of Tyneside, 1800–1850,' in *Trans. R. Hist. Soc.*, 1970.)

3 Published Berwick, 1834. Rule IV is strikingly worded: 'No cow to be admitted, unless in a thriving condition, nor to be entitled to the benefit of the Club after twelve years of age.'

and distress led to much socially ameliorative activity in early 19th-century Britain, and exhibited more adventurous and varied enterprise than the official poor law agencies. Governments were well aware of the importance of local charitable enterprise, but were also determined to do nothing by public means that might diminish the enthusiasm of local societies and individuals to carry on their philanthropic activities; activities which enriched the life of the donor while bringing relief to the afflicted. Indeed government ministers could often find themselves in the dilemma of being faced with a need for relief measures, yet fearing that state intervention might do more harm than good by discouraging local energies and activities. A good example is the reaction of government to distress in certain parts of the country resulting from industrial unemployment in the later 1820s.

Government aid—direct and indirect

It was common in such periods of social trouble for local dignitaries to press on the central government the need for exceptional intervention to relieve local distress. Such requests were to recur again and again. They faced ministers with the question: should public money be used to bolster up ailing elements in the economy? Would the appearance of the central government in the role of protective fairy godmother inhibit local effort and enterprise? Faced with conflicting pressures and arguments Peel, as Home Secretary, adopted in the late 1820s a compromise policy which fits in well with our earlier analysis, and which meant in practice that central government was doing more in the way of combatting distress in the later 1820s than it has usually been given credit for. A certain amount of money was doled out in direct subvention of especially hard-hit areas. On 20 April, 1826, for example, Peel authorised in the King's name grants of £1,000 each to Macclesfield and Blackburn; they were given explicitly as royal assistance and encouragement to local relief measures.[4]

This was not, however, the government's main or only resource. Appeals for donations by the Manufacturers' Relief Committee, an unofficial relief agency with headquarters at the City of London Tavern, were officially backed by the central government by various methods, including the issue of successive formal King's Letters

---

[4] Public Record Office, H.O. 43/34

appealing for help to the committee's work. Home Office Papers make it clear that the central government, chary and hesitant about large-scale direct expenditure to relieve distress caused by industrial unemployment, was much happier to work behind the scenes in close collaboration with this ostensibly unofficial agency. C. J. Blomfield, Bishop of Chester and later Bishop of London, who was closely associated with the work of this committee, was one of Peel's main advisers and informants on these matters, and in June 1828 they were in correspondence about unemployment among Spitalfields silk workers.[5] Peel felt that government could not intervene to bail out the declining silk industry at Spitalfields, hard hit by the development of more efficient production elsewhere in Britain, but he suggested the diversion of City of London Tavern Committee funds 'under judicious regulations, to the temporary relief of the Weavers'.

The Home Office often referred local correspondents directly to the City of London Tavern Committee, at the same time hinting privately to the Committee that its resources could usefully be employed in giving help to the district concerned; undoubtedly an intimate connection existed in the later 1820s between central government and the committee's work. In July 1828, when the committee's leaders were uncertain what policy to adopt in relation to their existing £57,000 balance, a meeting was held with the Prime Minister, the Home Secretary, and the Chancellor of the Exchequer, which resulted in a policy of bold expenditure, with a reasonable assurance that a subsequent public appeal would replenish the coffers.[6] In its letters to local applicants for help the Government repeatedly emphasised the superior advantages of voluntary local relief work. Here is Peel writing to the Blackburn magistrates in July 1828[7] that ministers were

'strongly impressed with the conviction that the direct interference of the Government for the relief of the unemployed Poor (even if the Pecuniary means existed) would be much less effectual than the exertions which are made locally in concert with the Committee at the City of London Tavern—and might probably by relaxing those exertions do serious harm.'

Certainly local relief measures—the provision of public works to give temporary employment, the establishment of soup kitchens and other palliatives—regularly appeared on local initiative to relieve distress caused by large-scale industrial unemployment. In confining

---

5 H.O. 40/34.
6 H.O. 41/7: Peel/Bishop of Chester, 24 April, 1828.   7 *Ibid.*

most of the responsibility for ameliorative measures to dynamic local forces, primed by occasional government grants and aid channelled through an ostensibly independent charitable agency, government may have been reaching the best compromise possible in the light of the complex pressures and considerations involved. Nevertheless the preference for non-official action is a marked one, and reflects more general aspects of relief activity in early 19th-century Britain, in which unofficial charity exceeded public poor law activity.

VI. CONCLUSIONS

Can any general conclusions be drawn from the foregoing discussion? The picture that emerges is of a society by no means devoid of care for its less fortunate members, but one in which the ameliorative measures and agencies reflected the existing society. A highly unequal society facing a period of unusually rapid change had already in the previous century begun to expand its voluntary measures for the relief of distress. As the 19th century advanced, hospitals and dispensaries, asylums and schools rapidly increased in number, and as more information on social problems became available there was continued willingness among the propertied classes to support new agencies of relief. For most of the century the private sector of relief was more active and enterprising than the official poor law,[1] though there were many links between the two, not least among the persons directing these activities at local level.

Needless to say, it would be wrong to leave an idyllic conception of early 19th-century Britain. If much suffering was administered to, and much voluntary help given, the period also saw other poverty and suffering which went largely unattended. In this respect it probably differed little from earlier periods. Not everything was done in early 19th-century Britain to relieve poverty that could have been done; not everything that was done was done well. Many men were heartless or inconsiderate, though perhaps not more so than in other periods. Not all charitable activity was carried out from the loftiest of motives. Social emulation, fear of hell-fire and the desire to establish a good credit balance above, and the desire to forestall social troubles by palliative measures—all these motives took their place beside the very large amount of genuine kindliness and humanity which the period presented.

---

[1] A point broadly accepted in Lord Beveridge's *Voluntary Action*, 1948.

When all necessary reservations have been made, however, we may conclude with Macaulay that his generation was doing *more* to relieve poverty and distress than any previous age had done. Those efforts were largely at the expense, in money and energy, of the propertied ruling classes whose dominance and power were never seriously shaken in that period. It may well be, as the Committee of the Newcastle Ragged School believed, that the charitable activities of the propertied classes did 'strengthen and consolidate the bonds of civil society'. But it does not look as if most of the charitable activity of that period was inspired by machiavellian plans to disarm disaffection; most of it proceeded rather from the desire to alleviate poverty and mitigate distress.

The activities discussed here formed part of the foundations for the very considerable achievements of British society in the 19th century, a rare example of a society absorbing massive social, economic and political change and enormous population expansion with remarkably little conflict and bloodshed. The achievement is not particularly easy to explain, but part of the explanation lies in the existence of many links of sympathy and co-operation between the different segments of that society. Individually the links were often frail and tenuous, but in total they were to prove much stronger than the strains which threatened to break the cohesion of the community. Philanthropic activity formed part of this complex pattern, perhaps a larger part than has often been realised. The activities and experiments in private relief operations in the early 19th century were an important stage in the evolution of more enlightened social policies, and did much good at a time when the need for such help was urgent, and the state did not possess the resources to interfere competently in this sphere.

It may be pertinent to end with another passage from Macaulay's third chapter.

'We too shall, in our turn be outstripped, and in our turn be envied. It may well be, in the twentieth century, that the peasant of Dorsetshire may think himself miserably paid with twenty shillings a week; that the carpenter in Greenwich may receive ten shillings a day; that labouring men may be as little used to dine without meat as they now are to eat rye bread; that sanitary, police and medical discoveries may have added several more years to the average length of human life; that numerous comforts and luxuries which are now unknown, or confined to a few, may be within the reach of every diligent and thrifty person. And yet it may then be the mode to assert that the increase of wealth and the progress of science have benefited the few at the expense of the many. . . . '

FURTHER READING

Books

Owen, David, *English Philanthropy 1660–1960*, Harvard University Press, 1965.

Simey, M. B., *Charitable Effort in Liverpool in the 19th Century*, Liverpool University Press, 1951.

Woodroofe, Kathleen, *From Charity to Social Work*, Routledge & Kegan Paul, 1962.

Young, A. F., and Ashton, E. T., *British Social Work in the Nineteenth Century*, Routledge & Kegan Paul, 1956.

Articles

Flinn, M., 'The Poor Employment Act of 1817', *Economic History Review*, Vol. XIV, 1961.

Harrison, B., 'Philanthropy and the Victorians', *Victorian Studies*, Vol. IX, 1965–6.

Roberts, D., 'How Cruel was the Victorian Poor Law?', *Historical Journal*, Vol. 6, Part 1, 1963.

Henriques, U., 'How Cruel was the Victorian Poor Law?', *Historical Journal*, Vol. 11, Part 2, 1968.

McCord, N., 'The Implementation of the 1834 Poor Law Amendment Act on Tyneside', *International Review of Social History*, Vol. 14, No. 1, 1969.

5. Welfare before the Welfare State

C. G. HANSON

Lecturer in Economics,
University of Newcastle upon Tyne

THE AUTHOR

C. G. HANSON was at Felsted School, Essex, before spending two years in the Royal Artillery. He took his BA in Economics at Cambridge in 1958 and then went into the printing industry for $3\frac{1}{2}$ years. He was appointed temporary lecturer in Economics at the University of Newcastle upon Tyne in 1962. He is still at Newcastle, specialising in industrial relations and researching into the development of trade unions and trade union law over the past century.

£5½ and £7 million.[3] But the population of central London at that time was less than a tenth of the total population of England and Wales.[4] Thus it may reasonably be supposed that the annual expenditure of private charities over the country as a whole ran into tens of millions of pounds. This compares with a total expenditure on public poor relief of £5.8 million in 1861 and £7.9 million in 1871.[5]

The Charity Organisation Society, founded in 1869, had limited success in living up to its name, but it had a good deal of influence on public policy in the late 19th century through its outspoken secretary, C. S. Loch. For members of the Society, social advance depended on an increase in individual responsibility. It followed that they were opposed to indiscriminate alms-giving, whether from private or public sources.

'True charity therefore implied sympathy and understanding on the part of the donor and was fulfilled not in a single act but in a continuing relationship.'[6]

The nature of that relationship, and the differences between private and public welfare, were described by Mr Gardiner, a witness to the Royal Commission on the Aged Poor of 1895:

'Charity pensions are quite on a different footing, at any rate in the case of pensions provided by the Charity Organisation Society. They are always taken every week to the old people by some lady visitor. She will have three, four or five pensioners on her list, and she will visit them in a friendly way, taking them in the summer time flowers, and in the winter time little comforts, which, of course, they could never receive at the hands of a poor law official . . . Those visits brighten their lives very much, and they are very good for the visitor who pays the visit as well as for the poor person who receives it.'[7]

Today there are more than 1¼ million old-age pensioners living alone. They collect their state 'welfare' (i.e. cash) by paying a weekly visit to the post office. Perhaps those who saw good in private charity and who worked in the way described above were not quite so foolish or uncharitable as some writers would have us believe.

Private charity has come in for much hostile criticism in the 20th century by many who are indulgent of the imperfections and defects of state welfare. For example, it has been argued that private charity 'did a good deal to mitigate the weight of misery borne by the poor of London, but in the unsystematic and indiscriminate way in which much of it dribbled

---

[3] Hawksley, *Charities of London*, p. 6, quoted in D. Owen, *English Philanthropy*, Harvard University Press, 1965, p. 218.

[4] G. M. Young (ed.), *Early Victorian England*, Oxford University Press, 1934, pp. 22 and 62.   [5] *Report of the Royal Commission on the Aged Poor*, 1895, p. x.

[6] D. Owen, *op. cit.*, p. 227.

[7] *Report of the Royal Commission on the Aged Poor*, 1895, p. lii.

out, it also did something to fasten on them the habit of dependence on charity, considering it, in fact, as no more than their due.'[8]

Again, it has been suggested that the attitude of the private social worker to the poor sometimes became a 'patron-client relationship'.[9] Some people may think that private charities are likely to be more discriminating than state agencies, and that these two criticisms can be just as valid of 20th-century state welfare as of 19th-century private welfare.

The most telling argument against the adequacy of private charity was the amount of poverty which still existed in the 1890s. On the other hand, the most telling argument against the expansion of state welfare was the evidence that people *were* becoming more responsible under the existing system. What was this evidence?

III. THE GROWTH OF THE FRIENDLY SOCIETIES

Apart from private charity and public relief, the principal agents for the provision of welfare in Britain before 1908 were the friendly societies. They had enjoyed steady and continuous growth since the end of the 18th century, and with the increase in living standards in the second half of the 19th century their membership became widespread. But how widespread? In any debate about the need for state welfare, the effectiveness and extent of independent welfare organisation are crucial questions. These are questions which must be examined in detail, not least because some existing estimates of the extent of friendly society membership seem to be too low.

Misinterpretation of the statistics

It is easy to misinterpret information regarding the extent of friendly societies. Confusion can arise on at least three counts. First, the official statistics gave only part of the picture because registration with the official Registrar of Friendly Societies was voluntary, not compulsory. It was well known that large numbers of societies did not register but, in the absence of detailed research, estimates of the membership of *unregistered* societies cannot be more than informed guesses. There was, then, always the danger that the official figures, which referred solely to membership of *registered* societies, would

---

8 D. Owen, *op. cit.*, p. 218.
9 *Ibid.*, p. 227.

be mistaken for the total membership of *all* societies. More will be said later about the likely membership of unregistered societies.

Secondly, there has been confusion because of the wide variety of friendly societies. There is plenty of room for argument about exactly what type of organisation should count as a friendly society. This problem, too, will be considered below.

Thirdly, there is room for disagreement about the proportion of friendly society members among the working population because of differences of view about the normal age at which young men joined the societies. It has been stated that 19 'may be taken as a normal entering age for the societies',[1] but it seems likely that this statement is wrong. The friendly society with the largest membership in the second half of the 19th century was the Manchester Unity of Odd Fellows, an affiliated society with branches all over the country. S. Daynes, a spokesman for the society, told a Royal Commission in the early 1870s that 'The period of joining benefit societies is 24 or 25 years of age; of course a very great number of persons join before that age, but you may assume 24 as the age'.[2] After all, it would be reasonable to suppose that in their late 'teens and early twenties many young men, even earnest Victorian young men, had matters other than the provision of sickness and death benefits on their minds. Unless there is positive evidence that young men began to join at an earlier age as the century drew on, it is right to take Daynes' statement as correct and to compare the total number of friendly society members with the male population of 24 and over.

Benefits and membership

We return, then, to the two major outstanding problems: which types of friendly society should be included in the figures, and how widespread were unregistered societies?

The benefits provided by most friendly societies were two—sickness benefit and death benefit. The sickness benefit was normally payable while a member was unable to work. As the 1874 Commission was told by an experienced actuary: 'it is not sickness in a medical point of view at all that friendly societies provide against, it is incapacity for labour'.[3] The statistics showed, as one would expect, that as

---

[1] B. B. Gilbert, *The Evolution of National Insurance in Great Britain*, Michael Joseph, 1966, p. 167.

[2] *Second Report of the Royal Commission on Friendly Societies*, 1874, question 201.

[3] *Ibid.*, question 1,082.

people grew older, and especially after the age of 65, their incapacity for labour increased. There was no standard retirement age in the 19th century. People worked as long as they were able to, and many friendly society members took great pride in keeping off the benefits. Normally the sick benefit was reduced to a half rate after 6 or 12 months' continuous sickness. Thus, typical benefits in the Manchester Unity of Odd Fellows, for a payment of 6d a week, were 9s a week for the first 12 months' sickness, and 4s 6d for all sickness after 12 months' continuous sickness; £9 at the death of a member and £4 10s at the death of a member's wife. If a member's health broke down completely at any age he would, therefore, receive what amounted to a pension of 9s a week for the first 12 months and 4s 6d a week thereafter.

In addition to friendly societies proper, 'collecting societies' were rapidly expanding their membership in the late 19th century. As the Registrar of Friendly Societies pointed out in his report for 1896, these were really much more akin to industrial assurance societies, like the Prudential, than to ordinary friendly societies of the type described above. Payments of 2d or 3d a week insured a sum of a few pounds at death. The Registrar's tabular statement makes the difference between friendly societies and collecting societies clear, although it is too hard on the latter (Table II).

TABLE II.—COMPARISON OF FRIENDLY AND COLLECTING SOCIETIES' FUNCTIONS

Friendly Societies	*Collecting Societies*
Combine relief in sickness with life insurance.	Limited to life insurance; relief in sickness discontinued except in some cases to original members.
Monthly or, in some cases, fortnightly meetings the rule.	Meeting, whether district or general, practically disregarded by members.
Management inexpensive; officials generally appointed by intelligent consent of members.	Management rarely costing less than 40% of premium income; members practically excluded from voice in election of managers.
Promoted and conducted for benefit of members.	Promoted and conducted for benefit of managers.

In his annual report the Registrar commonly included 'collecting societies' and various other types of society under the general heading of 'Friendly Societies'. In the 1902 report, for example, total membership under the general heading of 'Friendly Societies' was 12,807,378; but of this total, collecting societies accounted for no less than 6,678,005, or more than half. In a widely circulated book, first published in 1905, it was stated that 'The Friendly Societies have 12,000,000 members'.[4] This was the total figure, and grossly over-states the number of registered friendly society members proper. These can be more accurately defined as the number of members of what the Registrar called 'Ordinary Friendly Societies' and 'Societies having branches'. Their membership is set out in Table III.

TABLE III.—MEMBERSHIP AND FUNDS OF 'ORDINARY FRIENDLY SOCIETIES' AND 'SOCIETIES HAVING BRANCHES,' 1891–1909*

	No. of members (million)	Amount of funds (£million)
1891	4·2	22·7
1899	5·2	32·7
1909	6·2	48·2

Sources: The figures for 1891 are derived from the Registrar's *Report* of 1892 which provides information for England and Wales (p. 45), and from E. W. Brabrook, *Provident Societies and Industrial Welfare*, Blackie and Son, 1898, p. 55, which provides information for Scotland and Ireland. Figures for 1899 and 1909 are from the Registrar's *Reports* of 1901 (p. 29) and 1910 (p. 37) respectively.

* The figures are for registered societies in Great Britain and Ireland.

So much for the steadily growing membership of registered friendly societies proper. What of unregistered societies? As already suggested, estimates here can never be better than informed guesses. But an informed guess based on the best available evidence is better than no estimate at all. The most thorough investigation of friendly societies ever undertaken was that made by the Royal Commission on Friendly Societies of 1874. They faced exactly the same problem of ascertaining the number and membership of unregistered societies as later investigators. When E. W. Brabrook, the Registrar of Friendly Societies, was questioned in 1893 by the Aberdare Com-

---

[4] L. G. Chiozza Money, *Riches and Poverty*, Methuen, 1905, p. 49.

mission about the membership of unregistered societies, he referred to the estimate of the 1874 Commission that 'the extent of unregistered societies was as large as that of the registered societies'. This estimate was based on detailed research which compared the *total* number of friendly societies in Lancashire and their membership with the number of *registered* friendly societies in that county and their membership, Lancashire at that time having more registered friendly societies and a larger membership than any other county.[5] Brabrook then went on to say:

'I think there is good reason to suggest that no change, at any rate in the direction of greater proportion of registry to non-registry, has taken place since that time. The law clerk of my office went down a few days ago on an expedition into Norfolk to look after some societies which had made default in making returns and sending the valuations prescribed by law, and he found in the villages through which he had to pass that there was a considerable number of unregistered societies, and he found in many cases that old registered societies which had existed for nearly a century or more ago, had been dissolved and their places taken by unregistered societies; so that I think it is beyond a doubt that the sphere of unregistered societies is exceedingly large.'[6]

Brabrook had made a similar point in evidence to the Royal Commission on Labour in 1892. Using the 1890 figures, and allowing for overlapping membership because some men joined two or three societies, he suggested then that there were more than 3 million members in registered societies and another 3 million in unregistered societies, and went on:

'If you add to those the members of the trade unions who are not also members of a friendly society (I do not know how many they may be, but there must be some out of the 871,000 members of trade unions), you get a very large population indeed who are members in one shape or another of a friendly society or trade union, and who are providing by their own exertions for sickness and a small sum for funeral expenses at death. It would look as if there was really merely a kind of residuum left of those who are in uncertain work or otherwise, and are not able to insure in some shape or another.'[7]

The census of 1891 showed a total of 7.1 million males over the age of 24 in England, Wales and Scotland; if a fifth of the 20–24 age group is added to that figure—284,000—we arrive at 7.4 million as the maximum possible extent of friendly society membership. The evidence suggested to Brabrook that 6 million of these men were

---

[5] *Fourth Report of the Royal Commission on Friendly Societies*, 1874, Appendix iv.

[6] *Evidence to the Royal Commission on the Aged Poor*, 1895, question 11,039.

[7] *Evidence to the Royal Commission on Labour*, 1893 (Sitting as a whole), question 1,331.

members of friendly societies proper. Bearing in mind the constant criticism by Booth and other reformers about the provision of welfare, it is understandable that Brabrook was astonished by his own conclusions. Asked whether the numbers he had given included the members of co-operative societies, he replied:

'No, I was speaking entirely of those who were insured for sick pay and for funeral money; and I confess that I am so startled by the result that I give it with the utmost possible reserve.'[8]

A careful assessment of the best available evidence suggests that it is quite possible that Brabrook's opinion was correct. By the 1890s the number of adult males who were not insured against sickness (and thereby to some extent against old age) and death of their own initiative was a small minority. Furthermore, as friendly society membership grew proportionately more rapidly than the population, the number uninsured was a constantly diminishing minority.

In the struggle for the introduction of more extensive state welfare benefits it is possible to portray the friendly societies as the obstinate and vested interest of a part of society which was acting against the interests of society as a whole. That is what Professor Gilbert seems to be trying to do, by making the friendly societies appear exclusive bodies, largely restricted to the better-paid skilled workers. He emphasises, for example, that some societies, among them the popular Hearts of Oak, maintained a minimum income limit.[9] It is true that the Hearts of Oak, whose membership rose from 175,000 in 1892 to 350,000 in 1905, *had* maintained a minimum income limit of 24s a week, and that certain dangerous or unhealthy trades had been excluded. But the Rothschild Committee of 1898 was told that 'these several restrictions have been abrogated'.[10] Generally speaking, societies which wished to grow, and most of them did, could not afford to be exclusive, and varying rates of contributions and benefits were tailored to suit most members of the community The only condition of membership was a sufficiently regular income to pay a contribution of a few pence (normally between 4d and 9d) a week. This was not a particularly severe condition for most working-class families at the turn of the century, and by that time, far from being

---

[8] *Evidence to the Royal Commission on Labour*, 1893 (Sitting as a whole), question 1,332.
[9] B. B. Gilbert, *op. cit.*, p. 166.
[10] *Report of the Committee on Old Age Pensions*, 1898, Appendix H, p. 154.

123

an exclusive vested interest in society, the friendly societies practically *were* society.[11]

Error in Beveridge's calculations

The reader may perhaps think that too much has already been made of the problems associated with the statistical analysis of friendly society membership But for those who are interested in a high degree of accuracy it is necessary to say a little more about the friendly society statistics, especially Table III which is concerned with their membership and funds from 1891 to 1909.

The Table shows that the number of 'registered friendly society members proper' was 6.2 million in 1909. And yet, in a detailed study of friendly societies, Lord Beveridge writes that 'In 1910 there were about two and three quarter million persons in affiliated orders and nearly another two million in friendly societies of other types giving sick pay',[12] i.e. a total of about 4¾ million members. How is the discrepancy between 6.2 million members in 1909 and 4¾ million in 1910 to be explained? Not by mass resignations from the friendly societies in 1910, but in the following way.

It is in the nature of a statistical series that it should be reorganised from time to time. The registrar of friendly societies reorganised the statistics for registered societies in 1910. Before 1910 the two main categories were 'Ordinary Friendly Societies' and 'Societies having branches' or 'Orders and their branches' (Beveridge's 'affiliated orders'). In 1909 the membership of these two categories was 3.5 million and 2.7 million respectively, or together 6.2 million. But in 1910 the first category, 'Ordinary Friendly Societies', was sub-divided into eight separate categories as shown on the opposite page.[13]

It could be reasonably argued that some of these categories were not friendly societies in the strict sense of the term, because they did not pay a sick benefit. This group might have included the deposit societies, which were more akin to savings banks than to clubs, the death and burial societies and the 'Other Societies'. Membership of

---

11 Professor Gilbert is not the only writer who under-estimates the extent of the activities of the friendly societies in this period. Dr Pauline Gregg, in *A Social and Economic History of Britain, 1760–1965,* practically ignores the societies after 1874. (Below, pp. 135–136.) Given this sort of treatment of the societies during the period of their most luxuriant growth, perhaps it is hardly surprising that the impression is widespread among teachers and students that welfare was virtually non-existent in Britain before the state began to provide it in 1909.

12 W. H. Beveridge, *Voluntary Action*, Allen and Unwin, 1948, p. 76.

13 *Report of the Registrar of Friendly Societies for 1911*, p. 41.

Type of Society	No. of Members (million)
Ordinary Benefit Societies	1.29
Deposit Societies	0.38
Death and Burial Societies	0.86
Widows and Orphans Societies	0.11
Dividing Societies	0.33
Juvenile Societies	0.16
Friendly Society Asylums and Convalescent Homes	0.04
Other Societies	0.40
Total	3.57

these three categories totalled 1.64 million. It seems likely that Beveridge ignored these categories in arriving at his estimate of friendly society membership in 1910.

But, it may be asked, does this not mean that all the figures in Table III, which are the only ones available before 1910, give an exaggerated impression of friendly society membership? The answer to that question is 'Yes'. But this does not invalidate the conclusions which were drawn from that Table and its accompanying evidence. Those conclusions were, first, that there was a steady and substantial increase in the provision of voluntary welfare in the period under discussion, and, second, that by the 1890s a large majority of adult males were members of friendly societies proper.

In connection with these conclusions it should be pointed out that, although in his *Voluntary Action* Lord Beveridge makes it clear that a distinction should be made between registered and unregistered societies,[14] by the time he comes to discuss friendly society membership in 1910 he seems to have forgotten the existence of the unregistered societies. Beveridge's estimate of 4¾ million refers solely to the members of *registered* friendly societies, and the unwary reader would be led astray by it.

The extent of cover

An analysis of the extent and function of the friendly societies raises certain pertinent questions. What were friendly societies doing to

---

[14] Beveridge, *op. cit.*, p. 26.

provide their members with old-age pensions? And what was their attitude towards state pensions?

Since the reduced sick benefit practically became a small old-age pension for elderly, incapacitated friendly society members, the financial burden of their elderly members became increasingly serious for the friendly societies as life expectancy increased in the second half of the 19th century. The societies were well aware of this problem. The simple solution would have been to insist that all new members paid a contribution high enough to entitle them to a pension of, say, 5s a week at the age of 65, with the sick benefit automatically coming to an end at that age. Unfortunately, this simple solution was not available. The societies were operating in a competitive environment and, although they had been attempting for some time to encourage their members to subscribe for old-age pensions (or 'deferred annuities' as they were correctly called), these attempts had met with little success. For example, the Manchester Unity of Odd Fellows had begun a scheme for deferred annuities in 1882; but by 1893 only 530 out of their 700,000 or so members had joined.[15] This may seem surprising, but in fact it was not.

People can provide for their old age in a variety of ways. All of these require an act of saving, but the saving may be put to different uses. One man may save to buy a pair of cottages, living in one and letting the other. Another may take out an endowment assurance policy maturing at age 65. Another may accumulate a healthy bank balance, or, in the 19th century, a bag of gold sovereigns sewn into the mattress or hidden under the floorboards. The deferred annuity may seem the most obvious way of providing for old age, but in several respects it is unattractive.

Unless the cost is to be heavy, the decision to subscribe for a deferred annuity, beginning at the age of 65, must be taken before a man is 30. This means that the subscriber is committing himself to a risky course of action for 35 years or more. The risk is, of course, that he will die before, or soon after, he reaches the age of 65. If a married man dies before that age, unless he has covered himself for a widow's benefit, which would involve an extra charge, his saving is fruitless. Thus few married men will subscribe for deferred annuities unless compelled or offered a considerable inducement to do so. For them, this is a matter of simple common-sense. The friendly societies would have liked their members to have subscribed for

---

[15] *Evidence to the Royal Commission on the Aged Poor*, 1895, question 11,561.

deferred annuities. But there was little or no likelihood that on their own they could overcome the reluctance of their members to do so. Most families preferred other forms of saving, especially endowment assurance. For example, the manager of the Prudential Assurance Company stated in 1896 that under a table for deferred annuities published in 1882 there were only 37 policies in existence; but under a table for life endowment assurance policies which matured at age 65, first published in 1895, there were already 400,000 policies at risk with an average premium of 2d a week.[16]

Why then did the friendly societies oppose state pensions? Before attempting to answer that question something must be said about the growth of saving and the various schemes for state pensions which were being discussed before the state finally stepped in.

IV. THE GROWTH OF SAVING AND THE PRESSURE FOR STATE PENSIONS

Deferred annuities were unpopular as a means of providing for old age, but savings were increasing at a rapid rate. The Registrar of Friendly Societies published figures for the funds of

> Building Societies
> Friendly and Collecting Societies
> Co-operative Societies
> Trade Unions and other Workmen's Societies
> and
> Railway, Trustee and Post Office Savings Banks.

Total funds of these organisations were increasing as shown in Table IV A. In addition, the life assurance industry was flourishing (Table IV B).[1]

Upward trend in saving

Much of this saving was being done by the middle classes and well-paid artisans. One indication of this is that the funds of ordinary life companies in 1899 amounted to £238 million, while the funds of industrial life companies (those which sold policies for a weekly premium of a few pence collected at the door) were only £19 million.

---

[16] *Report of the Committee on Old Age Pensions*, 1898, Appendix VIII, p. 186.

[1] *Statistical Abstract of the UK* for 1903 and 1912.

TABLE IV.—TOTAL FUNDS OF SOME SAVINGS INSTITUTIONS, 1891–1909

A. SOCIETIES AND SAVINGS BANKS*

	Total funds (£ million)
1891	213
1899	340
1909	460

* Those whose figures were published by the Registrar of Friendly Societies.

B. LIFE ASSURANCE COMPANIES

	Life and Annuity funds of Ordinary and Industrial Life Companies established in the UK (£ million)
1891	180
1899	257
1909	379

But the trend was in the right direction. By 1909 the funds of industrial life companies were £43 million. Thus it was not unreasonable for those who believed in increased individual responsibility as the best remedy for poverty to argue that even the lower-paid were becoming more thrifty and responsible.

It is easy to become so obsessed with Booth's discovery that 30.7 per cent of the people of London were living in poverty that the corollary—that 69.3 per cent were living 'in comfort', as Booth put it—is ignored. There were a few occupational pension schemes in the 1890s, and some craft trade unions were operating their own pension schemes, of which the largest was that of the Amalgamated Society of Engineers under which more than 80,000 members were insured for a pension of up to 10s a week. But the majority of workers were not insured for a pension. In old age they went on working as long as they could. If they fell sick, most men (but very few women) could claim their friendly society benefits. Apart from those, old people were dependent on their savings, if any, on their children, on private charity or, in the last resort, on public relief. In these circumstances it was very likely that, as the wealth of the nation increased and as the politicians began to compete more and more strenuously for the votes of the people,[2] the provision of state old-age pensions would become a live issue of public debate.

Proposals for state pensions in the 1890s

In the 1890s no less than three official Commissions or Committees investigated the problem of state pensions. A Royal Commission on the Aged Poor, chaired by Lord Aberdare, was set up in 1893 and reported in 1895; a Committee on Old Age Pensions chaired by Lord Rothschild was set up in 1896 and reported in 1898; and a Select Committee on the Aged Deserving Poor, with Mr H. Chaplin, MP, as chairman, was set up in 1899 and reported the same year.

All the main points of principle were discussed by the Aberdare Commission, and the later committees drew heavily upon its report. Both Charles Booth and Joseph Chamberlain, two of the chief protagonists of state old-age pensions, were members of the Commission and gave evidence to it. In addition to their schemes, 10 others were considered, including the scheme for compulsory insurance which Canon Blackley had submitted to a select committee in 1885–7. It would be true to say that all the then current proposals for state pensions were considered by the Aberdare Commission.

As one would expect, the first task of the Commission was to analyse the problem of poverty in old age. The relevant statistical information, drawn from the census for 1891, is shown in Table V.

TABLE V.—NUMBER OF PAUPERS AND TOTAL POPULATION OVER 65 IN ENGLAND AND WALES, 1891

	Popula-tion over 65	Indoor Paupers		Outdoor Paupers		Total Paupers	
		Number	per cent	Number	per cent	Number	per cent
One-day count	1,372,601	63,352	4·6	205,045	14·9	268,397	19·5
Twelve-months count	1,372,601	114,144	8·3	287,760	21·0	401,904	29·3

Source: *Report of the Royal Commission on the Aged Poor*, 1895, p. xii.

---

[2] The vote had been extended to a majority of adult males only in 1884.

Two main lessons can be learned from these figures. First, over any reasonable period of time nearly 30 per cent of all people over 65 found themselves obliged to accept poor relief. Second, a large majority of elderly paupers were assisted outside, as opposed to inside, the workhouse, which meant that they were virtually provided with a small pension on the rates.

It could have been, and was, argued that for such a proportion of the elderly to have recourse to the poor rates was 'a scandal upon our civilisation'.[3] However, the point was rightly made that many of the elderly indoor paupers were 'in poor law establishments because their sickness and infirmities made it difficult for them to live in ordinary conditions outside'.[4] It was, therefore, true to say that this large number of the aged poor were 'practically patients in state hospitals'.[5] There is no doubt that the belief was widely prevalent that under the then existing system the aged deserving labourer had nowhere to end his days except the workhouse. This belief was not borne out by the facts. The investigations of the Commission and the evidence given to it, as the report put it, 'conclusively demonstrates the fallaciousness of this popular opinion'.[6] The number of deserving aged persons who were in workhouses for reasons other than sickness or infirmity was few. The Commission considered the special problems of women, and reported that it believed it was 'distinctly exceptional for aged women who can properly be relieved outside to be obliged to come into a workhouse'.[7]

Proposals for pensions divorced from Poor Law

Nevertheless, the extent of poor relief among the aged was *prima facie* evidence that at least a substantial minority of elderly people were living in poverty. It was because of this that so many schemes had been put forward for state pensions removed from the poor law, so that no stigma should be attached to them.[8] The two schemes which attracted most attention from the Aberdare Commission were those proposed by Charles Booth and Joseph Chamberlain. They were very different from each other.

---

[3] *Evidence to the Royal Commission on the Aged Poor*, question 12,170.
[4] *Report of the Commission*, p. xv.
[5] *Ibid.*   [6] *Ibid.*, p. xvi.   [7] *Ibid.*, p. xvii.
[8] Details of all these schemes, including Booth's and Chamberlain's, may be found *ibid.*, pp. lxix–lxxxiii.

Booth's scheme

Booth's scheme, which had first been put forward in 1891, was as simple as it was expensive and ambitious. Every person on attaining the age of 65, rich or poor, was to be given a pension of 5s a week for the remainder of his or her life out of public funds. The total cost of this proposal was thought to be about £18 million for England and Wales and an additional £6½ million for Scotland and Ireland, but there would have been a saving of about £2 million on poor relief for those over 65. Thus the total additional cost would have been about £22½ million. This may seem a modest enough figure to a present-day reader. In the fiscal year 1969–70, for example, the total current expenditure of the British government, including national insurance expenditure, was £14,800 million, or 42 per cent of the net national income for 1969 of £34,900 million. Expenditure on pensions alone in 1969 was £1,609 million. But in the 1890s government expenditure, and of course taxation, were on a different scale. In 1895 total gross expenditure by the central government was £100.9 million, or 7 per cent of the net national income of £1,447 million. Because the government believed in a balanced budget, at least in peace time, the acceptance of Booth's proposals would have meant an immediate, very large increase in taxation.

Booth had suggested in 1891 that 'Taxation . . . can be arranged to fall in true proportion to income'. Later he amplified this and, by the time he gave evidence to the Commission in 1893, had written of extra taxes of ½d a pound on sugar, 2d on tea and 3d on the income tax.[9] Again, today 3d on the income tax sounds a modest enough proposal but in 1893 income tax was 7d in the £. Thus Booth was proposing an increase of over 40 per cent! The yield of income tax in the fiscal year 1893–4 was £15.5 million.[10] Booth, therefore, was proposing to raise £6.6 million from direct taxes on the wealthy (those with less than £160 a year—the vast majority—were exempt from income tax) and the balance (about £16 million) from indirect taxes on the general population.

Because his scheme was so expensive, few people took Booth's proposals seriously in 1895. Apart from their cost, the most telling argument against them was that put forward by a Mr Grout who told the Commission: 'The idea of pensioning a millionaire, as I think, would be simply ridiculous'.[11]

---

[9] *Evidence to the Royal Commission on the Aged Poor*, 1895, question 10,923.
[10] L. G. Chiozza Money, *op. cit.*, pp. 284–292. [11] *Report of the Commission*, p. lxx.

Chamberlain's scheme

Chamberlain's scheme, which had been originally worked out with some fellow members of parliament, and was sometimes called the scheme of the Parliamentary Committee, was for voluntary, assisted insurance. Chamberlain told the Commission that his scheme contemplated ' "three cases, in which persons desirous of making provision for old age, and voluntarily prepared to do so, can be helped by this State Pension Fund" '. In the first case the insurance was to be for an annuity of 5s a week from the age of 65. The insurer was required to pay a cash deposit of £2 10s at or before the age of 25 and after that age an annual cash payment of 10s up to the age of 65. These payments in themselves would have provided an annuity of only about 3s a week, so there was a considerable element of subsidy. The second case was similar, but with higher payments and benefits, the main one being provision for widows and children in the event of death after the third payment and before the age of 65. But it was from Chamberlain's third case that he anticipated by far the largest result. It involved the co-operation of the friendly societies. The provision was

'"that any person after depositing 30s if male, 25s if female, into the Post Office, and insuring in any society [i.e., friendly society] for £6 10s [i.e., 2s 6d a week] or £3 18s [i.e., 1s 6d a week] respectively, shall have their pension doubled by the State at the age of 65".'

The cost of this scheme would have depended on the number who took advantage of it. If everyone joined, the cost would have been about £5 million, but it was thought that it would be very much less than that. Chamberlain's scheme was much more closely tailored to the spirit of the decade than Booth's, and there was a good deal of support for it from various witnesses to the Commission. But there were also many objections to it, of which three were the most telling. The first was that those who would take advantage of such a scheme 'would be limited in numbers and would be mainly confined to the higher strata of the working classes'.[12] Second, the scheme would not begin to help the aged until 40 years after its introduction. And third, there would be a need for the state to interfere to some extent in the affairs of those friendly societies through which it would in effect have been guaranteeing a pension, to ensure that they did not become insolvent. Bearing these three points—and one further one—

---

12 *Report of the Commission*, p. lxxviii.

in mind, the Aberdare Commission had little hesitation in rejecting Chamberlain's proposals.

The further point concerned the Commission's terms of reference. It had been asked to consider

'whether any alterations in the system of poor relief are desirable, in the case of persons whose destitution is occasioned by incapacity for work resulting from old age, or whether assistance could otherwise be afforded in those cases.'

The job of the Commission was to concern itself with those old people who were unable to provide for themselves in old age, and not with the elderly as a whole.

Booth's scheme was too dear; but a voluntary contributory scheme would not give help to those who most needed it, and in any case the friendly societies refused to co-operate. To return to the question asked earlier—why this refusal? After all, the cost of sick pay for their elderly members was already becoming an embarrassingly heavy burden for them. It has been suggested that 'such a programme should have been welcomed [by the societies] but surprisingly it was not'.[13] Was it really so surprising? The friendly societies were the embodiment of the Victorian ethic of self-help, and that ethic was still strong in the 1890s. To them at that time any general scheme of pensions paid from the public purse was a form of 'universal pauperisation' or a 'huge outdoor relief system', as Booth's proposals were described, while a contributory scheme involved unacceptable government interference in their affairs. Perhaps, too, they saw state pensions as simply the first step in the wholesale provision of welfare by the state, a policy which would undermine their structure, or at the best stunt their growth.

Birth of state pensions

Despite the stalemate in 1895, public interest in state pensions steadily increased and forced the setting up of the Select Committee in 1899, which made the first official recommendation for a pension scheme: a 5s a week payment to be made partly out of the poor rates and partly from the Exchequer to the 'deserving' aged poor, after an investigation of the applicant's need and character by the local board of guardians. This was really an extension of out-door relief for the so-called 'deserving' aged poor. But the campaign for state pensions was gaining momentum; it came to an abrupt halt with the outbreak

---

[13] B. B. Gilbert, *op. cit.*, p. 179.

of the Boer War in October 1899, but was resumed after peace had been made in June 1902. In that year the resistance of the friendly societies to state pensions began to crumble and their national conference passed a resolution endorsing state pensions 'to all thrifty and deserving persons of 65 years of age and upwards where unable to work and in need of the same'. Social and political attitudes were changing, and the Government's hand was eventually forced by two events which clearly demonstrated these changes—the large increase in the Labour vote in the 1906 general election, and two by-election results in July 1907, in traditionally Liberal constituencies, in which a Labour and a Socialist candidate were elected.

The government publicly committed itself to state pensions in January 1908, and the Old Age Pensions Act was passed in that year. Under the Act non-contributory, selective pensions were provided to people who could meet two main tests: a test of age (over 70) and a test of means (less than 12s a week). Initially there was, too, a poor relief disqualification, under which persons could not receive a pension if they were receiving poor relief or had done so since 1 January, 1908. However, this disqualification was allowed to lapse at the end of 1910. The means test was on a sliding scale, with the pension increasing in five stages of 1s from a minimum of 1s a week for those with an income of not more than about 12s a week to a maximum of 5s a week for those with an income of not more than 8s a week. By 1913 the pension was being drawn by 968,000 people; the 1911 census had shown that 1.5 million were over 70 in that year, so almost two out of three were eligible under the rules. And 93.6 per cent of the pensioners were drawing the full pension. The cost of state pensions in the fiscal year 1912–13 was £12.1 million for the UK, and the saving on poor relief for paupers over 70 was £1.1 million. Thus the net cost of the state scheme after two years of operation was £11 million.[14]

The 1908 Old Age Pensions Act was only one measure among many which have together made for a massive extension of state welfare in the 20th century. It was followed, in 1911, by very different schemes for state unemployment and sickness insurance, which required contributions. The sickness, or health, contribution was 9d a week for an adult male, the worker paying 4d, the employer 3d and the state 2d (Lloyd George's 'ninepence for fourpence'), and the unemployment scheme was on a similar basis.

---

14 H. J. Hoare, *Old Age Pensions*, P. S. King, 1915, *passim*,

Slow revolution

These changes were slow to come about because they were part of a major change, if not a revolution, in fundamental attitudes about the role of the state and the relationship of the individual to the state. One example of this change in attitudes was the rise in the maximum rate of income tax from 2d in the £ in the 1870s to 19s 7d in 1950.

It was hardly surprising that those who wished to change the orthodox views of the late 19th century should have been stubbornly opposed by those who sincerely held those views; in the same way today, those who think that a reaction against the expansion of state welfare is overdue will be stubbornly opposed by those who subscribe to 20th-century orthodoxy.

Contemporary misunderstanding of 19th-century welfare

Why has the misapprehension of the 19th century gone for decades without being contested?

The short answer to this question is that there have always been *some* scholars and writers who have attempted to present a balanced picture of economic development in 19th-century Britain. Outstanding among them is Sir John Clapham. whose three-volume work, *An Economic History of Modern Britain*, published by the Cambridge University Press between 1926 and 1938 and covering the period 1820–1914, is a masterpiece which is never likely to be seriously challenged. But this is a bulky, expensive work which the rapidly increasing number of sixth-formers and undergraduates who are studying economic history will not normally buy.[15] They are much more likely to use Dr Pauline Gregg's *Social and Economic History of Britain 1760–1970*,[16] which is reasonably priced and would appear to cover ideally the syllabus for an 'A'-level or university course. This book's popularity is indicated by the fact that between 1950, when it was first published, and 1971 it went through six editions and was reprinted seven times. But popularity is no evidence of quality, and I consider that Dr Gregg's is a bad book which presents an unbalanced view of social and economic development in the 19th century. It is right to give an example of this imbalance.

---

[15] The price of the complete work in 1972 was £20.45. Some useful details of *registered* friendly societies between 1885 and 1910 are given in the third volume, *Machines and National Rivalries (1887–1914)*, 1938, pp. 504–7.

[16] Sixth edn., published by G. G. Harrap at £2.80 in 1971.

Like many other social historians, Dr Gregg seems to want to contrast the evils and miseries of life in a 19th-century capitalist environment with the pleasures and joys of life in a 20th-century welfare state. If this premise is correct, and welfare was in short supply before 1909, one would expect her to say very little about institutions which were the chief providers of welfare for the masses—the friendly societies—before the state began to expand into the welfare business. That expectation is justified. Dr Gregg provides a good deal of information about the development of the friendly societies up to 1874.[17] Later we are told about the introduction of state health insurance and pensions in 1911 and 1908.[18] But what had happened to the friendly societies between 1874 and 1908, their period of peak expansion? About that there is a minimum of information.

In a curious chapter, enigmatically entitled 'The End of "Victorian Prosperity" ', in which it is stated that the British 'working classes in the last two decades of the century were better off than ever before, measured both by the standard of real wages and by the percentage of unemployment',[19] the only mention of the friendly societies is contained in the statement 'There was a growth of Friendly Societies and savings banks'.[20] No statistics are given, nor a hint of the scale on which the societies were expanding.

In her preface Dr Gregg acknowledges her debt to the Webbs, the Hammonds and Sir John Clapham, but to say that the Webbs and the Hammonds on the one side and Sir John Clapham on the other would be uneasy bed-fellows would be a serious under-statement of their different approaches to 19th- and early 20th-century social and economic history. What Dr Gregg has done, in effect, is to accept the deterministic view of history held by the Webbs and the Hammonds, the view that social progress is synonymous with the expansion of the role of the state, but at the same time she has filled in the many gaps in their coverage of the period, especially on the economic side, by using Sir John Clapham's work. Her book is conclusive proof that the quality of a book is determined not so much by the sources a writer uses as by the way in which he or she uses them.

---

17 Fifth edition, pp. 314–320.
19 *Ibid.*, p. 381.

18 *Ibid.*, p. 484 and p. 490.
20 *Ibid.*, p. 367.

V. IMPLICATIONS FOR PRESENT-DAY THINKING

If the friendly societies feared that the expansion of state welfa would stunt their growth, it seems that their fear may have been justified. The total membership of registered friendly societies fell from 6.2 million in 1909 to 4.8 million in 1970, and the membership of the Manchester Unity of Odd Fellows fell from 770,000 in 1897 to 276,000 in 1969, while the total population rose by almost exactly 50 per cent between 1901 and 1970. But if the friendly societies and their allies feared that the expansion would eliminate private welfare organisations and destroy the inclination of citizens to provide for themselves outside the ambit of the state, experience shows that their fear was not justified.

Today private charities still flourish and achieve excellent results in relation to their available funds. At the same time the total of private savings has reached record levels: for example, the life and annuity funds of ordinary life companies and industrial companies established in the UK had increased from £379 million in 1909 (Table IV) to £10,938 million in 1968. And private health and pension schemes are growing rapidly. Indeed, it seems that in the latter there is to be found a close parallel, albeit in different circumstances, to the earlier growth of the friendly societies.

Total membership of occupational pension schemes rose from 8 million in 1957 to 12.2 million in 1967, of which 9.9 million were men, representing 65 per cent of all male employees.[1] Brabrook suggested in 1892 that 'merely a kind of residuum' was left outside the friendly societies.[2] In the 1970s it is not unreasonable to foresee a situation in which the number of adult males who are not insured for occupational pensions will also be 'merely a kind of residuum'.

The state's role in welfare

Today no-one would dispute that it is for the state to provide a welfare safety net for those who need it; nor would anyone dispute that the level of the net ought to be raised as the nation grows richer. Disagreement arises about whether the state should do more than this, and if so, what else it should do.

The growth of friendly societies at the turn of the century and occupational pension schemes in recent years both illustrate the

---

[1] Government Actuary, *Third Survey Occupational Pension Schemes*, HMSO, 1968, p. 8.

[2] Above, p. 122.

same principle: that the instinct of groups of people to provide independently for their welfare where a need exists and the means are available is amazingly strong. This instinct is a good one. The state can respond to it in two ways. It can encourage it, by granting tax concessions for independent welfare schemes and in other ways; or it can discourage or suppress it, deliberately or inadvertently, by expanding state welfare and increasing taxation still further.

The first way is the right way, but at present there are no grounds for optimism that this way will be chosen. In the 1960s both political parties began to favour graduated, or wage-related, state contributions and benefits. This means that the better-off pay more and receive more from the state. The policy of the 1908 Old Age Pensions Act, under which money was transferred from the wealthy and the working generation to the elderly poor, has been practically stood on its head: the state now promises the largest pensions to those who are manifestly capable of providing for themselves if they wish to do so. With the rapid development of wage-related contributions and benefits in the past decade, the politicians seem to have joined in a competition, or a conspiracy against the public, to see how quickly they can dispose of every sound principle of state welfare policy. As for the public, they must surely be in a state of confusion about what is going on.

FURTHER READING

Suggestions for further reading in chronological order of publication:

1. *Report of the Royal Commission on the Aged Poor* (the Aberdare Commission), C.–7684, HMSO, 1895.
The lucid majority report of 87 pages and the memoranda and minority reports of 30 pages together provide a complete range of opinions about the way in which provision should be made for the aged poor. On the one hand the majority reported that 'We are of opinion that no fundamental alterations are needed in the existing system of poor relief as it affects the aged' (p. lxxxiii) and on the other Henry Broadhurst, MP, recommended the introduction of a universal (or at any rate to persons whose income did not exceed £3 a week) non-contributory state pension of 5s a week (p.c).

2.   Brabrook, E. W., *Provident Societies and Industrial Welfare*, Blackie and Son, 1898.
A useful account of the development of some voluntary welfare societies by an expert contemporary witness. Brabrook was the Registrar of Friendly Societies and Trade Unions.

3.   Wood, G. H., 'Real Wages and the Standard of Comfort since 1850', *Journal of the Royal Statistical Society*, Vol. LXXIII, 1909. This classic article has recently been re-published in E. M. Carus-Wilson (ed.), *Essays in Economic History*, Vol. 3, Edward Arnold, 1962.

4.   Clapham, J. H., *An Economic History of Modern Britain: Machines and National Rivalries (1887–1914) with an Epilogue (1914–1929)*, Cambridge University Press, 1938.
Clapham's book wears its scholarship lightly. It is a delight to read and possesses an admirable table of contents and index.

5.   Beveridge, W. H., *Voluntary Action*, Allen and Unwin, 1948.
A useful book on voluntary welfare which unfortunately is out of print today.

6.   Gilbert, B. B., *The Evolution of National Insurance in Great Britain: The Origins of the Welfare State*, Michael Joseph, 1966.
A detailed and scholarly account of the expansion of state welfare between 1906 and 1912. But see my comments above, pp. 119 and 123.

6. The Classical Economists, Industrialisation, and Poverty

A. W. COATS

Professor of Economic and Social History,
University of Nottingham

THE AUTHOR

A. W. COATS was born in 1924 and educated at Southall Grammar School, Bishopshalt School and University College, Exeter (now University of Exeter), where he graduated B.Sc.(Econ.) in 1948 and M.Sc.(Econ.) in 1950. He held an English Speaking Union Fellowship at the University of Pittsburgh, 1950–51, and spent the years 1951–53 at Johns Hopkins University (Ph.D. 1953). He has been at the University of Nottingham since 1953 and was appointed Professor and Head of Department of Economic and Social History in 1964. He has been visiting Professor of Economics at Virginia and Stanford Universities, and has also taught at Columbia and Wisconsin. During the academic year 1972–3 Professor Coats will be a Fellow of the Netherlands Institute for Advanced Study in the Humanities and Social Sciences at Wassenaar.

Professor Coats has contributed some 40 articles to the learned journals in Britain, Europe and the USA and has edited (with Ross M. Robertson) *Essays in American Economic History* (Arnold, 1969); *The Classical Economists and Economic Policy* (Methuen, 1971); and the *History of Economic Thought Newsletter*. He is a member of the editorial board of *History of Political Economy*. He is writing an official history of the American Economic Association, and completing a biography of the American economist, *Henry Carter Adams, The Making of an American Economist*.

He is married with three children.

I. INTRODUCTION

Any brief account of the classical economists' ideas about so wide-ranging and complex a subject as industrialisation and poverty must necessarily be highly selective. Even on a restricted definition, the category 'classical economics' embraces ten or a dozen individuals, most of whom were prolific authors.[1] Moreover, their collective life-span extended over a century and a half of significant economic and social transformation, from 1723 to 1875, and only the most abstract and speculative of philosophers could have been unaffected by contemporary events.

Protracted controversy

There has, admittedly, been protracted controversy about the precise relationship between classical economics and the circumstances of the time.[2] But, as a group, the economists were continually seeking to understand the world around them, and they were eager to influence current and future economic and social policy. Even some of their more general theories were decisively influenced by recent events. For example, the Ricardian rent theory, which was formulated almost simultaneously in 1815 by Ricardo, Malthus and West, has with some justification been regarded as an *ex post facto* rationalisation of the Napoleonic wartime experience. And both their theories and their policy proposals were repeatedly in the forefront of public discussion.

During the century that separated Smith's *Wealth of Nations* (1776) from Cairnes's *Leading Principles of Political Economy Newly Expounded* (1874), the classical doctrines were repeatedly and

---

[1] The principal figures normally regarded as members of the classical 'school' are Adam Smith (1723–1790), Jeremy Bentham (1748–1832), Thomas Robert Malthus (1766–1834), David Ricardo (1772–1823), James Mill (1773–1836), Robert Torrens (1780–1864), Sir Edward West (1782–1828), John Ramsay McCulloch (1789–1864), Nassau William Senior (1790–1864), John Stuart Mill (1806–1873), John Eliot Cairnes (1823–1875). Some authorities would question the inclusion of Bentham, while others would wish to extend the list, for example by adding Thomas de Quincey (1785–1859) and Karl Marx (1818–1883).

[2] A valuable recent contribution to this discussion is Neil de Marchi, 'The Empirical Content and Longevity of Ricardian Economics', *Economica*, Vol. XXXII, August 1970, pp. 257–276. He argues that Ricardo's system was not incompatible with contemporary facts; that both Ricardo and J. S. Mill aimed to produce statements with refutable content; and that while Mill occasionally ignored inconvenient facts, he did not deliberately suppress historical evidence in order to protect Ricardo's economics.

bitterly attacked by a wide variety of critics, including poets, novelists, journalists, propagandists, politicians, professors, clerics, factory owners, trade unionists, and other economists. While these attacks helped to create an *esprit de corps* among the defenders of the main British doctrinal tradition, there were nevertheless important differences of opinion among them on method, theory, and policy. These differences inevitably complicate the task of summarising their views. Moreover, disagreements among the *cognoscenti* periodically attracted public attention and threatened to undermine the scientific reputation of political economy.[3] Indeed, by the mid-1870s matters had become so serious that when the Political Economy Club held a dinner in London to celebrate the centenary of *The Wealth of Nations* a writer in the *Pall Mall Gazette* commented that the economists 'had better be celebrating the obsequies of their science than its jubilee'.[4]

'Bouquets as well as brickbats'

The climate of opinion was, of course, not universally hostile: there were bouquets as well as brickbats. Yet in the five or six decades after Waterloo there was a discernible growth of individual and collective self-consciousness among the classical economists, part of a process that would nowadays be termed professionalisation. When Thomas Carlyle derided 'the gloomy professors of the dismal science', he over-rated the academic status and content of their work. But the trend towards academic economics was growing irresistibly, so much so that since the 1870s there have been few outstanding contributions to economic science by men untrained in universities. In the process of professionalisation the polemical, ideological, and practical ingredients in political economy were gradually repressed as attention was increasingly focussed on theoretical and technical questions. This change must be borne in mind when considering the classical economists' views on such a broad theme as industrialisation and poverty, for these subjects

---

[3] When the Earl of Limerick complained of 'the crude opinions of the professors of political economy, no two of whom are agreed in the doctrines of their sect', James Mill questioned whether they could be called a sect if there was no agreement among them (cf. *Parliamentary History and Review*, 1826, p. 691). For a more extended account of the economists' scientific reputation see A. W. Coats, 'The Role of Authority in the Development of British Economics', *Journal of Law and Economics*, Vol. VII, October 1964, pp. 85–106.

[4] Quoted by William Stanley Jevons, 'The Future of Political Economy', *Fortnightly Review*, Vol. XXVI, 1876, p. 190.

cannot be confined within the conventional boundaries of economic science. The changes in the economists' aims and self-image affected their writings in more subtle ways than changes in the economic and social environment, and failure to take both these dimensions into account has seriously misled some commentators.

'Industrialisation' broadly defined

Throughout this essay the term 'industrialisation' will be taken to include not only the narrowly economic and technical changes within the manufacturing sector during the industrial revolution, and the concomitant developments in industrial organisation, occupational distribution, and in the level and composition of national income; it also encompasses the wider influence of these changes on the social structure and the prevailing habits, values, beliefs and attitudes.

The classical economists' writings touch upon many facets of this complex process. Since it is impossible to consider them all, attention will be concentrated on a few central themes, such as the changing balance between agriculture, manufacturing and commerce; the role of machinery and inventions; changes in the relative wealth and power of the social classes; and the predicament and prospects of the labouring population.

II. STRUCTURAL CHANGES IN THE ECONOMY

When John Stuart Mill published his magisterial *Principles of Political Economy* in 1848, agriculture was still the leading occupation in Britain. But by this time agriculture's share in the national income was falling, and the focus of classical economics had shifted markedly since the *Wealth of Nations*, largely in response to the changing structure of the economy. Adam Smith attached so much importance to the role of agriculture in the economy that he has sometimes been viewed as a follower of the French Physiocrats, even though he decisively rejected their belief that the agriculturalist alone produced a 'produit net'.

Smith's 19th-century disciple, J. R. McCulloch, regarded Smith's statement that a given capital employed in agriculture puts more productive labour into motion than an equivalent sum invested in manufacturing or commerce as 'the most objectionable passage in

F

The Wealth of Nations'.[1] And a vivid, if somewhat exaggerated, impression of the differences between the two men is conveyed by the critic who protested that McCulloch

'was ready to turn the whole country into one vast manufacturing district filled with smoke and steam engines and radical weavers, and to set adrift all the gentlemen and farmers now constituting our agricultural population'.[2]

Classical theory of economic growth

It is hardly surprising that manufacturing occupied an increasingly prominent role in the works of Smith's 19th-century followers, and the theoretical reasons can be suggested by a brief account of the Malthus-Ricardo discussion of the 1815 Corn Law. This was a significant episode in the development of the classical theory of economic growth, for the theory essentially rested on the fundamental relationship between population and the food supply. For two or three decades after Malthus first published his notorious *Essay on Population* (1798) there were widespread fears that population increase was outstripping agricultural output. The inevitable consequence would be that food prices (especially corn) would continue to rise, leading to a rise in money wages and a concomitant fall in the rate of profit, not only in agriculture but throughout the economy. Since profit constituted the incentive to capital accumulation, which was the mainspring of economic growth, a fall in the rate of return would discourage investment and, if it continued, eventually bring about the 'stationary state'. Thus while economic prosperity was associated with a constant or rising output of food-stuffs *per capita*, any serious check to investment while population expansion continued would eventually depress living standards and cause general distress, especially among the poor.

This account of the classical theory is, of course, over-simplified, and individual members of the school differed in their interpretations of the growth process.[3] To Ricardo it seemed obvious that restrictions

---

[1] McCulloch, *Outlines of Political Economy* (ed. J. McVickar), New York, 1825, p. 94.

[2] J. L. Mallet, *Political Economy Club*, Centenary Volume. Minutes of Proceedings (London, 1921), Vol. 6, p. 234. For McCulloch's reservations about the factory system, below, pp. 154–155.

[3] For example, it was becoming apparent by the mid-1820s that although the British population continued to grow rapidly, food prices were low enough to cause widespread complaints from the farming community. By 1828 McCulloch had abandoned his former belief in the Malthusian 'law', probably under the influence of Senior. They were subsequently joined by Torrens who, while continuing to regard population increase as a threat to the labourer's standard of living, rejected Malthus' theory as

on corn imports merely made matters worse by raising food prices, whereas cheap food imports would help to counteract the pressure of population on food supplies. In Parliament in 1820, Ricardo said that

'he conceived the duty of government to be, to give the greatest possible development to industry' by removing 'restrictions on trade, and other obstacles of that description.'[4]

Most of the later classical economists agreed, which helps to explain their support for free trade. But Malthus, who attached much more importance to agriculture than his contemporaries, argued vigorously in favour of a balanced economy, claiming that 'the principles of political economy' should be subordinated to the higher end of 'the happiness of society'. Society's gains from an indefinite extension of manufacturing might be counterbalanced by several disadvantages, he contended, including

'a greater degree of uncertainty in its supplies of corn, greater fluctuations in the wages of labour, greater unhealthiness and immorality owing to a larger proportion of the population being employed in manufactories, and a greater chance of long and retrograde movements occasioned by the natural progress of those countries from which corn had been imported.'[5]

This passage reveals Malthus's sensitivity to the problems of industrialisation which were to figure more and more prominently in the later classical writings. In defending restrictions on corn imports he recognised that he was making an exception to his general support for the free-trade principle. But while ostensibly resting his case on the grounds that dependence on foreign food would lead to economic instability and would seriously weaken the

---

'not conformable to experience'. (Cf. D. P. O'Brien, *J. R. McCulloch. A Study in Classical Economics*, London, 1970, pp. 314–319; M. E. A. Bowley, *Nassau Senior and Classical Economics*, London, 1937, pp. 117–126; and Robert Torrens, *The Principles and Practical Operation of Sir Robert Peel's Act of 1844 Explained and Defended*, 2nd edn., London, 1857, Appendix B, p. 83.)

[4] P. Sraffa (ed.), *Works and Correspondence of David Ricardo*, Cambridge, 1952, Vol. V, p. 68.

[5] Malthus, *An Essay on Population*, Everyman edn., London, 1914, Vol. II, p. 119. Malthus enlisted Adam Smith's support for this view by quoting the following passage from the *Wealth of Nations*: 'Capital which is acquired to any country by commerce and manufactures is all a very uncertain and precarious possession, till some part of it has been secured and realised in the cultivation and improvement of its lands.' (Cannan edn., London, 1904, Vol. I, p. 393: Malthus misquoted the original.)

nation in time of war, it is clear that he also feared the social and political consequences of a significant decline in the landed class.[6]

In this respect Malthus's disagreement with Ricardo is striking. Although Adam Smith had asserted that the interest of the landlord, unlike the merchant manufacturer, was 'strictly and inseparably connected with the general interest of society', Ricardo saw the landlord as a parasite, even as an enemy of progress.[7] Moreover, he denied that there was any necessary conflict between agriculture and manufactures:

> 'Nations grow old as well as individuals; and in proportion as they grow old, populous, and wealthy, must they become manufacturers. If these things were allowed to take their own course, we should undoubtedly become a great manufacturing country, but we should remain a great agricultural country also ... There would always be a limit to our greatness, while we were growing our own supply of food; but we should always be increasing in wealth and power, whilst we obtained part of it from foreign countries, and devoted our own manufactures to the payment of it.'[8]

Material wealth and social welfare

As we shall see, Ricardo and his successors were by no means unaware of the defects of an industrial society. Nevertheless, they retained their fundamental faith in the benefits of economic progress.

---

[6] Malthus also feared that a surplus of savings would develop with the growth of industrialisation and argued that, as landlords had a high propensity to spend, their 'unproductive consumption' would counteract or minimise the dangers of periodic 'gluts', i.e. crises resulting from a deficiency of aggregate demand. It was this aspect of Malthus's thought that led J. M. Keynes to regard him as a precursor of his own *General Theory of Employment, Interest, and Money* (1936). (Cf. Malthus, *Principles of Political Economy*, New York, 1951, p. 361 ff.)

[7] Adam Smith had described rent as a 'monopoly price', stating that landlords 'love to reap where they never sowed'; but Ricardo, Senior, and J. S. Mill adopted a more positively anti-landlord standpoint. According to Mill, 'They grow richer, as it were in their sleep, without working, risking, or economising. What claim have they, on the general principle of social justice, to this accession of riches?' (*Principles of Political Economy, with some of their applications to Social Philosophy*, Toronto, 1965, Vol. II, pp. 819–20.)

[8] Ricardo's *Works, op. cit.*, Vol. V, p. 180. As is so often the case, Adam Smith may be cited in support of this view also: 'England . . . is perhaps as well fitted by nature as any large country in Europe, to be the seat of foreign commerce, of manufactures for distant sale and of all the improvements which these can occasion.' (*Wealth of Nations*, I, p. 391.) Whatever may be the interpretation of this passage, the contrast between Ricardo and Malthus is clearly evident from the following extract: 'According to all general principles, it will finally answer to most landed nations, both to manufacture for themselves and to conduct their own commerce. That raw cottons should be shipped in America, carried some thousands of miles to another country, unshipped there, to be manufactured and shipped again for the American market, is a state of things which cannot be permanent.' (*Essay on Population*, Vol. II, p. 90.)

The Classical Economists, Industrialisation, and Poverty

Like their 18th-century predecessors, David Hume and Adam Smith, who associated the expansion of commerce with the advance of civilisation, they were convinced that material wealth was an essential pre-requisite of social and cultural welfare. As McCulloch observed:

'Where wealth has not been amassed, individuals, being constantly occupied in providing for their immediate wants, have no time left for the culture of their minds; so that their views, sentiments, and feelings, become alike contracted and illiberal. The possession of a decent competence, or the power to indulge in other pursuits than those which directly tend to satisfy our animal wants and desires, is necessary to soften the selfish passions; to improve the moral and intellectual character; and to ensure any considerable proficiency in liberal studies and pursuits. And hence, the acquisition of wealth is not desirable merely as the means of procuring immediate and direct gratifications, but is indispensably necessary to the advancement of society in civilisation and refinement.'[9]

As these remarks show, the classical view of economic development was not narrowly constricted. Among later members of the school, John Stuart Mill was by far the most perceptive commentator on the relationship between wealth and welfare. Unlike his predecessors he did not view the stationary state with 'unaffected aversion'; indeed, he regarded the competitive 'trampling, crushing, elbowing and treading on each other's heels' merely as 'disagreeable symptoms of one of the phases of industrial progress', and looked forward to the stationary state as a time when cultivation of the 'art of living' would replace the 'art of getting on'.[10] The English needed instruction not in 'the desire of wealth' but in

'the use of wealth, and appreciation of the objects of desire which wealth cannot purchase . . . Every real improvement in the character of the English, whether it consists in giving them higher aspirations, or only a juster estimate of the value of their present objects of desire, must necessarily moderate the ardour of their devotion to the pursuit of wealth.'[11]

Pervasive influence of Adam Smith

One of the main analytical reasons why manufacturing figured so prominently in later classical writings was the belief that it offered scope for increasing returns, as contrasted with the prevalence of diminishing returns in agriculture.[12] This distinction had been fore-

---

[9] *Principles of Political Economy*, Edinburgh, 1843, pp. 8–9.
[10] *Principles, op. cit.*, Vol. II, pp. 754, 756.　　　[11] *Ibid.*, Vol. I, p. 105.
[12] This is not the place to examine the analytical confusions in the classical treatment of the laws of returns. There is a brief account in Edmund Whitaker, *A History of Economic Ideas*, New York, 1940, pp. 383–403.

shadowed in *The Wealth of Nations*, where Smith placed enormous stress on the division of labour as a source of productivity gains and new inventions; and he had acknowledged that there was little scope for the division of labour in agriculture. Smith paid comparatively little attention to mechanisation, a fact that has led some commentators to suggest that he was oblivious to the industrial revolution which was gathering momentum before his very eyes;[13] and it is an inadequate excuse to say that his *magnum opus* did not appear until 1776, for scholars now agree that the warm-up period lasted several decades.

Smith's presumed insensitivity to his surroundings is all the more surprising in view of his reputation as a keen observer, for economic and social historians have long regarded his writings as a mine of valuable information about contemporary life. However, a careful recent re-reading of Smith's works has shown that he was more aware of the importance of factory production and machine technology than has usually been supposed.[14] It cannot be claimed that he foresaw the remarkable transformation of manufacturing that was to occur in the next half-century or so; but these developments were by no means incompatible with his optimistic view of economic growth, a process in which his recognition of the possibilities of manufacturing and commercial expansion occupied a central place. As a modern commentator has observed:

'Smith's long-term prognosis for capitalism is centred upon its capacity for generating technical change and thus substantially raising *per capita* income. This capacity, in turn, is made by Smith to depend overwhelmingly—indeed one may almost say exclusively—upon the division of labour and the consequences flowing from it.'[15]

---

13 For example, R. Koebner, 'Adam Smith and the Industrial Revolution', *Economic History Review*, Vol. XI, April 1959, p. 382: 'There was not a line in his [Smith's] book anticipating such transformations as were to take place in mechanised production and transport.' Indeed, 'apart from having no inkling of many technical innovations which lay ahead and of the forms of organisation by which they were to be exploited— Adam Smith had been rather unfavourably disposed towards those elements of society who were to organise mechanised production and to divert it into the channels of commerce.'

14 Cf. Samuel Hollander, 'Adam Smith and the Industrial Revolution: A New View', unpublished paper delivered at the History of Economic Thought Conference, Manchester, September 1971. The substance of the argument will appear in Professor Hollander's forthcoming book, *The Economics of Adam Smith* (University of Toronto, 1972). He would probably agree with Karl Marx that 'what characterises him [Smith] as the political economist of the period of manufacture is the stress he lays on the division of labour.' (*Capital*, Everyman edn., London, 1930, Vol. I, p. 367, n. 3.)

15 Nathan Rosenberg, 'Adam Smith on the Division of Labour: Two Views or One?' *Economica*, Vol. XXXII, May 1965, p. 128.

As we have noted, there was little scope for the division of labour in agriculture.

Smith not only emphasised the productivity-increasing effects of manufacturing but also its adverse social consequences. In an oft-quoted passage he remarked that a worker employed on a few simple operations under the division of labour

'has no occasion to exert his understanding or to exercise his invention.... He naturally loses, therefore, the habit of such exertion, and generally becomes as stupid and ignorant as it is possible for a human creature to become.... His dexterity at his own particular trade seems ... to be acquired at the expense of his intellectual, social, and martial virtues. But in every improved and civilised society this is the state into which the labouring poor, that is, the great body of the people, must necessarily fall, unless government takes some pains to prevent it.'[16]

Although Smith advocated state aid to education as a means of counteracting these adverse social effects, there is no doubt that the main impact of this passage was to draw attention to the dangers of dehumanising the labour force, a process that was to become a major feature of the socialist, sentimentalist and literary indictment of 19th-century industrialisation.

Nor did Smith sugar the pill when he

'recognised the existence of a hierarchy of inventions involving varying degrees of complexity, and requiring differing amounts of technical competence, analytical sophistication and creative and synthesising intellect.'

For this implied not only continuing technical progress, but also a growing social as well as technical division of labour, whereby those with higher skills and attainments (and presumably superior initial opportunities) would form the upper ranks of society, thereby becoming 'thoroughly insulated from the ravages of the division of labour' experienced by the labouring class.[17]

Effects of mechanisation on employment

On the whole Smith's followers paid comparatively little attention to the direct effects of mechanisation and the division of labour upon the workers' outlook,[18] for they were mainly concerned to

---

[16] *Wealth of Nations*, Vol. I, pp. 7, 8; Vol. II, p. 177 ff.

[17] Rosenberg, *op. cit.*, pp. 131, 134, 138.

[18] However, McCulloch protested at Smith's account: 'Nothing can be more marvellously incorrect than these representations. ... The weavers and other mechanics of Glasgow, Manchester and Birmingham, possess infinitely more general and extended information than is possessed by the agricultural labourers of any country in the Empire'. (*Outlines of Political Economy, op. cit.*, pp. 100–101. In the 1870 edition of his *Principles of Political Economy*, p. 89, he quoted Malthus in support of his view.)

stress the productivity-increasing results of the expansion of manufacturing.[19] There was, however, considerable interest in the effect of machinery on the level of employment, especially after Ricardo's dramatic *volte face* in the third (1823) edition of his *Principles of Political Economy and Taxation*. In the first two editions (1817 and 1819) he had assumed that machinery was beneficial to all members of the community, and did not even consider the possibility of technological unemployment. Indeed, Ricardo persuaded McCulloch to abandon his earlier opinion that the introduction of machinery had an initially depressing effect on wages. In the third edition, however, Ricardo accepted the argument of John Barton's pamphlet *Observations on the Condition of the Labouring Classes* (1817) that machinery might not only cause temporary hardship to labourers by creating unemployment, but that there might also be a permanent displacement of labour.

While most of Ricardo's classical associates conceded the temporary ill-effects,[20] they were both embarrassed by, and hostile to, his contention that there could be permanently harmful consequences —an idea enthusiastically endorsed by Karl Marx.[21] It is unnecessary

---

[19] Thus John Stuart Mill's famous outburst was untypical: 'Hitherto it is questionable if all the mechanical inventions yet made have lightened the day's toil of any human being. They have enabled a greater population to live the same life of drudgery and imprisonment, and an increased number of manufacturers and others to make fortunes. They have increased the comforts of the middle classes. But they have not yet begun to effect those great changes in human destiny, which it is in their power and in their futurity to accomplish.' (*Principles, op. cit.*, Vol. II, pp. 756–7.)

Generally speaking, the popularisers of political economy stressed the productivity of machinery and neglected its social effects, while the working-class press complained that the economists 'persisted in regarding human beings as soulless instruments in a great machine.' (Cf. R. K. Webb, *The British Working Class Reader 1790–1848*, London, 1955, pp. 99–100.)

[20] For example, while acknowledging the harmful effects of the power loom on the employment of hand-loom weavers, Senior ridiculed general attacks on machinery, commenting 'and when it has been made penal to give advantages to labour by any tool or instrument whatever, the last step must be to prohibit the use of the right hand.' (*Three Lectures on The Rate of Wages*, London, 1830, p. xiii.) Torrens complained of the 'fundamental and dangerous errors' in Ricardo's third edition, adding that his deviations had 'retarded the progress of the science' by exposing disagreements among its practitioners. (*An Essay on The Production of Wealth*, London, 1821, pp. xi–xii.) Elsewhere he protested vehemently about the hardships suffered by the hand-loom weavers, but while agreeing that the ill-effects of mechanisation were usually only temporary, he granted Senior's exception in the case of machines worked by horses, which permanently diminished the subsistence (i.e. wages fund) available for labourers' consumption. He even advocated the establishment of a national fund to assist workers displaced by machinery. (*On Wages and Combination*, London, 1834, pp. 34–44.)

[21] 'One of Ricardo's greatest services is that he realised that machinery is not only a means for producing commodities, but also a means for producing "redundant popula-

to specify the details of Ricardo's analysis, which are complex and confusing;[22] but it is worth noting that although Ricardo explicitly warned against state action to discourage technical progress, which he regarded as generally beneficial, J. S. Mill insisted that if technological advances diminished the wages fund, as Ricardo suggested, 'it would be incumbent on legislators to take measures for moderating its rapidity'.[23]

The social consequences of factory employment

The classical economists displayed somewhat more uncertainty about the effects of factory production and urbanisation than about other aspects of industrialisation, and with the passage of time the general tone of their writings became somewhat less optimistic. As might be expected, Malthus expressed profound misgivings, arguing that the unavoidable variations of manufacturing labour constituted one of the principal causes of pauperism.

Nor did he expect to see any substantial improvement in urban manufacturing communities.

'It is undoubtedly our duty, and in every point of view highly desirable, to make towns and manufacturing employments as little injurious as possible to the duration of life; but after all our efforts, it is possible that they will always remain less healthy than country situations and country employments; and consequently, operating as positive checks, will diminish in some degree the necessity of the preventive check.'[24]

In his *Essay on Population* Malthus reproduced a detailed account of the evils of child labour in cotton mills from Aikin's *Description of the Country from Thirty to Forty Miles around Manchester* (1795), and in general the classical economists were enthusiastic supporters of legislative restrictions on children's work in factories.[25] However,

---

tion".' Marx considered that Ricardo's renunciation of his earlier opinion on machinery reflected 'the scientific impartiality and love of truth characteristic of the man.' (*Capital, op. cit.*, I, pp. 434, n. 1; 469, n. 2; II, p. 697, n. 1.)

[22] For example, Mark Blaug, *Ricardian Economics*, New Haven, 1958, pp. 64–74; also O'Brien, *op. cit.*, pp. 302–306.

[23] Blaug, *op. cit.*, pp. 69, 73.

[24] *Essay on Population*, Vol. II, pp. 63, 256. In this context the 'positive checks' to population growth meant the high death rate in towns; the 'preventive checks', which Malthus advocated as the most desirable method of restraining excessive population increase, referred to 'moral restraint', chiefly through the postponement of marriage.

[25] With respect to restrictions on adult labour the position was more complex: cf., for example, Mark Blaug, 'The Classical Economists and the Factory Acts', *Quarterly Journal of Economics*, 1958, reprinted in A. W. Coats, *The Classical Economists and Economic Policy*, London, 1971, pp. 104–122.

they were reluctant to support legislative interference with adult working conditions, and although Senior's *Letters on The Factory Act* (1837) is often cited as evidence of their uncritical attitude towards the factory system, it was by no means a typical expression of opinion.[26] Nor was Senior's notorious contention that profit was earned in the last hour of work, so that a reduction of hours would be ruinous to employers.[27] McCulloch, in particular, who wrote extensively on the subject of factory conditions over a protracted period, expressed a variety of opinions at different times. While admitting the possibility that factory work was pernicious, he bitterly attacked the 1832 House of Commons Report on Factory Conditions which, he said, 'contains more false statements and exaggerated representations than any other document of the kind ever laid before the legislature'. He conceded that

'great inattention to cleanliness, and some revolting abuses, have existed in some factories, particularly of the smaller class . . . ; but the instances of abuse bear but a small proportion to the total numbers; and, speaking generally, factory work-people, including non-adults, are as healthy and contented as any class of the community obliged to earn their bread by the sweat of their brow.'[28]

Elsewhere, however, he acknowledged that the domestic system was morally superior to the factory, because those who worked at home, especially if they owned their own goods, were free from corruption

---

26 Senior claimed that hours of work in cotton factories were not excessive, the work was light, working conditions were not overcrowded, and the employees were healthy. 'The factory work-people in the country districts are the plumpest, best clothed, and healthiest-looking persons of the labouring class that I have ever seen. The girls, especially, are far more good-looking (and good looks are fair evidence of health and spirits) than the daughters of agricultural labourers.' However, he was shocked by the housing conditions in Manchester (as contrasted with the good houses at Hyde), which explained why the workers there were 'sallow and thinner'. (*Letters on The Factory Act*, 2nd edn., 1844.) In this edition he reproduced a long letter from Leonard Horner, the government factory inspector, contesting many of Senior's opinions and producing contradictory evidence!

In contrast to Senior, Torrens complained that the congregation of workers in factories ruined their health and destroyed their morals, and demanded a reduction of hours of work 'to save the infant labourer from the cruel oppression of excessive toil'. (Cf. *The Principles and Practical Operation of Sir Robert Peel's Act, op. cit.,* p. 24; and *Letters On Commercial Policy,* London, 1833, p. 72.)

27 *Letters on the Factory Act, op. cit.,* p. 4. Other members of the Political Economy Club rejected Senior's view on the ground of his faulty economic analysis.

28 *A Statistical Account of the British Empire,* 2nd edn., 1839, Vol. I, p. 669. Later on the same page he declared, of Manchester, Glasgow and Leeds, 'whatever may be the state of society in these towns, . . . *it would have been ten times worse but for the factories.'* (Italics in original.) Recent historians have generally agreed that the 1832 Factory Report was partisan and inaccurate.

by contamination with unworthy persons in factories.[29] Moreover, they would be restrained by their parents, would benefit from the knowledge that they were working for themselves, and would reap the rewards of their labours. On the other hand, properly run factories could be schools for improvement, inculcating habits of industry and of orderly and regular conduct. Furthermore, cotton factory workers were less dependent on the vagaries of the climate than domestic workers, and were therefore in a superior condition.

'Some of them as are provident are in decidedly comfortable circumstances. Their money wages have somewhat declined since the peace, but they have not declined to anything like the extent that the prices of bread, beef, clothes, and almost every necessary and useful article have done; so that the manufacturing part of the population possess, at this time, a greater command over the necessaries and conveniences of life, and are in decidedly more comfortable circumstances, than at any former period.'[30]

McCulloch's views have been cited at length because they reveal some of the difficulties facing the classical economist who sought to draw general conclusions about the economic and social changes during his lifetime. In the 1820s McCulloch adopted an optimistic tone, conceding that the English workers were inflammable, turbulent and liable to be misled by radical demagogues, but regarding this as merely a symptom of the growing pains of an industrialising economy.[31] During the Chartist troubles of the 1840s, however, he began to question his earlier belief that the workers' violence would diminish as their intelligence grew, and by 1859 he was taking a far more pessimistic view of the situation.

'There seems, on the whole, little room for doubting that the factory system operates unfavourably on the bulk of those engaged in it. . . . It is certain, too, that the demand for the services of children and other young persons, and the ease with which factory labour may in general be learned, has had a powerful influence in depressing wages, and, consequently, in preventing the wonderful inventions and discoveries of the last half century from redounding so much to the advantage of the labouring classes as might otherwise have been anticipated.'[32]

---

[29] *Ibid.*, p. 639. D. P. O'Brien, *op. cit.*, p. 283, has remarked that McCulloch 'detested the domestic system which also ran counter to the need for division of labour and was harmful to children and oppressive', but his citations are drawn from earlier sources.

[30] *Statistical Account, op. cit.*, p. 663.

[31] 'Rise, Progress, Present State, and Prospects of the British Cotton Manufacture', *Edinburgh Review*, Vol. XCI, 1827, pp. 37–8.

[32] *Treatises and Essays*, Edinburgh, 1859, p. 455. Quoted by Blaug, *Ricardian Economics, op. cit.*, p. 242. The similarity between this remark and John Stuart Mill's comment on the effects of machinery (*supra.*, n. 19) is obvious.

Nevertheless, as his recent biographer has argued, McCulloch was less concerned about the factory system itself than its distributional consequences, which represented a threat to social order. Although he retained his fundamental optimism towards the process of economic growth, he began to share Malthus's earlier anxieties, recognising that manufacturing was subject to fluctuations in demand, and even wondering whether the manufacturing sector of the economy should have been kept smaller than the agricultural sector.[33]

Long-term economic and social trends

Although many historians have regarded the mid-19th century as the period of Britain's economic supremacy, when she was 'the workshop of the world', the later classical economists were far from complacent about either the current state of affairs or the long-term prospects. J. S. Mill and Cairnes feared that the gains from industrial progress might be counteracted by continued population growth, and despite their belief in the existence of increasing returns in manufacturing they were not convinced that technological progress in agriculture would be sufficient to offset diminishing returns from the land. Moreover, both authors considered that the rate of capital accumulation was threatened because England was one of those opulent nations where the rate of profit was 'habitually within . . . a hand's breadth of the minimum'.[34]

Partly under the influence of Edmund Gibbon Wakefield, some of the classical economists came to believe that the 'powers of production' were 'outgrowing the field of employment', and overseas colonisation was advocated by Torrens, Mill, and—to a lesser extent—Cairnes, as a means of providing outlets for capital investment and relieving population pressure at home.[35] Although Cairnes acknowledged that there was no tendency for the rate of wages to fall to a minimum, he argued that

'the fund available for those who live by labour tends, in the progress of society . . . to become a constantly smaller fraction of the entire national wealth'.

---

[33] O'Brien, *op. cit.*, pp. 284–5.

[34] Mill, *Principles*, Vol. II, p. 738. Cairnes expressed similar views in *Some Leading Principles of Political Economy Newly Expounded*, 1888 edn., pp. 217, 230, 274.

[35] On this subject Donald Winch, *Classical Political Economy and Colonies*, London 1965, *passim*; also R. N. Ghosh, *Classical Macroeconomics and the Case for Colonies*, Calcutta, 1967, *passim*. The quotation in the text is from Torrens, *The Budget. On Commercial and Colonial Policy*, London, 1844, p. 288. It forms part of a very extended account of contemporary economic distress.

The recent immense industrial progress, he claimed, had made comparatively little impression on the rate of wages and profits because improvements had largely affected commodities not consumed by the labourers; and where it had, their gains had often been only temporary owing to subsequent increases in population. The distribution of wealth was already uneven, and was becoming more so, with the consequence that 'The rich will be growing richer; and the poor, at least relatively, poorer'. The decline in the rate of profit did not necessarily mean that the capitalist class suffered, for their income depended on the rate of profit multiplied by the amount of capital, which might increase indefinitely. For the working class, however, co-operation was the only means by which they could emancipate themselves from dependence on capital and share in the 'gains and honours of advancing civilisation'.[36]

Like John Stuart Mill, who also displayed a sympathetic attitude towards co-operation, Cairnes sought a means of counteracting 'the separation of industrial classes into labourers and capitalists which now prevails'.[37] His social philosophy was less complex, and less tainted with reformist sentiments, than Mill's, and in this respect he serves as a more typical example of the long-run tendencies of classical economics. All traces of Adam Smith's concept of a harmony of interests had disappeared with Ricardo's conception of the inverse relationship between wages and profits, a proposition that led Marx to hail him as the

'last of the great exponents of the classical political economy', because he 'consciously made the conflict of class interests, the antagonism between wages and profits and between profits and land-rents, the starting-point of his investigations, while naively conceiving these antagonisms to be a social law of nature.'[38]

Contemporary social historians agree that clear-cut class divisions, though not necessarily irreconcilable class conflicts, emerged in Britain during the first two or three decades of the 19th century.[39] But while it is clear that the later classical writings reveal more sensitivity to the social and political stresses resulting from industrialisation than their predecessors', there is some danger of exaggerating the differences. Certain disharmonious remarks in *The Wealth*

---

[36] Cairnes, *Leading Principles, op. cit.*, pp. 281–289.   [37] *Ibid.*, p. 284.
[38] *Capital, op. cit.*, p. 867, from the author's Preface to the second German edition. For Marx's distinction between 'classical' and 'vulgar' political economy, *ibid.*, p. 55 n.
[39] For example, Harold Perkin, *The Origins of Modern British Society, 1780–1880*, London, 1969, especially Ch. VI, 'The Birth of Class'; also, from a very different standpoint, E. P. Thompson, *The Making of the English Working Class*, London, 1963, *passim*.

of Nations are sometimes cited (mistakenly) as evidence of Smith's embryonic Marxism;[40] but there is no denying the common strands of liberal political, moral, and social philosophy that run throughout the classical literature.

Optimism of classical economists

Although the classical economists lived at a time of serious economic instability, acute social tensions, and recurrent political disorders—circumstances which are nowadays often regarded as the inescapable accompaniments of rapid industrialisation—they retained their fundamental faith in the possibilities of progress. While they were themselves members of the middle class, and can properly be charged with over-rating the merits of their social stratum, their writings were remarkably free from expressions of class hostility. Indeed, the principal exception to this generalisation, James Mill, mainly directed his attacks at the aristocracy, not the labouring class, and he probably believed that reformers could only extract significant concessions from the governing classes when the workers seemed on the point of revolution.[41] Those modern commentators who have depicted the classical economists as uncritical defenders of the *status quo* have completely misinterpreted both their objectives and their historical significance. If they were, consciously or unconsciously, spokesmen for a particular class, it was the rising industrial and mercantile bourgeoisie, a social group that had not yet wrested the control of affairs from the landed interest, though it was gaining in economic and political strength throughout the first three-quarters of the 19th century.

---

[40] For example, in a primitive society which precedes the appropriation of land and the accumulation of capital 'the whole produce of labour belongs to the labourer'; but in an advanced society the landlord and the capitalist demand their shares, which Smith pointedly called 'deductions' from the produce of labour. In these circumstances, he added, 'rent and profit eat up wages, and the two superior orders of people oppress the inferior one'. And as if this were not enough to fan the flames of social discontent, he stated explicitly that 'civil government, so far as it is instituted for the security of property, is in reality instituted for the defence of the rich against the poor, or of those who have some property against those who have none at all'. (*Wealth of Nations*, I, p. 66; II, pp. 67, 207.)

[41] Cf. Joseph Hamberger, *James Mill and the Art of Revolution*, 1964, p. 115. According to R. H. Tawney, to James Mill 'the State is not a band of brothers, but a mutual detective society: the principal advantage of popular government is that there are more detectives, and therefore, presumably, fewer thieves'. (Cf. his Preface to the *Life and Struggles of William Lovett*, New York, 1920, p. xxi.) Mill was not, however, an unqualified admirer of the populace.

It is significant that the economists were attacked from both ends of the political spectrum. Conservatives regarded them as dangerous radicals, and it is said that Ricardo, a retired stockbroker and wealthy landowner, was denied the opportunity of becoming a JP because his views were too advanced. On the other hand, working-class leaders dismissed them as exponents of capitalist apologetics, and it is true that they regarded the poverty of the masses as a threat to social peace, believing that a rise in the average standard of living would give the workers a stake in the system.

In political affairs the classical economists were moderate reformers: on the whole they did not believe in universal suffrage, and they rejected schemes for popular control of government. Indeed their political outlook was ambivalent, since it combined distrust of the people's capacity for self-government with an even deeper distrust of the influence of strong central control.[42] In general, they were less interested in political freedom than economic freedom, mainly because they considered this was the indispensable prerequisite to personal freedom in other spheres of life, not only for the upper and middle classes but for all members of society.[43]

III. POPULATION, POVERTY AND WAGES

According to Adam Smith, 'no society can surely be flourishing and happy, of which the far greater part of the members are poor and miserable',[1] and this belief underlay the classical economists' preoccupation with the problem of poverty. Throughout their writings they displayed a genuine and consistent desire to raise the lower classes in the social and economic scale by a process that might be appropriately termed 'embourgeoisement'. Despite their fears of excessive population growth and the falling trend in the rate of profit, they were anxious to raise the average level of wages as high as possible since it would encourage the labouring classes to develop

---

[42] William D. Grampp, *Economic Liberalism*, Vol. II: *The Classical View*, New York, 1965, p. 55. The whole of Ch. 2, 'The Political Ideas of the Classical Economists', is relevant to the present discussion.

[43] This point has been especially emphasised by Joseph Cropsey, *Polity and Economy, An Interpretation of the Principles of Adam Smith*, The Hague, 1957, pp. x, 95. Though there were significant differences of emphasis between Smith and his 19th-century successors, their fundamental outlook was consistent.

[1] *Wealth of Nations*, I, p. 80.

a taste for the comforts and conveniences of life, a desire for respectability, and a spirit of emulation.[2] By raising the labourer's economic and social aspirations they believed his desire for self-improvement would be aroused and he would be more likely to develop qualities of self-reliance, thriftiness, prudence, and industriousness. The result would not only be to raise the productivity of labour, thereby providing the means to further economic gains, but also to enhance the quality of social, cultural, and political life.

Belief in benefits of laissez-faire

These ideas underlay most of the classical economists' policy recommendations, for as Torrens remarked, 'No plan of financial or commercial improvement can be so called unless it raises the real wages of labour'.[3] Impediments to the efficient use of scarce resources tended to reduce the rate of profit and check the accumulation of capital, and it was recognised that the approach of the stationary state was accompanied by a fall in the rate of wages as well as profits.[4] As government usually represented just such an impediment the economists were often opposed to and invariably sceptical towards state interference. From their standpoint *laissez-faire* was a progressive policy, since it entailed the reduction or removal of outmoded restrictions on economic freedom.[5] These reasons underlay their opposition to protection, excessive government expenditure, taxes on necessities, combination laws, factory legislation as applied to adults, and any other measures that were likely to reduce either the rate of wages or the incentive to capital accumulation. And as Joseph Schumpeter observed, their support for the 1834 Poor Law Amendment Act

'tallied well with their views on population and wages. It tallied still better with their almost ludicrous confidence in the ability of individuals to act with energy and rationality, to look after themselves responsibly, to find work, and to save for old age and rainy days.'[6]

---

[2] Many of the matters touched on in the remainder of this essay are treated more fully in my paper 'The Classical Economists and the Labourer', originally published in E. L. Jones and G. E. Mingay (eds.), *Land, Labour and Population in the Industrial Revolution*, London, 1967, and reprinted in Coats, *op. cit.*, pp. 144–179.

[3] *Three letters to the Marquis of Chandos*, 1839, p. 38.

[4] For example, Malthus, *Essay on Population*, II, p. 92.

[5] The classical economists were not, of course, advocates of *laissez-faire* in any literal sense. See, for example, H. Scott Gordon, 'The Ideology of Laissez Faire', pp. 180–205, and the editorial introduction in Coats, *op. cit.*

[6] J. A. Schumpeter, *History of Economic Analysis*, New York, 1954, p. 402. An admirer of classical economic analysis, Schumpeter was nevertheless highly critical of

Schumpeter's comment is somewhat exaggerated; but it highlights the classical economists' tendency, so common among social reformers, to under-estimate the obstacles to the fulfilment of their hopes. Their belief in the labourers' capacity for self-improvement was partly a matter of faith; but it was also based on knowledge and reason. They were well aware that real wages were generally higher in England than on the Continent or in Ireland, and they argued that this difference was mainly due to the British worker's superior industry and skill. A reduction of average wage levels would, in due course, be followed by a loss of incentive and a reduction of labour effort (whether for psychological or physiological reasons, or both); and with lower productivity and income there would be less inclination to practice moral restraint. Conversely, a rise in real wages would not be followed by an instantaneous increase in population and the labour supply;[7] and if the higher level persisted there could be a permanent upward adjustment in the wage earner's conception of a decent and proper standard of life. In the repeated discussions of the relationship between wages and 'subsistence' it was generally accepted that subsistence was determined by social (i.e. customary) rather than economic forces, since the long-term equilibrium wage level was well above the bare physical minimum necessary for survival.

Population growth and restraint

Although belief in the more rigid and mechanical version of Malthus' population theory diminished considerably from the late 1820s, the fear of excessive population growth by no means disappeared and the economists attached increasing weight to the social and psychological motives for postponing marriage or restricting the size of family. McCulloch, in particular, stressed that a taste for luxuries, comforts and enjoyments 'should be widely diffused, and, if possible,

---

their social philosophy: 'No philosophy at all in the technical sense, unsurpassably shallow as a "philosophy of life", it [utilitarianism] fitted to perfection the streak of materialistic (anti-metaphysical) rationalism that may be associated with liberalism and the business mind.' (*Ibid.*, pp. 407–8.)

Not all the surviving classical economists approved of the 1834 Act: McCulloch was a determined opponent.

[7] Opinions differed as to the time-lag between a rise in real income and a consequent increase of population (whether through earlier or more numerous marriages or an increase in the progeny of existing marriages). An instantaneous response was sometimes assumed for reasons of analytical convenience, whereas in later writings, e.g. Senior, De Quincey and McCulloch, it was often explicitly stated that population adjusted itself only slowly to changes in real earnings.

interwoven with national habits and prejudices.' Indeed he declared that it was

'the great and leading defect in the lower classes, that they submit to privations with too little reluctance. Nothing ought to be more earnestly deprecated, than any change in the sentiments of the great body of the people, which may have the effect of inducing them to lower their opinion as to what is necessary to their comfortable subsistence. Every such degradation is almost sure to be permanent; in as much as wages would always fall in a corresponding ratio; . . .'[8]

No doubt this standpoint is naïve, for it reveals a serious inability to comprehend the true nature of the difficulties facing the labourer. Even so, it represents a notable advance in humanity and understanding over the opinions prevalent in the early 18th century, when it was considered advisable to reduce wages and maintain or raise the prices of provisions so that the pressure of necessity would compel the workers to be industrious.[9] In McCulloch's complaint that the labourers too readily 'submit to privations' we find another indication of progress beyond the less sympathetic views of an earlier epoch.

In their bitter opposition to the Speenhamland system of poor law allowances the classical economists repeatedly insisted that subsidies to paupers undermined the independence of the independent labourers, and modern commentators have too readily ridiculed their over-estimate of this precious quality. But in emphasising the value of independence they were expressing their middle-class prejudices against the paternalistic emphasis on the need for dependency and deference on the part of the lower orders.[10] In some quarters the 18th century fear that the labourers would become 'saucy' and develop ideas 'above their station' survived well into the 19th century; but it was increasingly on the defensive. As J. S. Mill observed, the distinguishing feature of mid-Victorian society was that 'the poor

---

[8] 'Combination Laws—Restraints on Emigration', *Edinburgh Review*, Vol. LXXVIII, January 1824, p. 333; 'Ricardo's Political Economy', *ibid.*, Vol. LIX, June 1818, p. 87.

In the gloomy conditions of the early 1840s, De Quincey maintained that 'the energetic spirit of the English working man' and his determination to retain his 'high domestic standard of comfort' was the sole barrier against the triple threat of machinery, child labour and Irish competition, which threatened to reduce him to 'the very basest human degradation ever witnessed amongst oriental slaves'. (*The Logic of Political Economy*, Edinburgh, 1844, pp. 147–8.)

[9] Cf. Edgar Furniss, *The Position of the Labourer in a System of Nationalism*, New York, 1920, *passim*; also A. W. Coats, 'Changing Attitudes to Labour in the Mid-Eighteenth Century', *Economic History Review*, Vol. XI, August 1958, pp. 35–51.

[10] A general treatment of this theme will be found in Perkin, *Origins of Modern British Society, op. cit.*, Ch. 2.

have come out of leading-strings, and cannot any longer be governed or treated like children. To their own qualities must now be commended the care of their destiny', and the prospect struck him as hopeful.[11]

Although the classical economists sometimes complained that the industrial and urban workers were riotous and disorderly, in their calmer moods they recognised this behaviour as an integral part of the progress of industrial society, and they vigorously supported educational provisions designed to narrow the gap between the middle and working classes. They viewed the lower orders not as opponents but as 'accessories to reform',[12] and it was precisely this outlook that blinded them to the difficulties of achieving their objectives.

Co-partnership the key

To historians who regard conflict as the inevitable and proper relationship between social classes their standpoint doubtless seems naïve and unrealistic; but it is clear that the economists believed the future of the labouring classes, as of society in general, depended on a kind of co-partnership between the well-to-do and the poor, in which the former provided an appropriate framework of laws and a rate of saving and capital accumulation sufficient to ensure a high demand for labour, and the latter exercised a proper degree of restraint over the growth of numbers. However unjust it might appear, moral restraint was unnecessary among the upper and middle classes for if they reproduced excessively they could afford to pay the price of their imprudence. Moreover their numbers were small so that a change in their behaviour would make no significant difference to the rate of population growth. Even before Malthus formulated his notorious 'law', it was recognised that numbers made a crucial difference both to the distribution of wealth and the growth of population for, as Edmund Burke noted in 1795:

'The labouring classes are only poor, because they are numerous. Numbers in their nature imply poverty. In a fair distribution among a vast multitude, none can have very much. That class of dependent pensioners called the rich, is so extremely small that if all their throats were cut, and a distribution made of all they consume in a year, it would not give a bit of bread and cheese for one night's supper to those who labour, and who in reality feed both the pensioners and themselves.'[13]

---

[11] *Principles*, Vol. II, p. 763.   [12] Cf. E. P. Thompson, *op. cit.*, p. 139.
[13] *Thoughts and Details on Scarcity, etc.*, in *Works* (1808 edn.), VII, p. 376: quoted by J. R. Poynter, *Society and Pauperism*, London, 1969, p. xiv.

The problem of pauperism

Although the classical economists' prescriptions were really designed for the upper and middle echelons of wage-earners, they were only too well aware of the existence of extreme poverty, disease, misery and degradation at the lower end of the scale. In times of special difficulty, as for example during the Napoleonic Wars, or in bad harvest or trade depression, they recognised the widespread extent of distress,[14] and this largely explains their general conviction that the the long-term equilibrium wage level was too low. They also gave eloquent descriptions of the sufferings of particular segments of the working class, especially the hand-loom weavers whose plight attracted national attention in the late 1830s and early 1840s.[15] The extreme poverty of the Irish peasantry was constantly held out as an awful warning of the consequences of excessive procreation and falling living standards, and despite their general suspicion of government interference in economic and social affairs they increasingly acknowledged the need for legislative controls of housing, sanitation and factory conditions.[16]

Modern commentators of all shades of opinion have criticised

---

[14] Two early examples may be given: James Mill's lengthy protest against Thomas Spence's under-estimate of the poor's hardships in *Commerce Defended*, 1808, pp. 80–3; and the repeated expressions of concern for the sufferings caused by bad harvests in Ricardo's speeches and his correspondence with Malthus, James Mill, and Hutches Trower. (Cf. Ricardo's *Works*, Vols. V and VII.)

[15] Nassau Senior probably wrote the Report of the Commission on the Condition of the Hand Loom Weavers: cf. Marian Bowley, *Nassau Senior and Classical Economics*, London, 1937, p. 258 ff., reproduced in Coats (ed.), *The Classical Economists and Economic Policy*, pp. 57–63. Torrens and McCulloch also wrote at length on this subject, and the latter gave many detailed accounts of the hardships of particular groups in his articles in the *Edinburgh Review* and in his *Statistical Account of the British Empire*.

[16] Senior became particularly concerned about bad housing, and recommended strong regulations: 'With all our reverence for the principle of non-interference, we cannot doubt that in this matter it has been pushed too far. We believe that both the ground landlord and the speculating builder ought to be compelled by law, though it should cost them a percentage on their rent and profit, to take measures which shall prevent the towns which they create from being the centre of disease.' (*Report of the Commissioners on the Condition of the Hand Loom Weavers*, P.P., 1841, p. 73.) In his lectures Senior argued that the State had a right not only to prevent a man from injuring others, but also from injuring himself by living in inferior housing. (Cf. Bowley, pp. 266–7.)

Readers in the 1970s may note that McCulloch not only advocated public control of ventilation, cleanliness, and fencing of machinery in factories, but also suggested that smoke control might be expedient in towns or populous neighbourhoods! (Cf. *Treatises and Essays on Money, Exchange, Interest, etc.*, 2nd edn., Edinburgh, 1859, p. 462.)

the classical economists, though in very differing degrees, for their failure to make constructive suggestions for relieving the hardships of the very poorest members of the community, and there is no denying that they failed to offer effective solutions for problems that have remained with us ever since. On this subject Malthus was by far the most important single voice, and unfortunately, as one recent judicious historian has observed, his work is especially difficult to interpret and evaluate.[17] As is well known, he and Ricardo advocated the *'gradual* and *very gradual* abolition of the poor law', not because he wished to plunge the pauper into actual want—which he recognised was so degrading that it 'palsies every virtue'—but because he believed that *fear* of want was the indispensable spur to industry, self-reliance, and self-improvement.[18] Although the major poor law reform in the classical period, the famous Amendment Act of 1834, did not accord with Malthus's recommendations, his writings exerted a profound impact on the whole subject of poverty and pauperism in the first half of the 19th century, and had a significant indirect effect on the course of policy.

At the close of an already extended essay it is obviously impossible to discuss this topic in detail, for it is complex and still controversial. Suffice it to say that the solution adopted in 1834 was fully in harmony with the principles of political economy and its related philosophy of utilitarianism, and it is undeniable that the Act failed to alleviate the problem it was designed to solve. The principle of 'less eligibility' was based on a fallacious analysis of the nature of poverty and the psychology of the poor, and it could never have worked effectively even had it been administered efficiently. What can be said for the classical economists' solution was that it sought to ameliorate the lot of the poor by adopting a long-run solution rather than any of the numerous ill-considered and sentimental proposals then under discussion. Its exponents realised that in the short-run it would cause hardship; but

---

[17] J. R. Poynter, *Society and Pauperism, English Ideas on Poor Relief, 1795–1834*, London, 1969, p. 110: 'Malthus's writings provoke prejudices; even today few can write about him without undue animus or admiration. The extreme vilification by early critics . . . was based on ignorance, or at least on misunderstanding and exaggeration. It can now be agreed that Malthus was no misanthrope, but a kind and benevolent man in his personal relationships, and quite sincere in his protestations that he deplored misery and welcomed such improvement as he thought possible. . . . [Yet] there was definite ambivalence in his writings. Malthus the sincere philanthropist was also the author of passages of harsh dogmatism and extraordinary insensitivity to human sufferings.'

[18] *Essay on Population*, Vol. I, p. 64; II, pp. 143, 177.

they sincerely believed that without reform the long-run hardships would be much more serious. J. S. Mill's remark that Malthus's ideas conflicted with 'those plans of easy beneficence which accord so well with the inclination of man, but so ill with the arrangements of nature'[19] could be applied to all the classical economists.

IV. SUMMARY: POSSIBILITIES OF FREEDOM AND PROGRESS UNDER INDUSTRIALISATION

As indicated at the beginning of this essay, it is no easy task to summarise the classical economists' ideas about industrialisation and poverty. Nevertheless, the attempt must be made if the reader is not to lose sight of the main themes among the many individual differences and shifts of opinion that occurred in response to the momentous economic and social changes of the time.

Principles and beliefs

The basic principles of classical political economy were derived directly from 18th-century liberal moral philosophy, with its emphasis on the value of individual freedom in all spheres of life, and its fundamental faith in the possibilities of progress. Admittedly this faith was severely tested under the novel and often alarming circumstances of 19th-century industrialisation in Britain. Indeed, it would be easy to compile a catalogue of statements and predictions from the classical economists' writings which, taken together and out of context, would convey an overall impression of unmitigated gloom and despondency. But that would be a false picture. While they acknowledged what are nowadays termed 'the costs of economic growth'—such as low wages, long hours, bad working conditions, child labour, technological unemployment, the dehumanising effects of the division of labour, and the existence of over-crowded, ill-constructed, and insanitary housing—they tended to under-estimate these features, and they undoubtedly believed that in the long run the benefits would far outweigh the disadvantages. This was not simply because higher productivity would lead to higher standards of material welfare, but because these resources could also constitute the means to higher levels of culture and civilisation.

---

[19] 'The Claims of Labour', *Edinburgh Review*, Vol. CLXIV, 1845, pp. 501–2. It could be said of Mill, as Schumpeter said of Ricardo, that he was 'above the unctuous phrases that cost so little and yield such ample returns'.

These goals could not, of course, be attained easily. The economists recognised the dangers of ignorance, political unrest, and class conflict; and from our safe distance we can see that while industrialisation undoubtedly brings substantial improvements in average living standards, it neither guarantees a just distribution of wealth nor the elimination of poverty and other concomitant social evils.

Naïve optimists, humane reformers

In many respects the classical economists' optimism, though rarely unqualified, was naïve; and in general it reflected their bourgeois background, standards and values. In particular it led them to under-estimate the hardships suffered by many wage earners and the obstacles to the improvement of their material and cultural standards. To their credit, the economists did not regard the problem of poverty as insoluble, as many earlier generations had done. But they offered few constructive proposals, and the most important single legislative enactment based on their ideas, the 1834 Poor Law Amendment Act, proved to be a lamentable failure.

It is, of course, easy to make excuses for them. Their intentions were good; the problem of poverty was unprecedented in its character and scale; they lacked adequate data; the administrative machinery was grossly inadequate, as were also the available financial resources; and at least they made a genuine effort at reform based on systematic reasoning—by contrast with many earlier emotional and utopian schemes. Despite their justifiable doubts about the efficacy of state intervention in economic and social affairs, the classical economists were neither spokesmen for dogmatic *laissez faire* nor uncritical apologists for the *status quo*, but moderate, humane, and liberal reformers. And yet when all due allowances have been made, it cannot be denied that their analysis of the problem of poverty was defective, their diagnosis inaccurate, and their recommendations ineffective.

Achievements under-estimated

Generally speaking, historians have under-estimated the classical economists' achievements. Attention has been focussed on the inadequacies of their social policy recommendations rather than on the power of their economic analysis, and of course many commentators have objected to their social and political preconceptions. At the same time, however, there has been a tendency to exaggerate their influence, and even to suggest that they directed society along the wrong 'economic and social paths'.[1] Such a criticism is meaningless unless a viable alternative solution is offered, one that is compatible with the ideas, resources, and practical possibilities of the time.

From our mid-20th century vantage point we have become more sceptical of panaceas, and more doubtful of the efficacy of government fiscal, financial, or employment policy, or in schemes designed to redistribute income or increase social welfare. And until we have demonstrated our superiority, it behoves us to be judicious and sympathetic in assessing earlier generations.

---

[1] Cf. Brian Inglis, *Poverty and the Industrial Revolution*, London, 1971, p. 10. This long and stimulating study, written in the humanitarian tradition of social history associated with Tawney, the Hammonds, and the Webbs, has one novel feature: an almost Ruskinian belief in the power and pernicious influence of economists. According to Mr Inglis, by 1820 political economy was virtually 'a new religion, and a new God', and 'the new Government was hypnotised by Malthus, and political economy'. Yet elsewhere, he concedes that 'ministers could put it to whatever purpose they needed' because the economists disagreed among themselves and offered differing, and sometimes conflicting, policy recommendations (pp. 230, 255, 402). Fortunately most present-day commentators are more sceptical of the influence of ideas and experts, and the whole question of the influence of economists and other intellectuals in the early 19th century is still *sub judice*. At this stage premature generalisation is harmful. (Cf. Poynter, *op. cit.*, p. 324 ff.; Coats, *op. cit.*, pp. 1–32.)

Part III

7. Friedrich Engels and the England of the 'Hungry Forties'

W. H. CHALONER
Reader in Modern Economic History,
University of Manchester

and

W. O. HENDERSON
Reader in International Economic History,
University of Manchester

THE AUTHORS

WILLIAM HENRY CHALONER, M.A., PhD., was born in 1914 and educated at Crewe Grammar School and the University of Manchester where he has been Reader in Modern Economic History since 1962. From 1939 to 1945 he was in the Press Censorship Division of the Ministry of Information.

Dr Chaloner's publications include *Social and Economic Development of Crewe 1780–1923* (Manchester University Press, 1950); *Vulcan 1859–1959: One Hundred Years of Engineering and Insurance* (1959); *People and Industries* (Frank Cass, 1963); and various translations, notably his collaboration with Dr W. O. Henderson on Engels (below). He has contributed articles to learned journals including *History Today*, *History*, *English Historical Review*, and *Economic History Review*. Hon. Ed., *Transactions* of the Lancashire and Cheshire Antiquarian Society.

He is married with three sons and lives at Oldham.

WILLIAM OTTO HENDERSON, M.A., PhD., was born in 1904 and educated at Nottingham High School, Downing College, Cambridge and the University of Hamburg. He has been Reader in International Economic History at Manchester University since 1963.

His numerous publications include *The Lancashire Cotton Famine, 1861–65* (1934, new edn. 1968); *Britain and Industrial Europe* (1954); (with W. H. Chaloner) a trans. of W. G. Hoffmann's *British Industry, 1700–1950* (1952 and 1955); (ed.) *Engels: Selected Writings* (1967); *The Industrialisation of Europe* (1969); (with W. H. Chaloner) trans. and ed., Friedrich Engels's *The Condition of the Working Class in England* (2nd edn., 1971).

He is married with three children and lives in Blackpool.

I. THE LEGACY OF ENGELS

In the first half of this century the view was widely held that the 1840s had been a period of acute misery and degradation for the English working classes, and that their conditions had been getting worse since the end of the Napoleonic wars. It could be argued that Friedrich Engels's book on *The Condition of the Working Class* played an important part in creating this legend. How did this come about?

Few intellectual partnerships can have had such momentous results as that of Marx and Engels, the fathers of 'scientific' socialism and communism. Although Friedrich Engels, the junior partner, was for a long time not as well known as Karl Marx, he had a considerable influence upon the formation of socialist propaganda in the second half of the 19th century. Recent celebrations in both Germanies of the 150th anniversary of his birth, and the reprinting of some of his works and correspondence, have now somewhat redressed the balance and we are able to judge more clearly and objectively his importance in the early socialist movement.

Manchester apprenticeship

Engels's visit to England from November 1842 to August 1844 marked the climax of the formative period of his career during which he was preparing himself for his life's work as a socialist agitator.

His apprenticeship in Manchester—for it was there that he spent nearly all his time—was important for two reasons. First, he became well acquainted with the manufacturing districts of the North of England and collected the material from which, on his return to Germany, he wrote *Die Lage der Arbeitenden Klasse in England* (*The Condition of the Working Class in England*). This work established his reputation among socialists as an expert on the social consequences of modern industrialisation. Secondly, his study of political economy bore fruit in an article in the *Deutsch-Französische Jahrbücher* (*Franco-German Yearbook*) in 1844, which criticised the theories of the classical economists.

When Marx first met Engels in Cologne in the autumn of 1842—Engels was then on his way to England for the first time—there were no signs of the future close relationship between the two young men. Marx was apparently suspicious of Engels's motives in approaching him, and this first meeting has been described as 'cool, even un-

171

friendly'. But when Engels saw Marx in Paris two years later, on Engels's return from England, the meeting was much more cordial. Marx recognised the extent of Engels's intellectual development since their previous meeting and was now more ready to accept him as a collaborator.

Traditional upbringing

Friedrich Engels was just 22 years of age when he visited England in 1842. His father was a prosperous cotton manufacturer in Barmen and Engelskirchen (Rhineland), and Engels grew up in a pious Prussian middle-class household where respect for Church and King was traditional. He received a grammar school education, but left before taking his final examination to enter the family business. Part of his early training was in the office of Consul Leupold in the cotton port of Bremen. Between October 1841 and October 1842 Engels served as a volunteer in the Guard Artillery in Berlin and always retained a lively interest in military affairs. By 1842 he was already strongly opposed to his family's political and religious views and, under the pen name 'Friedrich Oswald', contributed articles to the Cologne radical newspaper *Rheinische Zeitung*.[1] Two months after leaving the army he went to England to work in the office of Ermen and Engels, a Manchester firm of cotton spinners in which his father was a partner. He reached London at the end of November 1842 and went on to Manchester in the middle of December.

Unfortunately comparatively little is known of Engels's first stay in Manchester, because this visit had an important influence upon his career. Few letters written by Engels at the time appear to have survived and information concerning his activities is available only in his published writings and the subsequent recollections of people he met in England. His contributions to various periodicals and his book on the condition of the working classes indicate that Engels spent most of his time in Manchester. He claimed that in 20 months he got to know Manchester as intimately as Barmen and 'more intimately than most of its residents'.[2] He met several Chartists, including James Leach, whom he held in high esteem as 'an honest,

---

[1] Karl Marx was the editor of the *Rheinische Zeitung* from 12 October, 1842, to 17 March, 1843. It was the severity of the Prussian censorship that led him to give up his position as editor.

[2] *The Condition of the Working Class in England in 1844*, English translation, 1892, p. 42.

trustworthy and capable man'.[3] He also made the acquaintance of the secularist, Dr John Watts, whose lectures at the Owenite Hall of Science in Manchester he admired.[4]

Engels's intimate knowledge of the Manchester slums may have arisen from his friendship with Mary Burns, an Irish working girl who eventually became his mistress. His investigations took him to the cotton towns in the vicinity of Manchester. In 1843 he went to Leeds to see George Julian Harney, editor of the Chartist paper *The Northern Star*. He became friendly with his compatriot, George Weerth, a clerk in a Bradford wool textile firm, and it is possible that Engels visited the worst parts of Bradford in Weerth's company. He also visited London in the summer of 1843, where he met three German revolutionary agitators—Karl Schapper, Heinrich Bauer and Joseph Moll—who influenced his later intellectual development.[5] He does not appear to have visited other manufacturing districts such as South Wales, the Black Country, the Tyne, or the Clyde.

II. POLITICAL-LITERARY ACTIVITY

Published works

Engels cannot have devoted much time to completing his commercial training in Manchester, since he was busily investigating the economic and social condition of the factory workers, both by mastering the literature on the subject and by personal observation. During his short stay in England he contributed essays on current affairs to two radical periodicals published on the Continent—the *Rheinische Zeitung* (November–December 1842) and the *Schweizerische Republikaner* (May–June 1843)—and also wrote for Robert Owen's *The New Moral World* (November 1843–February 1844). Of more significance were the two 1844 articles in the *Deutsch-Französische Jahrbücher*,

---

[3] *Ibid.*, p. 135. James Leach was the author of an anonymous pamphlet entitled *Stubborn Facts from the Factories*, by a Manchester Operative, published by William Rashleigh, MP (London, 1844).

[4] By 1851 Engels had lost confidence in Watts. Engels wrote to Marx on 5 February, 1851, sneering at the part played by Watts in promoting the establishment of the Free Public Library in Manchester. He complained that Watts was actually 'on the best of terms with the Bishop of Manchester.' (*Karl Marx–Friedrich Engels Historisch-Kritische Gesamtausgabe*, Part III, Vol. I, 1929, Letter 60, pp. 140–3.) For Dr John Watts see *Dictionary of National Biography*.

[5] *Karl Marx–Friedrich Engels Historisch-Kritische Gesamtausgabe*, Part I, Vol. 4 (1932), introduction, p. xx, quoting a letter from Engels to Marx dated 6 May, 1868.

the socialist periodical edited by Runge and Marx and published in Paris. In the first he again criticised current conceptions of economic theory; in the second he reviewed Carlyle's *Past and Present*. In Engels's opinion this was the only book written in England in 1843 worth reading.

The main results of Engels's investigations in England appeared in the book he wrote immediately after returning to Barmen. He was, he told Marx on 19 November, 1844, 'buried in English newspapers and books from which I am putting together my book on the condition of the working classes in England'. The young author worked under difficult conditions. He was engaged in communist propaganda among the workers of Elberfeld and Barmen and the Prussian police were showing an unwelcome interest. He was involved in a love affair which appears to have ended abruptly. His relations with his father drifted from bad to worse. The elder Engels was deeply shocked to realise that his son had no intention of entering the family business or of attending a university and was devoting his time to revolutionary agitation. Engels postponed the breach with his family long enough to complete his book. At the end of January 1845 he was writing to Marx that he hoped to finish it 'in two or three weeks'. The preface and the dedication 'to the Working Classes of Great Britain' were dated 15 March, 1845. Two days later he complained he was living 'a veritable dog's life' in Barmen. Shortly afterwards he joined Karl Marx in Brussels.

Frustration and bitterness

The circumstances under which the book was written help to explain the fury of his attack on the English middle classes in general and the manufacturers in particular. At loggerheads with his family and watched by the police, he was an angry young man who vented his spleen in passionate denunciation of the factory system as he had newly seen it in England. The violence of his language and his failure to understand other viewpoints may be explained by the overwhelming sense of frustration he suffered in the winter of 1844–5.

The first edition of *Die Lage der Arbeitenden Klasse in England* was published in Leipzig in the early summer of 1845 by Otto Wigand. A study of a strike in the building trade in Manchester entitled 'An English Turnout'—described by Engels as an appendix to his book—appeared in the Bielefeld periodical *Das Westphalische Dampfboot* in January and February 1846. A reprint of *Die Lage der Arbeitenden Klasse in England*, with a new title page, was published in 1848. For the next 40 years no new German edition appeared. But in the 1880s German socialists took a new interest in the book. 'My friends in Germany,' Engels wrote on 10 February, 1885, 'say that the book is important to them just now because it describes a state of things which is almost exactly reproduced at the present moment in Germany . . .' Engels stated that 'a new German edition of my work is in actual preparation'. Two years later, however, Karl Kautsky was complaining that the book was still out of print and that many socialists had never read it. It was not until 1892 that a second German edition was published by J. H. W. Dietz of Stuttgart. Engels, now 72, made only a few minor changes in the book but added a new preface (dated 21 July, 1892).

English translation

Meanwhile in 1887 an English translation by Mrs Florence Kelley Wischnewetzky entitled *The Condition of the Working Class in England in 1844*[1] had been published in the United States. The translation was authorised by Engels who wrote a special preface (26 January, 1887) and an appendix (25 February, 1887) for it. In 1892 Mrs Wischnewetzky's translation was issued by a British publisher with a preface by the author (dated 11 January, 1892), which was reproduced as an article, 'England in 1845 and 1885', in the *London Commonweal* of 1 March, 1885. Mrs Wischnewetzky's translation has frequently been re-issued since 1892 without significant changes.

This translation leaves much to be desired. It is little more than a word-for-word transcript of the original. The reader can turn page after page before coming to a paragraph that resembles the normal style of an English writer. As Engels wrote it the book is full of lively and vigorous passages: they have been translated in a very pedestrian fashion; neither the spirit nor style has been recaptured. Engels himself was far from satisfied with the original draft and criticised Mrs Wischnewetzky severely.[2] No attempt was made to

---

[1] The words 'in 1844' in the title of the book appear only in Mrs Wischnewetzky's English translation and have never formed part of the German title. Mrs Wischnewetzky (1859–1926) was an American socialist of Irish origin. (D. R. Blumberg, *Florence Kelley*, New York, 1966.)

[2] In 1887 Engels complained to Sorge: 'She translates like a factory, leaving the real work to me.' (K. Marx and F. Engels, *Letters to Americans, 1848–1895*, New York, 1963, p. 182.) For the most recent version, see F. Engels, *The Condition of the Working Class in England*, translated and edited by W. O. Henderson and W. H. Chaloner (2nd edn., 1971).

render into acceptable English the subtler shades of meaning that no reader of the original German could possibly miss. Mrs Wischnewetzky's approach lacked the spark of imagination to illuminate the translation of a work dealing with issues that had aroused the young author's deepest emotions. No attempt has been made to correct wrong dates[3] or elementary arithmetical errors in the statistics.

There are graver faults. Many of the passages quoted by Engels at some length from English books and reports were not reproduced in the original English but were translated back into English from Engels's German version. A few passages were arbitrarily omitted without informing the reader that this had been done. It is astonishing that generations of English scholars have been prepared to use so unsatisfactory a translation, which continues to be reprinted in various forms.[4]

Standard exposition

In the late 1840s the first edition became well known in Germany, was widely reviewed, and is known to have been frequently discussed in various Prussian government departments. Karl Marx gave it high praise. In the first volume of *Das Kapital* he declared that

'the fullness of Engels's insight into the nature of the capitalist method of production has been shown by the factory reports, the reports on mines, etc., that have appeared since the publication of his book.'[5]

Later generations of socialists and communists accepted Engels's study as a standard exposition of the social consequences of industrialisation.[6] They argued that although many writers had described the condition of the English workers in the 1840s only Engels—with his unique insight into the development of historical processes—had shown how the rise of the factory system was an

---

[3] Althorp's Factory Act of 1833, for example, is dated 1834.

[4] For a left-wing criticism of the Henderson–Chaloner edition, see E. J. Hobsbawm, *Labouring Men*, 1964, Ch. 12; this article originally appeared in *Marxism Today*.

[5] Karl Marx, *Capital*, Vol. I (Everyman Edition, 1930), pp. 240–1 (note). There are many references to Engels's book in the Marx–Engels correspondence. For example, *Karl Marx–Friedrich Engels Historisch-Kritische Gesamtausgabe*, Part I, Vol. 4 (1932), introduction, pp. xiii–xiv.

[6] Lenin wrote: 'Engels was the first to say that not only was the proletariat a suffering class, but that, in fact, the disgraceful economic condition of the proletariat was driving it irresistibly forward and compelling it to fight for its ultimate emancipation.' (Karl Marx and Friedrich Engels, *On Britain* (Foreign Languages Publishing House, Moscow, 1953), preface to the Russian edition, p. xi.)

inevitable stage in the evolution of capitalist society; only Engels had adequately explained the changes that industrial capitalism had wrought in the relations between the moneyed middle classes and the property-less proletariat. The German socialist Franz Mehring in his biography of Marx declared that Engels's book on the English working classes was 'a fundamental socialist work' and considered that

'the most admirable and at the same time the most noteworthy historical feature of the book is the thoroughness with which the twenty-four-year-old author understands the spirit of the capitalist mode of production and succeeds in explaining from it not only the rise but also the decline of the bourgeoisie, not only the misery of the proletariat but also its salvation.'[7]

III. SOURCE OF ECONOMIC HISTORY

Towards the end of the 19th century Engels's book achieved a new significance. It came to be generally accepted by economic historians as an authoritative account of social conditions in England in the 1840s. To some extent this was fortuitous in that many other works on the England of the 1840s had long been almost unobtainable. The printed materials which Engels himself used—such as the writings of Ure, Gaskell, Kay and Leach—were out of print. Accounts by various other foreign investigators into English social conditions in the early Victorian era had been forgotten.[1]

From about 1895 onwards scholars pointed out that Engels was a contemporary foreign observer who described conditions he had seen with his own eyes. They cited his extensive quotations from parliamentary reports, books, pamphlets, newspapers and other contemporary sources. Here surely was a reliable witness whose evidence about conditions in the factories and the living conditions of factory workers deserved the closest attention. It might be assumed, too, that in dealing with matters upon which opinions were so divided in Britain, Engels as a German would be freer from bias than an English writer.

---

[7] Franz Mehring, *Karl Marx, The Story of his Life* (translated by E. Fitzgerald, 1936), p. 105.

[1] Mention may be made of Eugène Buret's *La misère de la classe ouvrière en France et Angleterre* (2 vols., 1840), C. E. Lester's two books on *The Glory and Shame of England* (2 vols., New York, 1841) and on *The Condition and Fate of England* (2 vols., New York, 1843), Léon Faucher's *Etudes sur l'Angleterre* (2 vols., 1845) and J. C. Cobden's *The White Slaves of England* (Buffalo, 1853).

G

Modern research into the growth of capitalism, the genesis of the Industrial Revolution and the rise of the factory system, suggests that Engels was not particularly well informed on these matters. In his historical introduction—based largely upon a book entitled *The Manufacturing Population of England* (1833), written by an obscure surgeon named Peter Gaskell (?1805–41)[2]—Engels contrasted the happy carefree craftsmen and yeomen of the 18th century with the downtrodden factory operatives and farm labourers of the 19th century. He seems to have believed that the period during which the 'domestic system' flourished in the days before the industrial revolution was a golden age free from the sordid social evils that characterised the factory system of the early 19th century. Few modern scholars would agree. Social conditions were far from ideal in the middle of the 18th century. There may have been some smallholders and craftsmen who were both prosperous and independent, but many of the domestic spinners and weavers of that period were as ruthlessly 'exploited' by the great clothiers as were the factory operatives by the manufacturers in the 1840s. Men, women and children worked long hours for low wages under the domestic system as well as under the factory system. Because the factories brought the workers under one roof it became possible to detect bad conditions that had formerly been hidden in many isolated cottages and workshops.

Limited sources

The widely accepted view that Engels was a competent observer of the England of the 1840s and gave a reliable report of what he saw requires modification. His knowledge of the English scene—gained in 20 months or so—was more limited than is sometimes supposed. Manchester and Salford, which dominate his graphic description of 'the Great Towns' (Chapter 2), were industrial centres he undoubtedly knew well. Even so, the account of Manchester by Léon Faucher, particularly as translated and edited by the Benthamite barrister, J. P. Culverwell, *Manchester in 1844* (1844, reprinted 1969), is much fuller and more balanced than Engels's description.[3] Engels appears

---

2 In his turn Gaskell had borrowed freely from Richard Guest's *Compendious History of the Cotton Manufacture*, 1823, for his description of the domestic system of industry in the countryside.

3 Even Faucher could be highly selective in his choice of the areas he commented on. As J. P. Culverwell acidly remarked in a footnote to his translation of Faucher's *Manchester in 1844*: 'We must also add that M. Faucher alights upon some of the most depraved portions of the population, which are, in reality, notorious only as exceptions, and holds them up to the reader as a fair specimen of the working population

to have visited Oldham, Rochdale, Ashton-under-Lyne and other Lancashire towns, and he crossed the Pennines to see Leeds, Bradford and Huddersfield. He also paid brief visits to London. On the other hand there is no evidence that he had any first-hand knowledge of such important centres of industry as Birmingham, Newcastle-upon-Tyne or Glasgow. His description of conditions in textile, particularly cotton, mills is almost certainly based upon personal inspection, but the information at his disposal on coalmining, ironworks and engineering was probably derived from readily available printed sources.

Engels over-simplified the many gradations of status and income among the manual workers. In his descriptions the worst-off tended to become the typical. He equated the progress of industrial capitalism with the intensification of pauperism, and helped to promote the unfounded legend that the new towns presented a polarisation of society between rich employers and a mass of underpaid wage slaves, minimising the numbers and influence of the middle classes of society. Examination of the many street directories of the period and the manuscript census returns shows this legend to be unfounded.

A detailed examination of the material upon which Engels relied shows a restricted range of sources. He drew heavily upon a small number of books and pamphlets by Dr J. P. Kay, Peter Gaskell, Dr Andrew Ure, J. C. Symons, Sir Archibald Alison and James Leach.[4] Two or three chapters are largely based upon the evidence printed in the well-known Factories Enquiry Commission of 1833–4 and the Children's Employment Commission of 1841–3. The newspapers upon which Engels chiefly relied were the *Manchester Guardian* and two radical organs—*The Northern Star* and the *Weekly Despatch*. He did not always consult the book or report in which a statement first appeared and was content to quote at second hand from a newspaper.

Engels's account of the condition of the workers in Britain in the 1840s was not always based strictly upon contemporary evidence. In his description of the insanitary state of Edinburgh, for example,

---

in general. A mode of special pleading, anything but desirable, in an impartial enquiry into so important a subject. Angel Meadow and St. George's road, are no more average specimens of the working classes in Manchester, than Billingsgate is a fair specimen of the social conditions of London' (p. 31).

[4] Dr J. P. Kay (later Sir James Kay-Shuttleworth), *The Moral and Physical Condition of the Working Classes employed in the Cotton Manufacture in Manchester* (1832); Dr Andrew Ure, *The Philosophy of Manufactures* (1835); J. C. Symons, *Artisans at Home and Abroad* (1839); Sir Archibald Alison, *The Principles of Population* (2 vols., 1840); and James Leach, *Stubborn Facts from the Factories, op. cit.*

he referred to an article by John Hennen in the *Edinburgh Medical and Surgical Journal* without stating in which year the article appeared. It had in fact been printed in *1818* and therefore dealt with a state of affairs existing a quarter of a century before Engels wrote.

There are numerous extracts from evidence presented to the Factories Enquiry Commission of 1833–4. The information in the first volume of this Commission's report described conditions before the passing of Althorp's Factory Act of 1833. Engels led his readers to believe that the grim picture of 1833 had not been materially altered by the 1840s. While he was right in publicising the difficulties experienced by factory inspectors in enforcing the law, he was wrong in assuming that virtually no improvements had occurred in the previous decade. Engels quoted from Kay-Shuttleworth's well-known pamphlet on the Manchester cotton operatives which had appeared in 1832, ignoring that even Francis Place, a champion of the workers, had criticised Kay-Shuttleworth for giving the impression that all workers had sunk to the same level of misery.[5] Engels leaves the reader with the impression that Kay-Shuttleworth's strictures on housing and sanitation were still valid in 1844. He does not appear to have appreciated, or took no account of, the significance of the reforms in local government in Manchester and other industrial towns since the passing of the Municipal Corporations Act of 1835. Many of the factory towns were beginning to put their house in order at the very time Engels was writing.[6]

---

[5] Giving evidence before the Select Committee on Education in 1835 Francis Place commented upon Kay-Shuttleworth's pamphlet: 'Yes, I know Dr Kay, and I believe what he says is correct; but he gives the matter as it now stands, knowing nothing of former times; his picture is a very deplorable one. I am assured that my view of it is correct by many Manchester operatives whom I have seen; they inform me that his narration relates almost wholly to the state of the Irish, but that the condition of a vast number of the people was as bad some years ago, as he described the worst portion of them to be now. Any writer or enquirer will be misled unless he has the means of comparing the present with former times.' (*Parl. Papers*, 1835 (no. 465), Vol. VII, p. 838 (quoted in Mrs M. D. George, *London Life in the Eighteenth Century*, p. 323).)

[6] Professor M. W. Flinn's observations in *The Listener* ('Friedrich Engels's Manchester', 3 February, 1972, pp. 140–2) do not, in our opinion, lay sufficient stress on the evidence that all sanitary reformers in the 1830s and 1840s tended to make for and to describe the worst spots in order to shock the public and the Government into action. They therefore presented exaggerated and horrifying, but also unbalanced, accounts of the state of the large towns and populous districts.

Professor Flinn's article gives a somewhat favourable impression of Engels's expertise as a social observer by concentrating on his remarks on public health and housing, and compressing the commentary on the other subjects covered in his book—working conditions, diet and animadversions on the middle classes—into only seven lines.

Lack of judgement

Even when Engels used strictly contemporary materials he showed little judgement in his assessment of the value of different types of evidence. He was determined to draw up an indictment of the factory system and any evidence was grist to his mill. Reports of somewhat dubious value in the radical press were quoted cheek by jowl with statements given on oath before a Royal Commission.

One example of Engels's lack of judgement is his allegation that one of the evils of the factory system was that it provided more employment for women and children than for men. In Manchester

'there are many hundreds of men who are condemned to do household duties . . . One may well imagine the righteous indignation of the workers at being virtually turned into eunuchs'.

His most striking illustration is based on evidence at several stages removed. It came from a letter written to Richard Oastler by a Leeds worker named Robert Pounder quoting a statement made to him by an acquaintance on tramp in search of work. Pounder's informant had called upon an old friend in or near St Helens alleged to be out of work and supported by his wife.

The situation described by Pounder was certainly not typical of St Helens in the early 1840s. St Helens and the surrounding country were not textile areas—St Helens's last cotton mill closed about this time—and few women were employed in the heavy industries which were characteristic of the town. Pounder's informant stated that his friend lived in a cellar; but cellar dwellings were rare in St Helens at this time. Only 16 were mentioned in the rate books for 1845 and they were not inhabited.[7] The evil to which Engels referred undoubtedly existed in some places in the 1840s, and there were women who were the breadwinners of the family. The case cited by Engels, however, was based upon third-hand evidence and referred to an area where female labour was exceptional.

Selected evidence

Another weakness of Engels's description of the working classes in 1844 was that the author sometimes repeated the carefully guarded assertions of cautious investigators as if they were proved facts. For example, Sir Archibald Alison estimated in 1840 that there were

---

[7] T. C. Barker and J. R. Harris, *A Merseyside Town in the Industrial Revolution: St. Helens 1750–1900*, 1954, p. 321.

between 30,000 and 40,000 prostitutes in London: it is typical of Engels that he should not only have given the higher rather than the lower figure but also have given the impression that the existence of 40,000 London prostitutes was an established fact. It was a guess on Alison's part: no accurate statistics on prostitution are available.

Engels seldom quoted either fully or accurately from his authorities. He generally gave abridged or garbled accounts of what others had written, yet these statements were enclosed in inverted commas as if they were precise quotations. In describing bad factory conditions or insanitary dwellings Engels's 'quotation' frequently gave more authority to his description than an accurate reproduction of the original statement would have done. A Dr Loudon, in evidence submitted to the Factories Enquiry Commission (1833–4), said:

'Although no cases presented themselves of deformed pelvis, varicose veins, ulcers in young people under 25 years of age, and some others of the diseases which have been described, yet these ailments are such as every medical man must expect to be the probable consequences of young people working, in some instances, nearly forty consecutive hours on those days of the week when night work was not expected; and they are recorded by men of the highest professional and moral character.'

Engels's briefer and adjusted version was:

'Although no example of malformation of the pelvis and of some other affections came under my notice, these things are nevertheless so common, that every physician must regard them as probable consequences of such working hours, and as vouched for besides by men of the highest medical credibility.'

When Engels gave an account of places he had visited his descriptions are vivid and probably accurate, but when he relied upon newspapers and other secondary sources of information he is less trustworthy. He was writing a political tract, not a scholarly monograph. He detested the factory system root and branch and was seeking evidence to condemn it. If a job demanded heavy physical labour Engels condemned the employer for ruining the health of his workers. If only light work were required, the factory owner was reducing his workers to nervous wrecks by making them perform excessively tedious and boring tasks. If the manufacturer provided no amenities for his workers he was denounced as an inhuman monster. If a mill owner built cottages for his artisans he was a greedy and tyrannous landlord. If a manufacturer built a school for the operatives' children he was trying to train a new generation of workers to be obedient capitalist slaves. To Engels

182

no employer could ever do right, but the factory owner was the particular villain of the piece.

IV. REVOLUTIONARY BIAS

Indictment of the bourgeoisie

The bias which marked every page of Engels's book was of a twofold character. First, he carefully selected evidence which strengthened his indictment of the English middle classes and he suppressed or explained away evidence which did not support his thesis of the innate wickedness of the bourgeoisie. Secondly, Engels habitually imputed base and unworthy motives to the factory owners. He accused them of grossly misusing their position to overwork their operatives, to ruin their health and to swindle them at every opportunity. For Engels the manufacturers were habitually greedy, immoral and hypocritical.[1]

The young revolutionary who denounced the cotton magnates for all manner of wickedness was himself learning to become a cotton manufacturer. When he returned to Manchester in 1850 he settled down with Ermen and Engels as a corresponding clerk and eventually drew 10 per cent of the profits in addition to his salary of £100 a year. When his father died in 1860 Engels became a wealthy man for he inherited his father's share of the Manchester business, worth £10,000. Four years later he became a full partner in the firm of Ermen and Engels. He was as much a capitalist as any other partner in a cotton firm. In the 1850s and 1860s, therefore, Engels led a double life. On the one hand, he was a prosperous middle-class businessman who joined the Albert and Schiller Clubs, attended fashionable concerts, and rode to hounds with the Cheshire Hunt. On the other hand, he continued his career as a communist writer and agitator and helped to finance Karl Marx's researches in the British Museum library which eventually bore fruit in the publication of *Das Kapital*.

---

[1] Engels himself was hardly a man of such saintly character as would entitle him to find fault with others. The man who so vigorously denounced the middle classes because of their alleged immoral habits himself kept the Irish working girl, Mary Burns, as his mistress for several years and, when she died, he carried on an equally irregular liaison with her sister Lizzie. It was only when she was on her death-bed that Engels eventually married Lizzie Burns.

183

Historical evidence

Between the 1880s and 1914—the age of Toynbee, the Webbs, the Hammonds—the study of the economic history of Great Britain was expanding rapidly both as an academic discipline and as a subject for popular text books, while the many other social surveys of the country in the 1830s and 1840s remained either untranslated or nearly forgotten. Joseph Chamberlain's Tariff Reform campaign in 1903 to re-introduce protection for British manufactured goods against imports and tax foreign food imports in the interests of British and Empire farmers, led to an upsurge of reminiscence about conditions in Britain before the repeal of the Corn Laws in 1846–49 and to the phrase 'The Hungry Forties'. According to the publisher T. Fisher Unwin, the phrase was first put into circulation by his wife, Mrs Jane Cobden Unwin, daughter of Richard Cobden, during the winter of 1903–4. It quickly became popular.[2]

Recent research has shown that for Great Britain the phrase was inaccurate. The mass of the people in the 1840s were no hungrier than in the 1820s and 1830s. The phrase can be applied justifiably only to the period of business depression, with its high unemployment rates and high food prices, from 1838 to the end of 1842. After 1842, under the influence of the railway boom of 1843–47 and rising levels of employment, the consumption per head of many articles of food and drink rose steadily.[3] It is understandable that Engels should have taken a gloomy view of the English scene when he arrived in this country towards the end of 1842, because Manchester had just emerged from the 'Plug Plot' riots of the previous August. The operatives were unsettled and their discontent was fanned by orators denouncing the new Poor Law of 1834 and advocating such varied panaceas as the People's Charter, Corn Law repeal and the Ten Hours Bill. It was only towards the end of Engels's visit that business really recovered under the stimulus of the railway boom.

As Sir John Clapham has pointed out, there is no evidence to suggest that, judged by the price of bread, the 1840s were any more 'hungry' than the 1830s or the 1850s. To take one example only, the increased consumption of sugar in the United Kingdom from 207,000 tons in 1844 to 290,000 tons in 1847 indicates a rise in living

---

[2] Jane Cobden Unwin, *The Hungry Forties: or Life under the Bread Tax*, 1904.

[3] W. H. Chaloner sets out the detailed evidence in *The Hungry Forties: a re-examination*, Historical Association pamphlet, 1957, revised 1967; also R. M. Hartwell, *The Industrial Revolution and Economic Growth*, 1971, pp. 313–60.

standards in those years. Peel's reform of the tariff, culminating in Corn Law repeal, contributed towards the reduction in the cost of living. Engels ignored such evidence.

He also refused to admit that other reforms had improved the lot of the workers. But the gradual reorganisation of town government following the Municipal Corporations Act of 1835, the reduction in hours worked by women and children in most textile mills (1833), the prohibition of female labour in the mines (1842), and the abolition of truck (1831)—all these were changes which, if they failed to fulfil the hopes of the more ardent reformers, and often took much enforcing, did contribute something to the wellbeing of the working classes. The very existence of such ample printed material showed that the conscience of the public was being aroused to the more blatant evils of the factory system.

V. CONCLUSIONS

To sum up: there are many contemporary books, pamphlets and reports which are more accurate and less biased than Engels's account of England in the 1840s. The significance of Engels's book lies in the light it throws upon the intellectual development of a young revolutionary who later became the close collaborator of Karl Marx. When he was preparing his manuscript Engels wrote to Marx:

'I shall present the English with a fine bill of indictment. At the bar of world opinion I charge the English middle classes with mass murder, wholesale robbery and all the other crimes in the calendar. I am writing a preface in English which I shall have printed separately for distribution to the leaders of the English political parties, to men of letters and to Members of Parliament. These chaps will have good cause to remember me.'[4]

This clarion call shows that Engels was writing a political manifesto and it is as such that his work should be judged.

SELECT READING LIST

Clapham, John H., *An Economic History of Modern Britain*, Vol. I: *The Early Railway Age, 1820–1850*, 2nd edn., 1930.
Harrison, J. F. C., *The Early Victorians, 1832–1851*, 1971.

---

[4] Engels to Marx, 19 November, 1844, in *Karl Marx–Friedrich Engels Historisch-Kritische Gesamtausgabe*, Part III, Vol. I, *Der Briefwechsel zwischen Marx und Engels, 1844–1853*, Berlin, 1929, Letter 2, pp. 4–8.

Best, G. F. A., *Mid–Victorian Britain, 1851–75*, 1971.

Chadwick, Edwin, *Report on the Sanitary Condition of the Labouring Population of Great Britain, 1842* (ed. M. W. Flinn), 1965.

Roberts, D., *Victorian Origins of the British Welfare State*, New Haven, Conn., 1960.

Briggs, A., *Victorian Cities*, 1963.

Ashworth, W., *The Genesis of Modern British Town Planning*, 1954.

Ward, J. T. (ed.), *Popular Movements, c. 1830–1850*, 1970.

Edsall, N. C., *The Anti-Poor Law Movement, 1834–44*, 1971.

Hovell, M., *The Chartist Movement*, 1918, latest edn., 1970.

8. Industrialisation and Poverty: In Fact and Fiction

J. M. JEFFERSON

THE AUTHOR

MICHAEL JEFFERSON is the Deputy Director of the Industrial Policy Group. He was born in 1940, and educated at Whitgift School and Kingswood School before reading Philosophy, Politics and Economics at University College, Oxford, and Business Administration at the London School of Economics, where he was a Manor Trust Scholar.

He is principally engaged in the preparation of papers published by the Industrial Policy Group, but has also written articles and signed Papers, including *Some Myths Concerning Competition* (1971), *Competition Policy and the Control of Restrictive Practices* (1972), and *Industry and the Mass Media* (1972). He has participated in broadcasts on 'The Determinants of Investment' and 'Investment and Economic Growth' for the Open University.

He is married, with twin sons, and lives in Windsor.

I. INTRODUCTION

The 'Condition of England' novels of the 1840s and 1850s continue to exert a powerful influence upon our attitudes towards the economic and social conditions of that time, and in no small way explain the antipathy which exists towards the industrialisation process and the industrial system. Earlier writers—Blake, Shelley, Southey, Wordsworth, Carlyle and Cobbett, for instance—had expressed opposition to industrialisation, and their writings influenced the novelists we will be examining. But it is the novelists who have been the most widely read. The novels were also written, almost without exception, by middle-class authors as social propaganda directed at middle- and upper-class readers with the purpose of changing attitudes and reforming practices.

Few of the novelists had any first-hand experience of their subject-matter. This, revealingly, was usually gleaned from official reports (Blue Books) and Parliamentary debates which had already taken place for the express purpose of exaggerating the problems in order to alleviate them by Statute. Most of the novelists recoiled from the violence and organised militancy which they associated with Chartism and the trade union movement, unlike numerous writers later in the century who would use the novel to express their political and social beliefs in a more working-class context. The novelists who touched upon industrial, urban, and agricultural poverty in the 1840s and 1850s (together with some novels published in the 1860s in the same genre) probably had a stronger impact because they did recoil from the violence associated with the Chartist Movement; because they did falter at outright sympathy for the aspirations of the militant working-men; and because, and this is closely relevant to the main theme of this essay, they claimed to be offering an accurate and representative description of the misery caused by industrialisation.

The theme may be conveniently summarised at this point. The 'Condition of England' novels which deal with the industrial system and industrial poverty are widely acclaimed as poor literature but good economics. Among the influential people who take this view are numbered a large proportion of literary critics whose knowledge of economics and economic history is necessarily limited, and who take pride in their hostility to industrialisation for reasons largely political. But I shall seek to show that, while we may agree the

189

novels under discussion are poor literature, they are also a poor guide to economic history. The final section points to evidence of how subsequent writers—'popular' economic historians and literary critics—have been excessively influenced by what they considered to be the economic and social accuracy and representativeness of the early Victorian novelists.

It may also be useful to set down here what the essay does *not* assert. It does not suggest these novels should not have been written or read. The novel as social or economic propaganda may serve a useful purpose at the time in alleviating conditions; and, used with discretion, may be a valuable indicator of contemporary attitudes and explain conditions to future generations. But in the hands of prejudiced, or ignorant, commentators the potentially useful may become positively harmful.

II. THE NOVEL AS FICTION

The best-known novelists whom we are concerned with here are Charlotte Bronte, Charles Dickens, Benjamin Disraeli, Elizabeth Gaskell, Charles and Henry Kingsley, Charles Reade and Frances Trollope. But it is important to make clear at the outset precisely which of their novels are considered and why some are left out of account; why several novelists are mentioned in passing, while others are not mentioned at all.

Two main classifications

The first distinction made is between those novels which discuss industrial poverty (implying a causal link between industrialisation and poverty) and those which discuss urban poverty more generally. This essay is principally concerned with industrial poverty, and therein lies the reason why references to Dickens are largely confined to *Hard Times*. The distinction is not always simple in 19th-century social propaganda literature, and this essay passes over the borderline at numerous points, but for the early Victorian period it is easier than for novels written towards the end of the century.

A second, more difficult, distinction is between the historical novel and the novel dealing with contemporary social conditions. One of the most illuminating novels of early 19th-century Manchester is Mrs Linnaeus Banks' *The Manchester Man* (1876), but Mrs Banks was born in 1821 and the novel is obviously historical and based largely upon research and family anecdote. George Eliot's novels are also historical, although in a number of cases little more than 30 years divided the events described from the date of publication, and not even *Felix Holt, the Radical* (1866) is relevant to our theme. The practice has nevertheless developed of treating a number of strictly historical novels, or novels largely historical in origin, as 'Condition of England' novels dealing with contemporary social conditions or relevant to those conditions. An obvious example is Charlotte Bronte's *Shirley* (1849), set in the first two decades of the 19th century. Less obvious, and rarely noted by critics, is Mrs Trollope's *Michael Armstrong* (1840), based upon a pamphlet describing—in a manner not corroborated by other evidence of the period—conditions in a Derbyshire mill in 1803–7.

Apart from novels on industrial poverty, similar examples are to be found, such as Douglas Jerrold's *St Giles and St James* (1851) which shifts from near contemporary settings to the 18th century and back again. Rural England is similarly treated in Richard Cobbold's *Margaret Catchpole, A Suffolk Girl* (1845). And the theme of a novel can become quickly outdated, as Charles Kingsley recognised within five years of *Alton Locke* (1850) being published. Yet, in spite of all these distinctions and problems, there has been a widespread tendency to class all these novels together as somehow related to the effects of industrialisation.

There are numerous indicators of the interest these novels and novelists have aroused. In most cases the novels themselves have never been out of print, unlike contemporary non-fiction works (with the sole and noteworthy exception of Engels's *The Condition of the Working Class in England* since its first English edition).[1] In very recent years new editions, many in paperback form, of several of these novels have become available in both Britain and the United States. Some of the less popular, long out of print, have recently been reprinted (Mrs Trollope's *Michael Armstrong, The Factory Boy*, in two hard-bound editions). Introductions to the new editions of these

---

[1] W. O. Henderson and W. H. Chaloner, in the introduction to their edition of Engels's classic work, offer as one explanation of why historians have tended to use Engels and ignore other contemporary works: 'Engels' book has been readily available since the 1890s while nearly all the other books, reports and pamphlets which have been mentioned have long been out of print and can be found only in the larger libraries.'
Engels: 'The Condition of the Working Class in England', translated and edited by W. O. Henderson and W. H. Chaloner, Blackwell, 1958, p. xix. (A new edition of this work has recently appeared—1971.)

novels in many cases reveal a belief that such fiction is a reliable guide for the historian. A notable French literary study of the novels, first published in 1903, has only now been translated into English.[2] And in numerous history text-books for the young frequent allusion is made to the novels.

Literary failings

Within the confines of this essay it would not, of course, be feasible to set down detailed or illuminating observations upon the literary merit of the novels we are concerned with. But for those not familiar with them, some brief comments may be in place.

Anyone reading the novels today will find the generality ill-constructed and badly written.[3] The notable exception is Charles Dickens's *Hard Times* (1854), of which F. R. Leavis has written:

'of all Dickens's work it is the one that has all the strength of his genius, together with a strength no other of them can show—that of a completely serious work of art.'[4]

For the rest, critics devote much attention to Mrs Gaskell's *Mary Barton* (1848), one of the most tediously constructed and cliché-

---

[2] Louis Cazamian, *Le Roman Social en Angleterre* (1903): translated by Michael Fido as *The Social Novel in England, 1830–1850*, Routledge and Kegan Paul (publication expected late 1972). Although an excellent translation of this important work, no attempt has been made in it to draw the reader's attention to many errors of literary and, more particularly, economic fact which the findings of research over the past 70 years have revealed. The author is grateful to the publisher for an advance proof copy of this book.

[3] One reason for this state of affairs is that stressed by P. J. Keating (in *The working classes in Victorian fiction*, Routledge and Kegan Paul, 1971, p. 4):

'The constant presence of social purpose in the working-class novel leads to a manipulation of the characters' actions, motives and speech, in order that they may be used finally to justify a class theory held by the author. However hard the novelist tries to suppress his sympathy, or hostility, his own class viewpoint becomes transparently clear, and the artistic value of the particular work suffers . . . Too often individual working-class scenes in Victorian novels are praised for their historical accuracy, while the total pattern and effect of the novel is either ignored or excused.'

[4] F. R. Leavis, *The Great Tradition*, Peregrine/Penguin Edn., 1962, p. 249. Few literary critics have shared Leavis's opinion, but increasing interest in the social novel has coincided with renewed interest in *Hard Times*. Although Edgar Johnson (*Charles Dickens: His Tragedy and Triumph*, 1953, Vol. 2, p. 801) described *Hard Times* as bringing 'to a culmination an orderly development of social analysis', it is nowadays more often regarded (in my view correctly) as demonstrating a change of attitude. For an interesting, but in other respects unbalanced, article on this point, cf. K. J. Fielding and Anne Smith: ' "Hard Times" and the Factory Controversy', *Nineteenth-Century Fiction*, Vol. XXIV, 1970, pp. 404–427.

ridden novels in the English language, whereas *North and South* (1855) is relatively ignored.[5] But not even *North and South* has quite the literary merit of *Cranford* (1853), *Cousin Phillis* (1865), or the exquisite *Wives and Daughters* (1864–6). Charles Kingsley's *Yeast* (1848) is devoid of any literary merit, except for the passage describing Lancelot Smith's riding to hounds at Whitford Priors. His *Alton Locke* (1850) is a much more interesting work, except for the Christian Socialist sermonising which is here less oppressive than in *Yeast* and *Two Years Ago*.[6] But Alton Locke is a tailor, suffering hardships which had long existed in his trade; a sweating system which Kingsley blames upon government contracts for the supply of military uniforms; and conditions which had much more in common with the domestic system than with the factory system. Few would consider *Shirley* the best novel by Charlotte Bronte.[7]

In *Sybil*, however, we do find Disraeli at his best. One goes from *Coningsby*, with its tedious propaganda for Young England, to *Sybil*, with a sense of relief. But Disraeli at his best is only a third-rate novelist.[8] Charles Reade, interesting as his descriptions of gaols and life in Australia are (in the latter respect just as interesting as Henry Kingsley's *Geoffry Hamlyn* or Marcus Clarke's later *For the*

---

[5] 'The weaknesses (of "Mary Barton") are, in fact, a most interesting revelation of the difficulties faced by Mrs. Gaskell and other "social problem" novelists of the mid-Victorian period, a testimony to the resourcefulness with which she tackled them but also, ultimately, a reflection of the limitations of an art which takes as its subject human problems on such a scale.' (Stephen Gill, introducing the Penguin Edition of *Mary Barton*, 1970, p. 21.)

Two literary critics give *Mary Barton* a very high rating because of its social concern, while being loathe to admit its literary failings: Kathleen Tillotson in *Novels of the Eighteen-Forties*, Oxford University Press, 1954, p. 202; and Raymond Williams in *Culture and Society, 1780–1950*, Chatto and Windus, 1958, pp. 87 ff.

[6] As E. Legouis and L. Cazamian put it (in *A History of English Literature*, J. M. Dent, Revised Edition, 1960, p. 1,143):

'Whereas a Tennyson disciplines his passion and curbs it to a search after perfect form, Kingsley with his facile but uncertain talent, his inability to realise the exact task of the artist, only succeeds in producing second-rate work in the various branches of literature towards which his disquietude of temperament prompts him to return.'

[7] ' "Shirley" is much more susceptible to criticism (than *Jane Eyre*) because Charlotte Bronte, in an attempt to write a novel that would give a picture of a certain society at a certain time, went outside the limits of her genius.' (Walter Allen, *The English Novel*, 1954, Pelican edition 1958, p. 90.)

[8] 'As a novelist Disraeli's limitations were many and obvious. His strength lay in his specialised knowledge; it would be almost true to say that he had to become a politician before he could become a novelist.' (Walter Allen, *ibid.*, pp. 158–159.)

For the late Sir Arthur Quiller-Couch, however, '*Coningsby* is the masterpiece'. (*Charles Dickens and Other Victorians*, Cambridge University Press, 1925, p. 196.)

Term of his Natural Life), is little better as a novelist.[9] In quite what class one puts Frances Trollope's *Michael Armstrong* (1840), the most outspoken attack on some aspects of the factory system, is difficult to say. From the literary point of view, it is quite the worst-written early Victorian novel in print.[10] A much better novel, though with references to poverty in London rather than concerned with industrialisation, is Henry Kingsley's *Ravenshoe* (1862).[11] But Henry Kingsley is generally considered a lesser novelist than his elder brother, Charles. The reason for this, even among literary critics, is largely and explicitly not because Henry Kingsley's books are less well-constructed and written, but because in Walter Allen's view: 'At least Charles Kingsley was conscious of the real situation of his time in one of its most important and least heeded aspects.'[12] Now it may be doubted whether, in the case of *Ravenshoe*, this is strictly correct. More generally, it implies that literary merit is secondary to social commentary in the novel, a proposition which is difficult to accept.

'Social conscience' criterion of merit

Recognising their lack of literary merit, critics have maintained interest in these novels because (it is claimed) they accurately depict social conditions during the Industrial Revolution, and the authors are judged on the social conscience they display.[13] Yet it seems

---

9 Sir Arthur Quiller-Couch was not being too unfair when he wrote:
'The tedious conclusion of the first of the long novels, "It is Never Too Late to Mend", with its avenging Jew and its wicked Bridegroom foiled at the church-door, is but stage-grouping and melodrama carried to the nth power.' (*Studies in Literature*, Cambridge University Press, 1918, p. 283.)

10 Lady Clarissa Shrimpton's meeting with the 'bull', and her 'rescue' by Michael Armstrong, was probably the most absurd episode of all time in an English novel.

11 One critic has written: 'I first read "Ravenshoe" at that period when absolute romance and absolute fact have to live together; and very turbulent partners they make. The appeal of the book was instant and permanent.' (C. K. B., *Academy*, 1901.)

12 Walter Allen, *The English Novel*, 1954 (Pelican Edition, 1958, pp. 209–210).

13 This is explicitly recognised time and again. Thus:
'Mrs Gaskell as a novelist is not quite easy to judge. One's first impulse is always to overpraise her, because there shines through her work the personality of a wholly admirable woman in harmony with the society in which she finds herself . . . It was, in a sense, a virtue in Mrs Gaskell that she did not know her place as a novelist, and very imperfect as "Mary Barton" and "North and South" are, it is on these novels that her reputation mainly rests. For her serenity existed side by side with a vigorous and courageous social conscience, of which these novels are the fine expression.' (Walter Allen (*Supra.*), pp. 182–183.)
and
'As an accurate and humane picture of working-class life in a large industrial town in the forties, "Mary Barton" is without rival among the novels of the time . . .

inherently improbable that the exercise of social conscience is a sound basis for accurate description of social conditions in the round.[14] Lord David Cecil, remarking on a limitation of Dickens, that his range is 'confined to those aspects of life which are susceptible of fantastic treatment', has written:

'It is this which led to the old accusation made by Trollope fifty years ago and by less intelligent people since, that Dickens is exaggerated. Of course he is; it is the condition of his achievement.'[15]

In varying degrees, the same is true of the other novels we are discussing. In judging its literary merit, or lack thereof, commitment and caricature in the novel is no bar to excellence. In assessing social and economic conditions, the criteria are different.

It may seem curious that literary critics have concluded that most of the 'Condition of England' novels are of little literary merit but accurate economic commentaries. *Prima facie*, one might assume that literary critics are not the best judges of the facts of economic history. But the attitude of the literary critics mirrors those of the novelists themselves.[16] Even when the novelist is attempting a well-

---

The strength of the rather tiresome and cliché-ridden central plot of the novel is that it does in some measure identify itself with this underlying image (of the Two Nations).' (Arnold Kettle, 'The Early Victorian Social-Problem Novel' in Boris Ford (ed.), *From Dickens to Hardy*, The Pelican Guide to English Literature, Vol. 6, 1958, pp. 179–180.)

Cf. also, Kettle's comment on *Alton Locke*.

' "Alton Locke" is, indeed, in the simplest sense of the term, a propaganda novel, a book designed to bring home to its readers the nature of a social situation and the author's remedies for it . . . "Alton Locke", for all its crudities and "dated" quality, for all its lack of the sort of art and intelligence one associates with those writers conscious of "the novel as an art form", can still move us today.' (*Supra.*, p. 184.)

[14] As P. J. Keating has pointed out (in *The working classes in Victorian fiction*, Routledge and Kegan Paul, 1971, p. 2):

'Most working-class novels are, in one way or another, propagandist. They are usually written by authors who are not working class, for an audience which is not working class, and character and environment are presented so as to contain, implicitly or explicitly, a class judgement.'

[15] David Cecil, *Early Victorian Novelists*, 1934 (Fontana/Collins edition, 1964, p. 34).

[16] For example, Disraeli wrote in *Sybil*:

' "I was reading a work the other day," said Egremont, "that statistically proved that the general condition of the people was much better at this moment than it has been at any known period of history."

"Ah! yes, I know that style of speculation," said Gerard; "your gentleman who reminds you that a working man now has a pair of cotton stockings, and that Henry the Eighth himself was not as well off. At any rate, the condition of classes must be judged of by the age, and by their relation with each other. One need not

rounded judgement, dissent if not derision has been the reward. We are in territory where, in the pursuit of truth, there can only be losers.

Mrs Gaskell has been the main sufferer in this respect. Of all the early Victorian novelists of repute, she was the only one to have long-standing personal experience of life in industrial Lancashire. Another Lancastrian, Mrs Linnaeus Banks, wrote of earlier events outside her direct experience.[17] So Mrs Gaskell's judgements have a particular importance:

'After a quiet life in a country parsonage for more than twenty years, there was something dazzling to Mr Hale in the energy which conquered immense difficulties with ease; the power of the machinery of Milton, the power of the men of Milton, impressed him with a sense of grandeur, which he yielded to without caring to inquire into the details of its exercise. But Margaret went less abroad, among machinery and men: saw less of power in its public effect, and, as it happened, she was thrown with one or two of those who, in all measures affecting masses of people, must be acute sufferers for the good of many. The question always is, has everything been done to make the sufferings of these exceptions as small as possible? Or, in the triumph of the crowded procession, have the

---

dwell on that. I deny the premises. I deny that the condition of the main body is better now than at any other period of history . . ." '
Disraeli's opinion is clearly that of Gerard. We may compare his view with that of G. R. Porter, one-time Chief Statistician in the Board of Trade:
'It cannot be necessary to adduce any evidence in support of this fact, which is obvious to every one who passes through the streets; so great indeed is the change in this respect, that it is but rarely we meet with any one that is not in at least decent apparel, except it be a mendicant, whose garb is assumed as an auxiliary to his profession.' (G. R. Porter, *The Progress of the Nation*, John Murray, 1847 Edn., p. 460.)
Mrs Trollope in *Michael Armstrong* challenged:
'Let none dare to say this picture is exaggerated, till he has taken the trouble to ascertain by his own personal investigation, that it is so . . . But woe to those who supinely sit in contented ignorance of the facts, soothing their spirits and their easy consciences with the cuckoo note, "*exaggeration*", while thousands of helpless children pine away their unnoted miserable lives, in labour and destitution *incomparably more severe*, than any ever produced by negro slavery".' (Italics as in original edition.)
Not even Mrs Trollope, I suggest, really believed Deep Valley Mill was typical. But Mrs Tonna went as far in *Helen Fleetwood* (1841):
'Let no one suppose we are going to write fiction, or to conjure up phantoms of a heated imagination, to aid the cause which we avowedly embrace . . . we will set forth nothing but what has been stated on oath, corroborated on oath, and on oath confirmed beyond the possibility of an evasive question.'
Similar claims are made by Richard Cobbold in *Margaret Catchpole* (1845). The claims are in one case largely justified, in Mrs Linnaeus Banks' *The Manchester Man* (1876).
[17] Manchester of the late 18th century in 'Forbidden to Wed'; the first three decades of 19th-century Manchester in 'The Manchester Man'.

helpless been trampled on, instead of being gently lifted aside out of the roadway of the conqueror, whom they have no power to accompany on his march?'

(*North and South*, Chapter VIII.)

This is one of the most revealing general statements in any of the novels we are discussing and, apart from the assertion that a few '*must* be acute sufferers for the good of many' (my italics), it seems unexceptionable. But it is rarely quoted. A passage frequently quoted, however, is where John Barton is bewildered and aggravated by seeing that 'all goes on just as usual with the mill-owners', who are not (apparently) bearing their share of the burden of depressed trading conditions: 'The contrast is too great. Why should he alone suffer from bad times?' Then Mrs Gaskell intrudes her own opinion:

'I know that this is not really the case; and I know what is the truth in such matters; but what I wish to impress is what the workman feels and thinks. True, that with child-like improvidence, good times will often dissipate his grumbling, and make him forget all prudence and foresight.'

(*Mary Barton*, Chapter 3.)

This passage has brought the literary critics down on Mrs Gaskell. She is criticised for being unable to 'empty herself of all her inherited middle-class attitudes'. Arnold Kettle has claimed that 'In her political and social *ideas*, it is true, Mrs Gaskell was a fence-sitter'.[18] But this criticism is unfounded. Mrs Gaskell is pained at the daily sufferings of the very poor in industrial Lancashire while, at the same time, able to contrast their condition with her wider knowledge of conditions, of causes and effects. The literary critics appear to resent Mrs Gaskell's judgements, not because they are unfounded or unbalanced, but because they conflict with the critics' ideology. Such an ideological viewpoint rejects the notion that John Barton could, through improvidence, be an agent of his own distress (perhaps it even rejects the notion that John Barton was foolish to give up his job to join a Chartist deputation). The evidence of first-hand observers at the time, and the judgement of specialist economic historians and statisticians, would back Mrs Gaskell,[19] on ground

---

[18] Arnold Kettle, *The Early Victorian Social-Problem Novel*, The Pelican Guide to English Literature, Vol. 6, p. 178. (Italics as in original.)

[19] For instance, J. P. Kay: 'It is melancholy to perceive, how many of the evils suffered by the poor flow from their own ignorance or moral errors.' (Introductory letter to the Rev. Chalmers, in *The Moral and Physical Condition of the Working Classes Employed in the Cotton Manufacture in Manchester*, 2nd Edn., 1832 (Frank Cass reprint, 1970, p. 5).) The Editors of *Industrialisation and Culture, 1830–1914*, an Open University Set Book for its Arts Foundation Course, have nevertheless remarked on Kay's 'rosy, rather complacent optimism' (p. 113).

unfamiliar to the literary critics. There is a middle ground between asserting that improvidence was not a significant factor and Dickens's Mr Filer who, in *The Chimes* (1844), seemed to believe improvidence was universal among the poor.

III. THE NOVEL AS ECONOMICS

Since there is widespread agreement that the 'Condition of England' novels are mostly poor literature, are the literary critics also correct in their belief that the novels are sound as economic history, presenting 'an accurate picture of working-class life'? On this point the novels must be judged by the criteria that trained economists and economic historians, by their study and experience, are best fitted to apply. And this is where views diverge. The nature of that divergence may be conveniently expressed in the words of Sir John Clapham:

'Stories assumed to be familiar are apt to become good nesting places for legend. Until very recently, historians' accounts of the dominant event of the nineteenth century, the great and rapid growth of population, were nearly all semi-legendary; sometimes they still are. Statisticians had always known the approximate truth; but historians had too often followed a familiar literary tradition. Again, the legend that everything was getting worse for the workingman, down to some unspecified date between the drafting of the People's Charter and the Great Exhibition, dies hard.'[1]

A. SOME GENERAL PROPOSITIONS

The literary tradition as set down in the novels is most conveniently examined, first, through the general propositions which are, broadly, made in all the 'Condition of England' novels that:

- (i) a Golden Age existed prior to the Industrial Revolution;
- (ii) the standard of living *in general* declined in the early period of industrialisation;
- (iii) the quality of life deteriorated as a result of industrialisation; and
- (iv) certain noxious doctrines, namely political economy as propounded by the Classical Economists, contributed to the sufferings of the industrial worker.

---

[1] Sir John Clapham, Preface to *An Economic History of Modern Britain: The Early Railway Age, 1820–1850* (Vol. 1), Cambridge University Press, 1926, p. vii.

In my view the first, second and fourth propositions are incorrect. No definitive judgement can be made on the third, but there are powerful arguments against it.

The evidence for the general propositions

The belief in a previous Golden Age was widespread throughout the 19th century. Before the 'Condition of England' novels we see such a view propounded by Burke, Cobbett, and—most influentially— by Carlyle. Subsequently Ruskin, A. W. Pugin, William Morris and Hilaire Belloc took a similar view. For most of these writers, the Golden Age had existed in Mediaeval England, conveniently forgetting serfdom, Wat Tyler's Rebellion, and much else besides.

Only Disraeli, in *Coningsby* and *Sybil* as is well known, embraced mediaevalism, although recognising a more recent deterioration as well. Thus Gerard, in *Sybil*, remarks that he 'became a man when the bad times were beginning'. For Charles Kingsley, Disraeli's mediaevalism is an absurdity (although, contrary to appearances, Kingsley seems not to have read *Coningsby* until after writing *Yeast*). Lancelot Smith, the hero of *Yeast*, remarks in a chapter added in 1851, upon

'that amusingly inconsistent, however well-meant, scene in *Coningsby*, in which Mr Lyle is represented as trying to restore "the independent order of peasantry", by making them the receivers of public alms at his own gate, as if they had been middle-age serfs or vagabonds, and not citizens of modern England.'

Quite where Kingsley stands on the existence of a more recent Golden Age is less easy to grasp. An old man in *Yeast* is found

'discoursing of the glorious times before the great war, "when there was more food than there were mouths, and more work than there were hands".'

Lancelot Smith finds it impossible to follow 'one of those unintelligible discussions about the relative prices of the loaf and the bushel of flour' and sighs:

'"Poor human nature! always looking back, as the German sage says, to some fancied golden age, never looking forward to the real one which is coming".'

Mrs Gaskell's viewpoint is more obvious. Alice, in *Mary Barton*, relates her idyllic Lake District childhood in a manner reminiscent of Wordsworth, and this is sharply contrasted with her life in a cellar-dwelling in industrial Manchester. In *Ruth* the Benson's servant, Sally, complains at the rise in price of eggs and butter since she was a girl; believes she could manage better on £3 per year in wages when she was young than the £7 and £8 per year that young servants receive as she speaks; and ends with the comment: 'we'n gone backwards and we thinken we'n gone forwards'.

Nor were these views confined to urban living conditions. Charles Reade opens his novel *It Is Never Too Late To Mend* (1853) with a statement on the decline in the profitability of farming, which sets the scene for George Fielding's withdrawal from his Berkshire farm and journey to Australia to seek his fortune, and Reade's concern with the penal system.

The influence of Carlyle is everywhere apparent in these attitudes,[2] nowhere more so than in Charles Dickens's *Hard Times*. The steeliness of Dickens's treatment of Josiah Bounderby and Thomas Gradgrind was directed, as Dickens put it to his friend Charles Knight:

'... against those who see figures and averages, and nothing else—the representatives of the wickedest and most enormous vice of this time—the men who, through long years to come, will do more to damage the real useful truths of political economy than I could do (if I tried) in my whole life.'

Dickens, if we exclude *The Chimes*, had previously written about social problems the incidence of which was lessening, if not past. For him, the Golden Age was still to come, and the main obstacle the industrial system. In *Hard Times* he strikes hard because he foresees the matters discussed in that novel becoming more acute over the years. At every point we see the industrial system and the business man under attack. And only rarely, as in the allusion to the effects of the Napoleonic Wars made by Charles Kingsley in *Yeast*, and the strong emphasis that Charlotte Bronte places upon the War's adverse effects upon the textile industry in *Shirley*,[3] are external influences upon industrial conditions and poverty recognised.

The 'Condition of England' novelists were also largely united in their belief that, even if the quality of life had not deteriorated in every respect as a result of industrialisation, the Industrial Revolution

---

[2] Carlyle's influence on the early Victorian novelists is summarised by Kathleen Tillotson, *Novels of the Eighteen-Forties*, Oxford University Press, 1954, pp. 150–156. For a more detailed study of the influence of Carlyle on Dickens cf. Michael Slater, 'Carlyle and Jerrold into Dickens: A Study of "The Chimes",' *Nineteenth-Century Fiction*, Vol. XXIV, No. 4, 1970, pp. 506–526.

[3] Cf. in *Shirley*: 'Madmen like Pitt, demons like Castlereagh, mischievous idiots like Perceval, were the tyrants, the curses of the country, the destroyers of her trade. It was their infatuated perseverance in an unjustifiable, a hopeless, a ruinous war, which had brought the nation to its present pass.' Though this is the view of Mr Yorke it is held by others at various points in the novel.

had scarred the environment and much else besides. In *Mary Barton*, Mrs Gaskell contrasts 'Green Hey Fields', to which the population of industrial Manchester escapes for fresh air, with life in tenement and cellar in the city. In *North and South*, Mrs Gaskell contrasts the earlier rural life of the Hale family with the industrial and urban squalor of Milton, to which the family later moves. In *Sybil*, *Hard Times*, *North and South*, and other novels, the traveller tops a hill only to find industrial chimneys, smoke and grime in the valley below. Charles Reade, in the opening passages of *Put Yourself In His Place* (1870), puts the point typically:

'Hillsborough and its outlying suburbs make bricks by the million, spin and weave both wool and cotton, forge in steel from the finest needle up to a ship's armour, and so add considerably to the Kingdom's wealth.

But industry so vast, working by steam, on a limited space, has been fatal to beauty: Hillsborough, though built on one of the loveliest sites in England, is perhaps the most hideous town in creation.'

Nell and her grandfather, in Dickens's *The Old Curiosity Shop* (1841), 'yearned for the fresh solitudes of wood, hill-side, and field . . . when the noise and dirt and vapour of the great manufacturing town, reeking with lean misery and hungry wretchedness, hemmed them in on every side, and seemed to shut out hope, and render escape impossible.'

And Charlotte Bronte, in the closing lines of *Shirley*, by indicating the process of change from unspoilt valley to industrial site of Fieldhead Hollow going on before the eyes of an old housekeeper, offers us an explanation of why there was concern even then that this aspect of the quality of life was in process of deterioration.

There were, of course, other aspects of the quality of industrial life which attracted attention. The disciplines of factory life and the living conditions of the industrial worker called forth much comment. Some of these more specific aspects are discussed below (pp. 213–229).

Only Mrs Gaskell is hesitant about blaming much of the evils of industrialisation upon Political Economy, although in explaining her attitude in the Preface to *Mary Barton* she suspects her account will clash with the views of the Classical Economists:

'I know nothing of Political Economy, or the theories of trade. I have tried to write truthfully; and if my accounts agree or clash with any system, the agreement or disagreement is unintentional.'

The other novelists are not so reticent. Disraeli refers to 'a spirit of rapacious covetousness, desecrating all the humanities of life' which has intensified since 1832 (*Sybil*). Sir Matthew Dowling in Mrs Trollope's *Michael Armstrong* suggests that: 'The political economists of the nineteenth century ought to erect a statue to Elgood Sharpton' (the owner of the appalling Deep Valley Mill). Charles Kingsley writes deprecatingly of 'the calculations of the great King Laissez-faire' in *Alton Locke*:

'the world ... is to be regenerated by cheap bread, free trade, and that peculiar form of the "freedom of industry" which, in plain language, signifies "the despotism of capital"; and which, whatever it means, is merely some outward system, circumstance, or "dodge" *about* man, and not *in* him.'

None of the other 'Condition of England' novelists, however, achieve quite the concentrated fury in their writing as Charles Dickens. Mr Filer reducing everything to 'a mathematical certainty' in *The Chimes*. In *Hard Times* Mr Gradgrind, whose sons are named Adam Smith and Malthus, writing

'in the room with the deadly statistical clock, proving something no doubt— probably, in the main, that the Good Samaritan was a Bad Economist.'

And the whole novel is the most terse and best-directed attack upon the prayer:

what you couldn't state in figures, or show to be purchaseable in the cheapest market and saleable in the dearest, was not, and never should be, world without end, Amen.'

(i) *A Golden Age*

Only the briefest indication may be given of the contrary or qualifying evidence to the picture portrayed by the 'Condition of England' novelists, but in the case of a Golden Age, as in most other general and specific propositions in the novels, reality seems to have been against the novelists.

Mediaevalism can be quickly passed by, for few would seriously hold such a view today. Professor D. S. Landes has dismissed it in conveniently chosen words:

'Many Britons would have stopped it [the Industrial Revolution] in its course, or even turned it back. For good reasons or bad, they were distressed, inconvenienced, or outraged by its consequences. They mourned a merrie England that never was. . .'[4] (1969).

---

4 D. S. Landes, *The Unbound Prometheus*, Cambridge University Press, 1969, p. 122.

George Unwin wondered whether

'In spite of all the noble eloquence and sound prophecy of Carlyle, those who know something of both periods may be permitted to doubt whether the twelfth century was any better than the nineteenth . . . If Carlyle had chanced on the records of Mellor (where Oldknow's factory was) as well as on Jocelyn's Chronicle he might have struck a juster balance between Past and Present.'[5] (1924).

Nor is there satisfactory evidence for a Golden Age immediately before the Industrial Revolution, in the 18th century. T. S. Ashton's *Economic Fluctuations in England, 1700–1800* (1959) is just one of many sources for the widespread dislocation and misery during that century, with its more frequent, irregular, if shorter, undulations than were apparent during the 19th century.[6] Dorothy George begins her classic work *London Life in the XVIIIth Century* (first published in 1925), with reference to the belief that the later 18th century is 'the beginning of a dark age' and continues:

'The social history of London obstinately and emphatically refuses to adjust itself to this formula. There is a cleavage, certainly, about the middle of the century, but it is improvement, not deterioration, which can be traced about 1750 and becomes marked between 1780 and 1820.'[7]

In manufacturing districts, at an early stage—even centuries earlier— child labour had been the norm. Daniel Defoe writes of Halifax before 1725: 'hardly any thing above four years old, but its hands sufficient to it self.'[8]

The effect of industrialisation upon women, often portrayed in engravings as almost unbelievably harsh, also suggests no previous Golden Age. Women had largely been engaged in productive work in their homes and in some form of domestic industry. As the major work on the position of women at this time, by Ivy Pinchbeck (1930), has put it:

'It has been generally admitted that women gained greatly by the transference of manufacture from the home to the factory. As Commissioner Hickson stated in his Report in 1840,[9] "domestic happiness is not promoted, but impaired by all members of the family meddling together and jostling each other constantly in the same room". Moreover, dust and oil and offensive smells were often the

---

[5] George Unwin (with chapters by A. Hulme and G. Taylor), *Samuel Oldknow and the Arkwrights*, Manchester University Press, 1924 (1968 edn., pp. 241 and 242).

[6] T. S. Ashton, *Economic Fluctuations in England, 1700–1800*, Oxford University Press, 1959, pp. 138–174.

[7] M. Dorothy George, *London Life in the XVIIIth Century*, Kegan Paul, 2nd Edn., 1930, p. 1.

[8] Daniel Defoe, *A Tour thro' the whole Island of Great Britain . . .*, 1726, Vol. III, p. 107 (Penguin Edition, 1971, p. 493).

necessary accompaniments of domestic industry; hence, however the industrial revolution may have affected the married woman's economic position in the home, it cannot be denied that it immensely improved all domestic conditions. Now that the home was no longer a workshop, many women were able, for the first time in the history of the industrial classes, to devote their energies to the business of home making and the care of their children, who stood to benefit greatly by the changed home conditions.'[10]

And alarming reports of overcrowding, insanitary conditions, collapsing houses,[11] and adulterated food are frequent in the 17th and 18th centuries. Among the many causes were Tudor and Stuart statutes which encouraged the multi-occupation and overcrowding of dwellings; and early Irish immigration.

In the world of ideas, too, there is no reason to assume decline. Edwin Cannan once gave a lecture on Adam Smith which ended with these relevant sentiments:

'[Adam Smith] elevated the conception of gainful occupation and investment from a system of beggar-my-neighbour to one of mutual service. . .

So we do not now think of work being done as by a slave for a master, and of business being engaged in as by a gambler to win gain at the expense of other players. We work for our wages and our salaries . . . The modern workman and the modern trader can practice virtue as well as a Greek philosopher, a mediaeval begging friar, or a twentieth century social reformer.[12]

(ii) *The standard of living*

Whether or not the material standard of living of working people *in general* declined as a result of industrialisation is a matter fiercely debated by economic historians and other writers upon industrialisation. By common consent among later writers, and the 'Condition of England' novelists themselves, industrialisation was certainly compatible with generally rising living standards after the middle of the 19th century. One only needs to look at the opening lines of George Eliot's *Felix Holt: The Radical*; or Charles Kingsley in his Preface to the fourth edition of *Yeast*, and the Preface to *Alton*

---

9 *Hand Loom Weavers' Report*, 1840, xxiv, p. 44.

10 Ivy Pinchbeck, *Women Workers and The Industrial Revolution, 1750–1850*, 1930 (1969 Edn., Frank Cass, p. 307).

11 Stanley D. Chapman, in editing a recently published symposium on *The History of Working-Class Housing* (David and Charles, 1971), has written: 'Individually, or in co-operative enterprise, the skilled beneficiaries of industrial change can be seen striving to reach superior standards of accommodation and domestic comfort . . .' (p. 11). Irish immigration, unemployment, and desultory habits, however, put difficulties in their way.

12 Edwin Cannan, 'Adam Smith as an Economist,' *Economica*, No. 17, June 1926, p. 134.

Locke of 1854, for confirmation of the novelists' views. Indeed, Kingsley's *Two Years Ago* (1856) has as a major theme that

'As for the outward and material improvements—you know as well as I, that since free trade and emigration, the labourers confess themselves better off than they have been for fifty years.'

and the experience of agriculture is, as we know from the Preface to *Alton Locke*, paralleled in industrial communities.

We are, therefore, concerned solely with what happened in the first half of the 19th century. The controversy has been turned by ideologues into a political matter of present-day relevance. Professor Hobsbawm has recently asserted:

'as we are perhaps once again learning today, a peculiarly harsh inhumanity entered the relationship between those who were and those who were not poor, with the development of capitalism'.[13]

This is a Marxist view, although from an economic historian who has produced some marginal qualifications to the view, which can still be safely accepted, that after the close of the Napoleonic Wars there was almost certainly a rise in the general standard of living, although it was not shared by all sections of the community. E. P. Thompson, who has been described as 'the most convinced pessimist' about standard of living changes in the early 19th century,[14] has wondered whether

'despite the heat which has subsequently been generated, the actual divergence between the hard economic conclusions of the protagonists is slight. If no serious scholar is now willing to argue that everything was getting worse, no serious scholar will argue that everything was getting better.'[15]

There is much truth in this opinion, for historians who take an optimistic view—based on the available statistical evidence[16] and a multitude of individual observations—have never claimed that *everything* was 'getting better', rather that *in general* things improved. The

---

[13] E. J. Hobsbawm, 'The Right to Live', *New Statesman*, 12 February, 1971; A. J. P. Taylor in *The Observer* (7 February, 1971) similarly remarked:
  'Many historical works leave a comfortable feeling that the past is all over and done with. This one provokes parallels with the present.' (p. 26)
[14] By R. M. Hartwell (Ed.), *The Industrial Revolution*, Nuffield College Studies in Economic History No. 1, 1970, p. 178.
[15] E. P. Thompson, *The Making of the English Working Class*, Pelican Edition, 1968, p. 228.
[16] Brian Inglis, 'The Poor Who Were With Us: Old Myths and New Views,' *Encounter*, September 1971, gives a misleading impression that N. J. Silberling's index of wholesale prices is the only statistical evidence on prices. Inglis correctly quotes Hartwell to the effect that all the various indices point in the same direction.

exceptions have always been recognised. J. L. and Barbara Hammond, writers in the pessimistic, literary tradition which stretches from Arnold Toynbee and the Webbs to Hobsbawm and Inglis in 1971, finally reached the fair conclusion in 1934:

'Statisticians tell us . . . that they are satisfied that earnings increased and that most men and women were less poor when this discontent was loud and active than they were when the eighteenth century was beginning to grow old in a silence like that of autumn. The evidence, of course, is scanty, and its interpretation not too simple, but this general view is probably more or less correct.'[17]

This conclusion is no more than the optimists have claimed. Thus T. S. Ashton (1949):

'I am of those who believe that, all in all, conditions of labour were becoming better, at least after 1820, and that the spread of the factory played a not inconsiderable part in the improvement. . . There were, however, masses of unskilled or poorly skilled workers—seasonally employed agricultural workers and hand-loom weavers in particular—whose incomes were almost wholly absorbed in paying for the base necessaries of life, the prices of which, as we have seen, remained high. My guess would be that the number of those who were able to share in the benefits of economic progress was larger than the number of those who were shut out from these benefits and that it was steadily growing.'[18]

And, if I may summarise the view of Dr Hartwell, who contributes his detailed arguments on this subject elsewhere in this collection (pp. 1–21):

'since the indices point in the same direction, even though the change cannot be measured with accuracy, (surely) the standard of living of the mass of the people in England was improving in the first half of the nineteenth century, slowly during the war, more quickly after 1815, and rapidly after 1840.'[19] (1967)

This is the traditional, and in my view correct, interpretation of the standard-of-living controversy.

The 'Condition of England' novelists gave a different impression, although Mrs Gaskell was inconsistent and could hold, in the passage from *North and South* quoted in Part II (above, p. 196), the traditional view. The divergence between the optimists and the pessimists is all the more surprising because solid contemporary evidence was in

---

17 J. L. and Barbara Hammond, *The Bleak Age*, Longmans, Green, 1934, pp. 3–4 (1947 Edn. Guild Books, p. 15).
18 T. S. Ashton, 'The Standard of Life of the Workers in England, 1790–1830', *Journal of Economic History*, Supplement IX, 1949, pp. 19 and 37–38. (Reprinted in F. A. Hayek (Ed.): *Capitalism and the Historians*, Chicago, 1954, pp. 128 and 159.)
19 R. M. Hartwell, 'The Rising Standard of Living in England, 1800–1850', in E. C. Black (Ed.), *European Political History, 1800–1850*, Harper and Row, 1967, p. 38.

favour of the optimistic interpretation. G. R. Porter had recorded (1847):

'It will be apparent, from the examination of the foregoing tables, that although at certain seasons all those who live by daily wages must have suffered privation, yet with some exceptions their condition has, in the course of years, been much ameliorated. The exceptions here alluded to are hand-loom weavers, and others following analogous employments, conducted in the dwellings of the workmen.'[20]

But, as we noted in Part II, the novelists did not allow the facts to stand in the way of their theories.* The references to the effects of the Napoleonic Wars on living conditions in *Shirley* and *Yeast*, while not having the power of similar references in Mrs Linnaeus Banks' *The Manchester Man* are, nevertheless, important. As was recognised at the time, and endured long in 19th-century memories, the War depressed the rise in living standards. James Thorold Rogers wrote in 1884:

'Thousands of homes were starved in order to find the means for the great war, the cost of which was really supported by the labour of those who toiled on and earned the wealth which was lavished freely, and at good interest for the lenders, by the Government. The enormous taxation and the gigantic loans came from the store of accumulated capital, which the employers took from the poor wages of labour, or the landlords extracted from the growing gains of their tenants.'[21]

And since much attention has been directed at the Lancashire cotton industry, it is worth recalling that this industry was particularly hard hit:

'the increased power of production, instead of improving the material welfare of the community, had to be devoted to the prosecution of the war.'[22]

(iii) *The quality of life*

Since the strongest arguments are on the side of those who believed that industrialisation caused a general improvement in material standards of living, and since the main exceptions were those workers in agricultural or pre-industrial forms of enterprise (the domestic, or putting-out, system), the pessimists have tended to shift their ground when pressed. Instead of persisting in their view

---

[20] G. R. Porter, *The Progress of the Nation*, 1847 edn., p. 459.

* Reference 16.

[21] James Thorold Rogers, *Six Centuries of Work and Wages*, Sonnenschein, 1884, p. 505.

[22] G. W. Daniels, 'The Early English Cotton Industry', Manchester University Press, 1920, p. 148.

that material standards declined, they argue that the quality of life deteriorated. Thus Mr E. P. Thompson:

'. . . it is perfectly possible to maintain two propositions which, on a casual view, appear to be contradictory. Over the period 1790–1840 there was a slight improvement in average material standards. Over the same period there was intensified exploitation, greater insecurity, and increasing human misery. By 1840 most people were "better off" than their forerunners had been fifty years before, but they had suffered and continued to suffer this slight improvement as a catastrophic experience.'[23]

In the final resort these are matters of judgement, and there remains an irresolvable contradiction between rising material standards and a concurrent increase in human misery. We may agree, the industrial archaeologists apart, that industrialisation caused scarring of the countryside. But its very prosperity and prospects attracted agricultural workers into the industrial towns, *a priori* evidence that they preferred the higher material standards to any assumed reduction in the quality of life. Where the balance of advantage lies no-one can say with certainty.

Two points may, however, be put against the belief in a deterioration of quality. First, although industrialisation may itself have been an inducement to population growth, it had the effect that

'What in the past had been a recurring surplus of population doomed to early death was in an increasing measure given the possibility of survival.'[24]

Second, the pessimistic view seems to be largely based upon a misconception about the role of competition which John Stuart Mill early recognised (1848):

'[Socialists] forget that wherever competition is not, monopoly is; and that monopoly, in all its forms, is the taxation of the industrious for the support of indolence, if not of rapacity. They forget, too, that with the exception of competition among labourers, all other competition is for the benefit of the labourers, by cheapening the articles they consume; that competition even in the labour market is a source not of low but of high wages, wherever the competition *for* labour exceeds the competition *of* labour.'[25]

And, therefore, the likelihood is that the competitive industrial system has created conditions in which a larger number of people

---

23 E. P. Thompson, *op. cit.*, p. 231.

24 F. A. Hayek, *Capitalism and the Historians*, Chicago, 1954, p. 16 (reprinted in F. A. Hayek, *Studies in Philosophy, Politics and Economics*, Routledge and Kegan Paul, 1967, p. 208).

25 John Stuart Mill, *Principles of Political Economy*, J. W. Parker & Son, Third Edition, Vol. II, 1852, p. 349.

can make a larger number of choices between alternative courses of action, some of which on any count provided the opportunity for improving the quality of human lives.

(iv) *Political economy*

Political economy has always had its outspoken critics. In an amusing lecture, Professor Jacob Viner once quoted several, of which the words of Lucy Aikin writing in 1830 are fairly representative:

'There is a pseudo science called political economy which dries up the hearts and imaginations of most who meddle with it.'[26]

The 'Condition of England' novelists, save for Mrs Gaskell, shared that view. They also shared the view that the doctrines of the Classical Economists, the policy of *laissez-faire* as they called it, were in good measure responsible for the miseries caused by industrialisation. This was a view revived by Arnold Toynbee in his influential lectures on the Industrial Revolution (1884):

'For the "Wealth of Nations" and the steam engine . . . destroyed the old world and built a new one.'[27]

Few allegations in economic history have been as misdirected as this attack on the Classical Economists and their expositions of Political Economy. In the lecture on Adam Smith to which we have already alluded, Edwin Cannan remarked that Smith's views

'involved that approval of high wages which marks off the economists from the more ill-disposed employers whom the socialists persist in supposing them to represent.' (p. 127),

and went on to say:

'Smith thus started the line of thought which was continued by what are called the classical economists. A recent writer has actually said that those economists "defended subsistence wages". Of all the libels upon them invented by socialist and semi-socialist writers this is about the worst. They may have been, they certainly frequently were, wrong about the causes of high wages, but they were always in favour of them.' (p. 128)

---

[26] Jacob Viner, 'The Economist in History', the Richard T. Ely Lecture, *American Economic Review*, May 1963, p. 8.

[27] Arnold Toynbee, *Toynbee's Industrial Revolution*, 1884 (1969 edn., David and Charles, p. 189). The 'Condition of England' novelists were interested in the effects of the Industrial Revolution rather than its causes. For an introductory essay on the latter, see R. M. Hartwell, 'The Causes of the Industrial Revolution: An Essay in Methodology', in R. M. Hartwell (ed.), *The Causes of the Industrial Revolution in England*, Methuen, 1967, pp. 53–79.

These views seem positive enough to be beyond doubt, and to most people familiar with the writings of the Classical Economists they would appear correct. Mr Brian Inglis has, however, recently written:

'the influence of the political economists made itself felt. Malthus's theory of population, reinforced by Ricardo's theory of wages, intimated that the labourer's income could not rise above subsistence level, except locally and for short periods.'[28]

Mr Inglis goes on to attack Lord Robbins's *The Theory of Economic Policy in English Classical Political Economy* (1953) on the grounds that what Lord Robbins

'did not show was the remarkable development by which classical economy, in the space of little more than a decade (*1817–29*), went through a revolution in which most of its original propositions were abandoned.' (p. 54—my italics)

That view is in fact false. Let us use Lord Robbins's quotations themselves to reject Inglis's hypothesis.

First, Adam Smith for the original proposition (1776):

'Servants, labourers and workmen of different kinds make up the far greater part of every great political society. But what improves the circumstances of the greater part can never be regarded as an inconveniency to the whole. No society can be flourishing and happy, of which the far greater part of the members are poor and miserable'.

Then Malthus in *1827*:

'I consider the labouring classes as forming the largest part of the nation, and therefore that their general condition is the most important of all.'

in answer to a question by the Emigration Commission on whether he thought it 'fitting that labour should be kept permanently in a state bordering on distress'.

Or Nassau Senior in the Handloom Weavers Report of *1841*, in which he wrote:

'With almost all [labourers] low wages produce immediate distress and want of employment immediate destitution. We do not believe that anyone who has not mixed with the working classes, we do not believe that we ourselves, can adequately estimate how much mental and bodily suffering, how much anxiety and pain, how much despondency and disease, are implied in the vague terms, "a fall of wages", or "a slack demand for labour".'

---

[28] Brian Inglis in *Encounter*, September 1971, p. 53. Inglis has made much of his hypothesis in his earlier book, *Poverty and the Industrial Revolution* (Hodder and Stoughton, 1970, especially pp. 146–151 and 159–162). In his views on this matter, as on some others, Inglis appears to owe much to E. P. Thompson's *The Making of the English Working Class*.

Or J. R. McCulloch in *1843:*

'High wages are advantageous only because of the increased comforts which they bring with them; and of these, an addition to the time which may be devoted to amusement is certainly not one of the least. Wherever wages are high, and little subject to fluctuation, labourers are found to be active, intelligent and industrious.'

Nor need we look far for confirmatory evidence from objective and informed academic sources of the correctness of Lord Robbins's viewpoint. Professor A. W. Coats, in a recent contribution (1971), wrote of the Classical Economists:

'As far as the labourer was concerned, they firmly believed that his lot could and should be improved ... [and] if their attitude to the lower orders was deficient in subtlety and sensitivity, it was neither hostile nor unsympathetic.'[29]

While Jacob Viner wrote (1927):

'Adam Smith was not a doctrinaire advocate of *laissez faire*. He saw a wide and elastic range of activity for government, and he was prepared to extend it even farther if government, by improving its standards of competence, honesty, and public spirit, showed itself entitled to wider responsibilities. He attributed great capacity to serve the general welfare to individual initiative applied in competitive ways to promote individual ends... His sympathy with the humble and the lowly, with the farmer and the labourer, was made plain for all to see.'[30]

The Classical Economists recognised that circumstances

'might justifiably lead in particular instances, transient or lasting, to major exceptions being properly made to the principle of non-intervention. This was true particularly of the later classical and neo-classical economists. They all expressly and vehemently disassociated themselves from the Manchester School and from those other fanatical exponents of *laissez faire* who proclaimed with much assurance and sometimes with the appearance of complacency that it was impossible for the state to assume any general and positive responsibility for the relief of even major distress without ultimately accentuating that distress.'[31]

I should perhaps add that Viner here is rather unjust towards the Manchester School. In the writings of Cobden, Bright, and the working-man Alexander Somerville (who edited *The Manchester School of Political Economy* after 1850) there is no absolute denial of the value of government activities. But they attacked the privileges

---

[29] A. W. Coats (ed.), *The Classical Economists and Economic Policy*, Methuen, 1971, pp. 177 and 178.

[30] Jacob Viner, *The Long View and the Short*, Free Press, Glencoe, Illinois, 1958, pp. 244 and 245.

[31] Jacob Viner, *The Intellectual History of Laissez Faire*, Second Henry Simons Lecture, University of Chicago, 18 November, 1959.

of the landed classes, such as the Game Laws, and it is revealing that it was the Tory (of a sort), Disraeli, who coined the phrase 'the Manchester School'. For T. S. Ashton it was a strange perversion that

'the men who had fought the battle against the exclusive interests of privileged classes and the claims of functionless property were stigmatised, alike by German and British writers, as the apostles of selfishness.'[32]

Their faults, Ashton believed, lay specifically in their opposition to the aspirations of trade unionism and the application of the Factory Acts to adult labour.

What emerges from a study of Political Economy and the writings of the Classical Economists is that there was nothing in principle, either in the theories or the writings, nor in the industrial system as such, that would necessarily create human misery or depress standards of living. To the extent that such things did happen they were empirical failings, rather than a general failure of the system or theory. The question therefore arises, how widespread were the specific examples of misery and declining standards as portrayed in the novels and elsewhere? Were they of such importance that the errors of the novelists and others in their general propositions became of little significance beside the justice of their particular complaints?

B. SPECIFIC CASES

The early Victorian novelists highlighted the conditions of the industrial worker at home and in the factory; the urban and agricultural poor; and the plight of workers in certain trades. In picking upon particular problems and abuses through the experiences of fictional characters the novelists unavoidably, for that is the form of the novel, dealt with particular cases. Through no fault of theirs, these cases have tended to be treated as more typical of the consequences of industrialisation and the industrial system than they are. Nowhere is this more true than in the textile industry, especially the Lancashire cotton industry, perhaps in part because the cotton masters epitomised the backbone of the Liberal Party and provided convenient whipping-boys for the outraged Tory landed interest and those who viewed persons engaged 'in trade' as beneath contempt. In pointing out the deficiencies of this picture, it is not suggested that

---

[32] T. S. Ashton, 'The Origin of "The Manchester School"', *Manchester School*, Vol. 1, No. 2, 1931, p. 26.

deplorable conditions were non-existent. But they were neither the whole story (or even typical), nor a necessary consequence of the industrial system. And it is incorrect to dismiss as barbarous an industrialisation process and industrial system which had empirical failings rather than deep-seated errors of principle.

1. The Lancashire cotton industry

Mrs Gaskell in *Mary Barton* and *North and South*, Mrs Trollope in *Michael Armstrong*, Mrs Tonna in *Helen Fleetwood*, Disraeli in *Sybil*, Charlotte Bronte in *Shirley*, and Dickens in *Hard Times* all touch upon the textile industry. Among the main points which come across, and more detailed treatment of conditions in industrial Lancashire will be found in Dr Rhodes Boyson's contribution to this Symposium (pp. 61–87), are:

(i) the deplorable living conditions in Manchester;
(ii) the sufferings of the unemployed; and
(iii) the ill-treatment of operatives by employers and overseers.

There can be no doubt that in some parts of Manchester—the Newtown, Ancoats, Central and Portland districts—conditions could be appalling. In *Mary Barton* Mrs Gaskell writes of the foetid smell and thick darkness of cellar dwellings, where there are

'three or four little children rolling on the damp, nay wet, brick floor, through which the stagnant, filthy moisture of the street oozed up.'

Disraeli writes of people emerging from their cellar-dwellings in the evenings for light and air. The unemployed, like John Barton, see 'by degrees the house stripped of its little ornaments'. Frequent references are made to the effect of machinery. 'Machines is th' ruin of poor folk' is a refrain in *Mary Barton*. In *Shirley* men speak of 'when hand-labour were encouraged and respected, and no mischief-maker had ventured to introduce these here machines, which is so pernicious'.

Death and violence are also ever-present. There are the poignant deaths of little Tom Barton and the Wilson twins in *Mary Barton*; of Bessy in *North and South*; and Michael Armstrong's mother in *Michael Armstrong*. There is the violence of the attack on Thornton's mill in *North and South*; the murder of Harry Carson in *Mary Barton*; the attacks on mills in *Shirley* and *Sybil*; attacks on non-unionists and strike-breakers by trade unionists in *Put Yourself in His Place*

I

and *Mary Barton*; the viciousness of overseers in *Michael Armstrong* and *Helen Fleetwood*; and the burning of a 'tommy-shop' and Mowbray Castle in *Sybil*. Much of the violence is exaggerated; for instance, Thomas Ashton is the only employer known to have been murdered about this time. Charlotte Bronte portrays a cordial and considerate employer in the character of Mr Yorke. Other novelists, even Mrs Trollope, are prepared to admit that some are considerate. But the overall impression in this, as in other matters, is that benevolence is very much the exception.

The other impression which is given is that the novelist is fully aware of the conditions about which he or she writes. But, as mentioned earlier, only Mrs Gaskell is a first-hand observer of long-standing, the rest mainly rely upon Blue Books and quick visits to the North. The method, as we shall discuss a little more fully below with examples from Mrs Trollope, Disraeli and Charles Reade, is open to severe criticism. For, as Dickens suggests in *Hard Times* when he writes of Gradgrind's 'blue chamber in its abundance of blue books': 'Whatever they could prove (which is usually anything you like), they proved there . . .'

Sir James Phillips Kay-Shuttleworth is generally acknowledged to be the most important source of evidence on living conditions in Manchester at the time. He wrote that conditions in central Manchester were not typical:

'the inhabitants of a great part of the adjacent townships are in a condition superior to that described in these pages. The most respectable portion of the operative population has, we think, a tendency to avoid the central districts of Manchester, and to congregate in the suburban townships.'[33]

And he added:

'Those districts where the poor dwell are of very recent origin. The rapid growth of the cotton manufacture has attracted hither operatives from every part of the Kingdom, and Ireland has poured forth the most destitute of her hordes to supply the constantly increasing demand for labour. This labour has been, in one important respect, a serious evil. The Irish have taught the labouring classes of this country a pernicious lesson . . . the contagious example of ignorance and a barbarous disregard of forethought and economy, exhibited by the Irish, spread.'[34]

He believed that

'The evils affecting the working classes, so far from being the necessary results

---

[33] J. P. Kay-Shuttleworth, *The Moral and Physical Condition of the Working Classes Employed in the Cotton Manufacture in Manchester*, 2nd edn., 1832 (1970 Reprint, Frank Cass, p. 20).   [34] *Ibid.*, p. 21.

of the commercial system, furnish evidence of a disease which impairs its energies, if it does not threaten its vitality.'[35]

and bemoaned the tendency for otherwise adequate incomes to be 'too often consumed by vice and improvidence.'

At the beginning of the 1840s, William Cooke Taylor wrote of his visit to Manchester and elsewhere in Lancashire:

'Contrary to general belief, experience has shown me that Manchester does not afford a fair specimen of the factory population in any of the conditions of its existence, and that the outward aspect of the place affords a very imperfect test of the state of trade in South Lancashire.'[36]

The factory system was not necessarily associated with hardship even in the eyes of its critics. Peter Gaskell, a surgeon, remarked in 1836 that many of those leaving the land for the industrial towns were generally more unhealthy and less strong than those they left behind, and remarked:

'Factory labour, in many of its processes, requires little else but manual dexterity, and no physical strength.'[37]

For some industrial workers factory discipline may have proved more burdensome than the discipline required for agricultural or domestic labour,[38] but the major problems lay in the fluctuations of trade (as had occurred in the pre-industrial age); the overwhelming number of immigrants into the industrial towns, attracted by the prospects of relative prosperity; and the tyrannical measures of some employers and overseers.

The problems and virtues were not all on one side, however. Numerous masters failed, and Professor R. C. O. Matthews has written:

'Employment of factory workers apparently moved more or less in line with that of the volume of output, growing steadily until 1840 and then declining. The fall in output in 1839 resulted in under-employment—short-time working—rather than the laying-off of hands. In 1841–2, however, the stoppage of mills threw many operatives completely out of work. Up till then the same considerations as prevented manufacturers from curtailing output impelled them

---

[35] J. P. Kay-Shuttleworth, *The Moral and Physical Conditions of the Working Classes Employed in the Cotton Manufacture in Manchester*, 2nd edn., 1832 (1970 Reprint, Frank Cass, p. 79).

[36] W. Cooke Taylor, *Notes of a Tour in the Manufacturing Districts of Lancashire*, 2nd edn., 1842 (reprinted in J. T. Ward, *The Factory System*, David and Charles, 1970, p. 39).

[37] P. Gaskell, *Artisans and Machinery*, 1836 (1968 Reprint, Frank Cass, p. 66).

[38] The dilemmas and difficulties are discussed by Sidney Pollard in 'Factory Discipline in the Industrial Revolution,' *Economic History Review*, 2nd Series, December 1963.

to provide employment to their workpeople, and it was generally agreed that entrepreneurs suffered much greater proportional loss in money earnings between 1837 and 1840 than the operatives did.'[39]

The enormous influx of largely unskilled, and largely Irish, labour did overwhelm Manchester. By the 1850s, however, rapid strides were being made in improving conditions, and by 1861 the death-rate in manufacturing towns was little different from that in non-manufacturing towns.[40] The importance of Irish immigration may be evinced from the chapter Engels devoted to it in *The Condition of the Working Class in England*. He wrote:

'The Irish had nothing to lose at home and much to gain in England.'[41]

Engels quoted estimates of 1 million Irish immigrants already in England by 1844 and 50,000 more arriving annually, and states: 'The majority of cellar-dwellers are nearly always Irish in origin.' Arthur Redford, the main authority on this subject in more recent years, agreed with contemporary accounts of its significance:

'The main social significance of the Irish influx lay in its tendency to lower the wages and standard of living of the English wage-earning classes.'[42]

Was this immigration and its effects the fault of the industrial system? Those who argue that it was must offer evidence that the restricted entry of immigrants and a larger number of deaths in Ireland would have been preferable. However lamentable the decline in living standards in parts of Manchester, the industrial system allowed more people the opportunity to avoid starvation and death in their native lands at a time when governments were unable, and perhaps unwilling, to intervene on any scale.

The treatment of employees by employers and overseers, whether in the cotton mills or other industries and trades, forms a subject of major interest to the 'Condition of England' novelists. In the most extreme descriptions of cruelty, by Mrs Trollope in *Michael Armstrong* and by Mrs Tonna in *Helen Fleetwood*, both novelists urge that they write without exaggeration. That claim is absurd, but where the

---

39 R. C. O. Matthews, *A Study in Trade-Cycle History: Economic Fluctuations in Great Britain, 1833–42*, Cambridge University Press, 1954, p. 144.

40 John Watts, *The Facts of the Cotton Famine*, Simpkin, Marshall, 1866, p. 96 (1968 Reprint, Frank Cass, p. 96).

41 Engels, *The Condition of the Working Class in England*, W. O. Henderson and W. H. Chaloner (eds.), 1958, p. 104.

42 Arthur Redford, *Labour Migration in England, 1800–1850*, Manchester University Press, 2nd edn., 1964, p. 159.

balance of truth lies, between the vicious examples drawn up by the novelists and the generous and considerate employers usually portrayed in the biographies, is difficult to judge with precision.

Opposing testimony is certainly available, and not only from the unusual case of Robert Owen. An early example is Samuel Oldknow, of whom George Unwin wrote in 1924:

'Perhaps the most convincing testimony to his open-hearted simplicity and disinterested benevolence—which are the vital and creative qualities in the founder of a community—is to be found in the instinctive confidence in them implied in the letters of all who had personal contact with him—his uncle the tea dealer, his managers and workmen, his friends in the business world.'[43]

Another was Thomas Ashton of Hyde, of whom Kay-Shuttleworth[44] wrote in 1832:

'This gentleman has erected commodious dwellings for his workpeople, with each of whom he has connected every convenience that can minister to comfort. He resides in their immediate vicinity, and has frequent opportunities of maintaining a cordial association with his operatives. Their houses are well furnished, clean, and their tenants exhibit every indication of health and happiness.'[45]

And Dr Rhodes Boyson has given a detailed account of the good living and working conditions enjoyed by employees of the Ashworths:

'The cottages erected by manufacturers were generally superior in every respect to those built by avaricious speculators, and Bank Top and Egerton cottages were superior to those of most cotton employers in size, building, and maintenance.'[46]

These seem to have been exceptional cases, and the general standard was no doubt somewhat lower. But how much lower no-one can say with precision. There is general evidence from Thackrah in 1832 that conditions in Manchester were worse than elsewhere:

'it appears that the labouring classes in that place are more dissipated, worse fed, housed, and clothed, than those of the Yorkshire towns.'[47]

---

[43] George Unwin, *op. cit.*, p. 241.

[44] I have refrained from invoking the support of Andrew Ure's *Philosophy of Manufactures* (1835) because Brian Inglis, in his recent *Encounter* article, has poured scorn on Ure's work for no very apparent reason. But there is much other evidence to hand, some of which is set down in this essay.   [45] *Supra.*, pp. 100–101.

[46] Rhodes Boyson, *The Ashworth Cotton Enterprise*, Oxford University Press, 1970, p. 118.

[47] C. Turner Thackrah, *The Effects of Arts, Trades, and Professions, and of Civic States and Habits of Living, on Health and Longevity*, 2nd edn., 1832, p. 146. (Reprinted in A. Meiklejohn, *The Life, Work and Times of Charles Turner Thackrah*, E. & S. Livingstone, 1957.)

What of the opportunities for workers to advance themselves? The working-class origins of cotton masters like Carson in *Mary Barton* and Thornton in *North and South* were no myth. As S. J. Chapman put it (1904):

'At a time when old social attachments were rapidly dissolving under the influence of the new spirit of enterprise, and before much capital was needed by an employer, it is not astonishing that labour moved with no great difficulty from one grade to another. Operatives easily became masters...'[48]

This social mobility was still much in evidence on the eve of the First World War,[49] a fact often difficult to appreciate when faced with such assertions as: 'The most profound and far-reaching consequence of the Industrial Revolution was the birth of a new class society'.[50] Social reality is difficult to fit into the Procrustean bed of mental attitudes based on theories of class conflict, yet social mobility and industrialisation coincided with a new and increasingly more equitable form of class society.

Other indicators of a potential or actual improvement in conditions were the savings accumulated by working men; the relationship between the use of cotton garments and the rise in standards of hygiene (emphasised by Dorothy George in *London Life in the XVIIIth Century*); and improvements in the fabric and lighting of the factories (emphasised by John Watts in *The Facts of the Cotton Famine*).

As for cruelty, it is worth quoting Peter Gaskell, a critic of factory conditions (1836):

'Much has been said as to the cruelty and injuries supposed to be inflicted upon children in mills. There is, however, but little ground for the extravagant accusations which have been made on these heads.'[51]

That there were cases of cruelty, more generally inflicted by spinners (even parents) than overseers and employers, seems to be well-founded. It is not to be complacent about cruelty, however rare, to assert that the claims appear to have been grossly 'extravagant'. This very exaggeration, combined with investigations into child

---

48 Sydney J. Chapman, *The Lancashire Cotton Industry: A Study in Economic Development*, Manchester University Press, 1904, p. 24.

49 S. J. Chapman and F. J. Marquis, 'The Recruiting of the Employing Classes from the Ranks of the Wage-Earners in the Cotton Industry,' *Journal of the Royal Statistical Society*, February 1912.

50 Harold Perkin, *The Origin of Modern English Society, 1780–1880*, Routledge & Kegan Paul, 1969, p. 176.

51 P. Gaskell, *Artisans and Machinery*, 1836 (1968 Reprint, Frank Cass, p. 167).

employment and working-hours, and the Factory Acts, all suggest that evil practices within the factory system were not beyond eradication.

The most extravagant tale of industrial cruelty, Mrs Trollope's *Michael Armstrong*, has been severely criticised by Dr W. H. Chaloner:[52] 'As an account of factory conditions in general *Michael Armstrong* cannot be said to justify the praise given it by some historians' (mentioning the Hammonds and Michael Sadleir in this connection, as will be done in Part IV). Deep Valley Mill is shown to be derived from John Brown's *Memoir of Robert Blincoe*, a pamphlet re-published in 1832 by a man Mrs Trollope met on her visit North, which describes conditions in Litton Mill, near Tideswell, Derbyshire, and owned by Ellice Needham (Elgood Sharpton). By the time Mrs Trollope was writing much had changed, not least the conditions of employment of the young following the Factory Act of 1833. But the events described in the *Memoir* do not fit a number of important facts that are known; they conflict with the reports of two magistrates (Joshua Denman and M. M. Middleton) who were not uncritical; and they do not fit the testimony of John Farey in his *Agriculture of Derbyshire*.

Far from being so profitable that the 19th-century political economists would raise a statue to Elgood Sharpton, as Mrs Trollope has Sir Matthew Dowling suggest, it was unprofitable even before Blincoe arrived there in 1803; and it remained so after his departure in 1807. And Blincoe makes false accusations against other employers known to be model, and in particular an unfounded attack on Samuel Oldknow. Dr S. D. Chapman has written off the *Memoir* in the following terms:

'the statement that the number of deaths was "such as to require frequent supplies of parish children to fill up the vacancies" hardly seems justified . . . The circumstances and style in which the pamphlet was written, the character of the author and, above all, the number of misrepresentations we have already discovered, clearly make the remainder of the work suspect . . . Litton, like the Radcliffe Bridge and Arnold Mills, was the victim of popular prejudice against the factory system.'[53]

---

[52] W. H. Chaloner, 'Mrs Trollope and the Early Factory System', *Victorian Studies*, December 1960.

[53] Stanley D. Chapman, *The Early Factory Masters*, David and Charles, 1967, pp. 207–209. Chapman refutes similar allegations against Davison and Hawksley's Arnold mill, originally recorded by William Stumbles, and presents detailed evidence in support of his claim that 'the partners were responsible and enlightened employers' but victims of prejudice against their political beliefs and the factory system. Dr Chapman's account also supersedes A. E. Musson, 'Robert Blincoe and the Early Factory System', *Derbyshire Miscellany*, February 1958, Part 2, pp. 21–27. This no longer seems as reliable as Dr Chaloner suggested (*ibid.*, note 15).

Dr Chapman had earlier written of 'the alleged sufferings of child apprentices' that

'although this subject has interested professional and amateur historians for four or five generations now, research has not been very productive.'[54]

2. Iron and steel industry

Two early Victorian novels deal with iron and steel-making, Disraeli's *Sybil* and Charles Reade's *Put Yourself in His Place*. For our present purposes, *Sybil* is the more important. *Put Yourself In His Place* is Reade's best 'Condition of England' novel and contains interesting passages on the unhealthy working environment of dry-grinders, wet-grinders, file-cutters, and saw-grinders. But its most memorable features are the murderous treatment meted out by trade unionists to the non-unionist hero of the book, and others.

Disraeli describes in lurid detail the people and town of Wodgate or Hell-House Yard. Its workers:

'As manufacturers of ironmongery, they carry the palm for the whole district; as founders of brass and workers of steel, they fear none; while, as nailers and locksmiths, their fame has spread even to the European markets, whither their most skilful workmen have frequently been invited.'

The 'Governor' of this fraternity, the so-called Bishop of Wodgate, otherwise known as Hatton, runs a dilapidated and multi-storeyed nail-workshop or Palace. His apprentices stand in particular fear of Mrs Hatton, each hoping that

'he might not be the victim singled out to have his head cut open, or his eye knocked out, or his ears half pulled off by . . . their bishop's gentle wife.'

Sheila M. Smith has investigated Disraeli's use of Blue Book evidence for his treatment of Wodgate, and in particular the evidence of Sub-Commissioner Richard Horne of the Children's Employment Commission. Horne, a friend of Dickens and later on the staff of *Household Words*, was directed to investigate 'the iron manufacturing district of Staffordshire and the contiguous counties'. Willenhall, some three miles from Wolverhampton, appears to have some features in common with Wodgate, although Disraeli also draws on Horne's accounts of other towns. Horne's account includes some alarming reports of living and working conditions, but Disraeli is found to have generalised from rare, solitary instances:

---

[54] Stanley D. Chapman, *The Early Factory Masters*, p. 174.

'Disraeli takes Horne's phrase "reservoir of leprosy and plague" but uses it in the plural to suit his more general picture of the place.'[55]

'Sometimes it [Disraeli's exaggeration] takes the form of significant omissions ... omits ... "redeeming circumstance", as Horne put it. Nor is there a day-school in Wodgate, although Willenhall has one, and in Willenhall redress of an apprentice's wrongs, although unlikely, is possible, whereas in Wodgate the wronged apprentice's case is completely hopeless. The novelist embroiders the Sub-Commissioner's comments on the drunkenness in Willenhall ... Describing the Wodgate apprentices, he [Disraeli] disregards Horne's remark that "there are many exceptions to the above mode of conduct among the masters of Willenhall. There are masters, not only the large but the smaller masters, who are both respectable and humane men, and who would not suffer any circumstances of poverty to render them brutal..."'.[56]

Horne hears of a single, but nevertheless horrifying, report of an apprentice being sold by his master:

'This enormity, emphasised as a rarity by Horne's shocked italics, is reported by Disraeli to be a common occurrence ... and the isolated case,

"An apprentice has been struck down insensible by a blow from the iron head of the hammer" (Horne) becomes in *Sybil*,

"they [i.e., the masters] are in the habit of felling them with hammers".'[57]

Sheila Smith sums up:

'In *Sybil* Disraeli, wishing to confront his sheltered readers with a startling picture of pagans in contemporary England, chose to depict the most shocking trade in the most shocking town.'[58]

I do not wish to underrate the notorious conditions in Staffordshire, associated not only with iron and steel but also coal mining. An inhabitant of Willenhall, Dr John Wilkes, remarked upon them as early as 1739.[59] But a balanced view must take into account such facts as that at the Crowley's factories:

'Very early in the eighteenth century a system of contributory insurance against death, sickness, and old age was compulsory on all workers; and a doctor, a

---

[55] Sheila M. Smith, 'Willenhall and Wodgate: Disraeli's use of Blue Book Evidence', *Review of English Studies*, Vol. 13, 1962, p. 370.

[56] *Ibid.*, pp. 376–377.

[57] *Ibid.*, p. 378.

[58] *Ibid.*, p. 379. Sheila M. Smith has carried out a similar exercise, revealing gross exaggerations, on Charles Reade's novels *It Is Never Too Late To Mend* and *Hard Cash*: 'Propaganda and Hard Facts in Charles Reade's Didactic Novels', *Renaissance and Modern Studies*, Vol. IV, 1960. She quotes *The Times* review of *Hard Cash* of 2 January, 1864: 'Eccentric fact makes improbable fiction, and improbable fiction is not impressive' (p. 135).

[59] W. H. B. Court, *The Rise of the Midland Industries, 1600–1838*, Oxford University Press, 1938, p. 97.

clergyman, and a schoolmaster were maintained jointly by the firm and its employees.'[60]

and

'In almost all cases houses were provided by the firm, either without charge or at low rents; fuel for domestic purposes was also generally supplied, and where this was not gratuitous or given at cost price, the workers helped themselves to it.'[61]

There was, nevertheless, a practice which had grown up, especially in this part of England, which was open to exploitation by unscrupulous employers—the truck system, by which wages were paid in part by tickets exchangeable for goods at the local 'tommy shop'. The hammered nail trade had been in decline since the 1820s:

'Before 1830, there were from forty to fifty firms largely engaged in this important trade. The nailmaker at that time received fair wages, had full work, and was generally paid in cash. It may safely be considered that about 1830 this trade began to decline, owing to the introduction of machine-made nails.'[62]

But

'Since 1842, the hammered nail trade has been subject to many numerous strikes, in fact, no other trade has suffered by so many . . . The secret of all such strikes arises from whole districts in which hand-made nails are manufactured having suffered from a truck-system of an oppressive and vicious character, which is the great injury of fair trading, and especially injurious to the workmen.'[63]

It is worth comparing this statement with T. S. Ashton's comment on factory conditions in Coalbrookdale: 'they contrast very favourably also with the hours of toil required to wring subsistence earnings from domestic nailmaking.'[64]

But the truck system is a different matter, and Disraeli makes much of it in *Sybil*, his account culminating in the burning of a tommy shop. Sir John Clapham found its incidence highly variable between trades, although he recognised that it was a very old evil in outwork industries. His impressions were that the possible range of abuse of the truck system was 5 to 10 per cent of British industry in the 1840s.[65]

---

[60] T. S. Ashton, *Iron and Steel in the Industrial Revolution*, Manchester University Press, 2nd edn., 1951, p. 196.   [61] *Ibid.*, p. 189.

[62] Ephraim Ball, 'The Hand-Made Nail Trade,' in Samuel Timmins (ed.), *Birmingham and the Midland Hardware District*, 1866 (1967 reprint, Frank Cass, p. 111).

[63] *Ibid.*, p. 114.   [64] T. S. Ashton, *op. cit.*, p. 194.

[65] Sir John Clapham, *An Economic History of Modern Britain: The Early Railway Age, 1820–1850*, Cambridge University Press, 1926, p. 565.

The system, in its form of outright compulsion upon employees to accept payment of wages in highly-priced goods, was practised mainly by the smaller employers in the hand-made nail trade of Staffordshire and surrounding counties; in framework knitting in Leicestershire and Nottinghamshire; and in hand-loom weaving in Gloucestershire. In the 1820s 'public policy pursued a course almost perfectly calculated to increase the prevalence of the truck system'[66] and depressed economic conditions in the early 1840s caused the system to spread, demonstrating that the 1831 Truck Act was ineffectual.

The system declined not as a result of legislation but because truck master and employee were no longer 'engaging in it because they could find no more attractive alternative.'[67] This resulted from a decline in the domestic trades; improved transportation; the growth of urban communities encouraged by the factory system; opposition from employees and trade unions; and the regular weekly payment of wages in cash. But although the system was open to abuse, it could be fairly said that Disraeli had highlighted its operation, yet again, in its worst form and in the worst place.

3. Coal mining

The working conditions of young people in the mines have been considered at length by Engels, J. L. and Barbara Hammond, and other non-fiction writers. Disraeli writes in *Sybil*[68] of

'troops of youth—alas! of both sexes . . . Naked to the waist, an iron chain fastened to a belt of leather runs between their legs clad in canvas trousers, while on hands and feet an English girl, for twelve, sometimes for sixteen hours a day, hauls and hurries tubs of coals up subterranean roads . . . Infants of four and five years of age, many of them girls . . . entrusted with the fulfilment of most responsible duties, and the nature of which entails on them the necessity of being earliest to enter the mine and the latest to leave it. Their labour indeed is not severe, for that would be impossible, but it is passed in darkness and in solitude.'

There is much truth in this dismal story, largely taken from the First Report of the Children's Employment Commission of 1842.

---

[66] G. W. Hilton, 'The Truck Act of 1831', *Economic History Review*, 2nd Series, April 1958, p. 471.　　　　　　　　　　　　　　　[67] *Ibid.*, p. 479.

[68] Surprisingly, coal mining has been relatively neglected in English fiction. The only well-known novel on the industry is W. E. Tirebuck's *Miss Grace of All Souls* (1895). Mrs Humphry Ward's *Sir George Tressady* (1896) makes some references to the industry, and the hero dies in a colliery disaster, but it is not a novel of the industry. There are, however, references to the industry in several works of children's fiction.

More detailed comments are in place, however. Engels himself pointed out that 'most of the children are over 8 years of age' (although some translators of *The Condition of the Working Class in England* have allowed their ideological commitment to run so far as to omit this sentence); and quoting G. R. Porter[69]—without acknowledgement—Engels showed that only 1,165 women under 20 years of age were employed in or around coal mines in 1841.[70] This was under 1 per cent of total employment in coal-mining in Great Britain. Total female employment (of all ages) was 2,350, or about 2 per cent of total employment in coal-mining.

Professor E. J. Hobsbawm has objected to this point on the grounds that: (a) 'it is blindness not to see that good men can be legitimately outraged' by small numbers of 'miserable wretches'; and (b) 'it is even greater blindness not to see the general abuse behind the exceptional examples which reformers and revolutionaries often (but by no means always) use to arouse public opinion against it.'[71] But his objections are unsound. First, there is no necessary conflict between outrage at the misery of the few and belief in the general and obvious material benefits of industrialisation for the many. Second, as Professor Hobsbawm largely admits, it is only by picking on 'the exceptional examples' that attacks can be made on the industrialisation process and the industrial system. The obvious conclusion is that, in principle and in general, industrialisation and the industrial system bring enormous and unmatchable benefits to the vast majority of people; but they did not bring those benefits to all, especially in the short term.

4. Agriculture and miscellaneous trades

There has been a widespread tendency to discuss conditions in activities outside the industrial system alongside those relevant to industrialisation, on the ground that they were contemporaneous. This has sometimes had the unfortunate effect of confusing conditions in the one with conditions in the other where no clear or close connection exists. And since we are concerned with the early Victorian novel, it is convenient to select for consideration agriculture

---

[69] G. R. Porter, *The Progress of the Nation*, 1847 edn., p. 78.

[70] Engels, *op. cit.*, p. 274. Engels's, and other, accounts suggest indifference of the coal-owners to their employees and safety. Widely held though this view is, Robert Galloway's *A History of Coal Mining in Great Britain* (1882) suggests it should be severely qualified (available in a David and Charles reprint, 1969).

[71] E. J. Hobsbawm, *Labouring Men*, Weidenfeld and Nicolson, 1968 edn., pp. 111–112.

(referred to in Charles Kingsley's *Alton Locke* and *Yeast*); tailoring (*Alton Locke* also); and chimney sweeps', or climbing, boys (Charles Kingsley's novel for children, *The Water-Babies*, and Dickens's *Oliver Twist*).

Kingsley concentrates on agricultural conditions in the 1840s, which are contrasted unfavourably with conditions before the Napoleonic Wars, although by the later 1850s he recognises that a vast improvement has occurred. There is much truth in his account, even if for some labourers in low-wage areas the general improvement which had occurred by the 1850s was largely due to improved housing conditions and 'the growing possibility of a better life in the towns'.[72] But the account differs from that of an influential group of writers on this subject, who have tended to focus on the era of parliamentary enclosure between about 1760 and 1830:

'due to the influence of Marx and his indication of the key significance of enclosure in his account of "the genesis of the capitalist farmer"; but it arose also from the supposed close relationship between parliamentary enclosure, contemporary changes in farming methods, and *the development of industry in the later eighteenth century*, a relationship discussed by Marx, Toynbee, Mantoux, and more recently Maurice Dobb. Marx indicted enclosure as the instrument by which the landlords . . . carried out a "systematic robbery of the communal lands" of the people with the object of creating large capitalist farms and *setting free "the agricultural population as proletarians for manufacturing industry"*.'[73] (my italics)

Some other highly influential writers have followed Marx's line—including J. L. and Barbara Hammond's *The Village Labourer* (1911); and Lord Ernle's *English Farming Past and Present* (6th edn., 1961). But more recent research shows that the so-called agricultural revolution stretched over centuries, rather than decades, and that there is a continuous development from the late middle ages:

'modern understanding of the slow pace of the "agricultural revolution" and of the effects of parliamentary enclosures does not, in general, support the old view that a major decline of small farmers occurred between 1760 and 1830. The land tax evidence, indeed, shows that the numbers of small owners tended to rise for much of this period . . . The major decline of small owners and of small farmers in general must have occurred before 1760, probably between about 1660 and 1750.'[74]

---

[72] J. D. Chambers and G. E. Mingay, *The Agricultural Revolution, 1750–1880*, Batsford, 1966, p. 147.

[73] G. E. Mingay, *Enclosure and the Small Farmer in the Age of the Industrial Revolution*, Macmillan, 1968, pp. 10–11.

[74] *Ibid.*, p. 31.

The reasons why the earlier writers in the literary tradition appear to have fallen into error is illustrated by a recent consideration of one of Lord Ernle's 'purple passages': 'Between 1813 and the accession of Queen Victoria falls one of the blackest periods'. Dr E. L. Jones has commented:

'The device whereby Ernle produced his alarming picture was the all-embracing generalisation. He described the experience of agriculturalists all over England, whatever their system of farming, from evidence (such as figures of distraints issued for debt) taken from the worst-hit districts in the very worst spells of distress.'[75]

It may be objected, with some justification, that these matters are not developed in the 'Condition of England' novels, but the method of taking extreme cases as the norm is common to both. For fictional sources one would do better to go back in time to Samuel Richardson's *Pamela*. But in one respect Kingsley's *Alton Locke* is of interest, for he gives the impression of absentee landlords, wasted and weed-strewn land, and a mass of labourers toiling away with

'their lack-lustre eyes and drooping lips, stooping shoulders, heavy, draggling steps, [which] gave them a crushed, dogged air, which was infinitely painful, and bespoke a grade of misery more habitual and degrading than that of the excitable and passionate artisan.' (*Alton Locke*)

Whereas Sir John Clapham has pointed out:

'There are figures in the census of 1831 which illustrate, with some precision, the extent to which really small farming had survived in Britain. They are entirely destructive of the view that, as the result of agrarian change and class legislation, an army of labourers toiled for a relatively small farming class.'[76]

And, as we have already observed, within five years of the first publication of *Alton Locke* Kingsley was remarking upon the transformation of agricultural conditions for the better.

5. Tailoring

But the main claim to fame of *Alton Locke* lies in its descriptions of conditions in tailoring in London, and the appalling dwellings south of the Thames where typhus could rage. Tailoring exhibited some of the worst features of the pre-industrial putting-out system, and is in stark contrast to the factory system; the trade had long been familiar with depression; and government was largely responsible for such decline in conditions as occurred after 1830.

---

[75] E. L. Jones, *The Development of English Agriculture, 1815–1873*, Macmillan, 1968, p. 11.   [76] Sir John Clapham, *op. cit.*, p. 113.

As early as 1747, tailors in London were 'as numerous as locusts, out of business three or four months of the year, and generally as poor as rats'.[77] And, although the more skilled workers appear to have earned high wages and to have experienced a rise in real wages after 1815,[78] comments by Francis Place in 1834 suggest that the problems of seasonal unemployment remained acute.

But for Charles Kingsley, as he expressed his views in *Alton Locke* and in his articles under the pseudonym 'Parson Lot',

'almost the worst feature in the whole matter is, that the Government are not merely parties to, but actually the originators of this [sweating] system.'

And Henry Mayhew, upon whom Kingsley relied in part for his information, quotes the moving account of a tailor working under a sweater:

'sweater's work is not as bad as Government work, after all . . . Government contract work is the worst work of all, and the starved-out and sweated-out tailor's last resource.'[79]

Some observers might have argued that the slop shops were even worse than government contract work, but the trade offers a telling contrast with life under the factory system.

There were also numerous trades in which conditions were deplorable due to the noxious materials used, and the inadequate precautions taken against their harmful effects. Often, as Charles Reade makes clear in *Put Yourself In His Place*, mean employers, immoveable trade unions, and short-sighted employees were united in opposition to improvements proposed by far-sighted employers to increase safety and longevity. As Dorothy George has emphasised, the physical strain of labour before the days of machinery is often forgotten:

'already in 1797 it was noted that Sheffield no longer abounded "in cripples and weak, deformed people", as it had when iron and steel were forged without the use of power. In London such trades as those of the anvil- and anchor-smiths must have put an enormous strain on human endurance . . . Adam Smith remarked that a London carpenter was not supposed to last in his utmost vigour above eight years . . . Hernia was very prevalent and [compared with 1842] in the eighteenth century must have been higher. . .

In 1747 we hear of works for making red and white lead in Whitechapel and

---

[77] R. Campbell, *The London Tradesman*, 1747, p. 193.

[78] M. Dorothy George, *London Life in the Eighteenth Century*, Kegan Paul, 2nd edn., 1930, p. 211.

[79] E. P. Thompson and Eileen Yeo, *The Unknown Mayhew*, Merlin Press, 1971, p. 221.

227

other places round London where the work was done by . . . labourers "who are sure in a few years to become paralytic by the mercurial fumes of the lead". A plumber's business was then carried on by working in molten lead and plumbers suffered much from paralysis. The glaziers' business also involved the melting of lead, and they were said to be more subject to the palsy than any other trade except the gilders and the plumbers. A glazier's apprentice complained in 1787 of having no proper bed, but being forced to sleep where the lead was melted.'[80]

6. Chimney sweeping

Much has been made of one trade which has certain similarities to the trades just referred to, chimney sweeping. The constant proximity of soot on unwashed or ill-washed bodies could cause cancer and other forms of illness, and the sleeping conditions of our glazier's apprentice had something in common with the experiences of some chimney-sweeps' apprentices, the climbing boys. Their plight was long recognised, from 1760 or thereabouts; and the experiences of Mr Grimes' apprentice Tom in Charles Kingsley's *The Water Babies*, and Oliver's fortunate avoidance of the clutches of Mr Gamfield in *Oliver Twist*, are widely known. For Mr Gamfield, when faced with an apprentice unwilling or unable to climb back down a chimney:

'there's nothink like a good hot blaze to make 'em come down with a run. It's humane, too, gen'lmen, acause, even if they've stuck in the chimbley, roasting their feet makes 'em struggle to hertricate theirselves.'

The reader is not surprised to learn that Mr Gamfield 'did happen to labour under the slight imputation of having bruised three or four boys to death already'. To Victorians the story was familiar, and its truth as illustrating some extreme cases was spread through the pamphlets of the Society for Superseding the Necessity of Climbing Boys and other literature, of which the most familiar account was Sydney Smith's *Edinburgh Review* article of 1819 reprinted in his *Works*.[81]

The practice of employing climbing boys dated back to the 17th century, and grew throughout the 18th. Jonas Hanway estimated there were 400 climbing-boys employed by master sweeps in 1785, and 150 by itinerant sweepers; David Porter estimated there were 500 climbing-boys in London in 1792; and Henry Mayhew estimated

---

[80] M. Dorothy George, *op. cit.*, p. 203.
[81] Rev. Sydney Smith, *The Works of the Rev. Sydney Smith*, Longmans, Brown, Green and Longmans, 1850 edn., pp. 265–272.

there were 370 chimney-sweeps' apprentices in London about 1850.[82] The main problems lay with the itinerant sweeps, and indeed a number of master chimney-sweeps were active in campaigning against the use of climbing boys from the earliest days of agitation. Yet despite the support of members of royalty and aristocracy, and ceaseless efforts at legislation, reform was extremely slow. In the long run, however, the solution lay in the offer by the Society for Superseding the Necessity of Climbing Boys of a gold medal to the person inventing a suitable apparatus for cleaning chimneys:

'In 1805 Smart received the gold medal for his invention and again in 1807, for his work in supervising the cleaning of more chimneys by machinery than any other contestant.'[83]

Success was only achieved after a long struggle, and it should be clear that machinery offered escape from the horrifying work of the children. But a recent book by Mr Brian Inglis, *Poverty and the Industrial Revolution*, has devoted the best part of 30 pages to the climbing boys without demonstrating any connection between their plight and the Industrial Revolution. A number of those who reviewed the book (in the *Sunday Telegraph*, *Observer*, and *Sunday Times*, for instance) seemed confused on the point, although the review in the *Daily Telegraph* mildly observed:

'Nowhere in this book is proper justice done to the achievements of the Industrial Revolution. The innocent reader might suppose from its pages that it was the Industrial Revolution which actually created poverty or which first heartlessly sent little climbing boys up chimneys. (In fact it must have helped to relieve them from this necessity.)'[84]

And Dr Hartwell in the *Spectator* averred that 'without debating the individual facts of Mr. Inglis's book, I would contest almost every generalisation as misleading or incorrect'.

C. SUMMARY

The ways in which the 'Condition of England' novels are seriously misleading on the economic and social realities of the time may be summarised as follows:

(i) the novels accept, in varying degrees and with the exception of the works of Charles Dickens, the belief in a Golden Age

---

[82] George L. Phillips, *England's Climbing Boys*, Harvard, 1949, p. 3. Outside London in 1817, William Tooke estimated, there were about 500 climbing boys. (J. L. and Barbara Hammond, *The Town Labourer*, Longmans, 1966 edn., p. 177.)
[83] *Ibid.*, p. 14.
[84] Colin Welch, 'Revolution Out of Perspective,' *Daily Telegraph*, 4 March, 1971, p. 6.

before the Industrial Revolution, for which there is no foundation;

(ii) they generally, although with some inconsistency, record a decline in the general standard of living which did not occur. Such decline as did occur was in specific, mainly non-industrial instances;

(iii) they suggest a decline in the quality of life under industrialisation, upon which no definitive judgement can be passed, but there are some powerful counter-arguments;

(iv) they lay some, occasionally much, of the blame for the miseries of industrialisation upon Classical Economists and their approach to political economy, an erroneous view into which numerous subsequent writers have fallen;

(v) in dealing with more specific instances—whether in the textile, iron and steel, coal, or other industries—the novelists took extreme cases from extreme places, and some novelists even misused evidence or used evidence containing misrepresentations and other types of error; and

(vi) the general effect of these exaggerations and occasional fabrications is to build up a largely false picture of the evils that industrialisation is supposed to have brought to the vast majority of the British people.

IV. THE CONTINUING TRADITION

The 'Condition of England' novelists were genuinely concerned about the sufferings of the poor, but they largely mistook their extent and cause. That so many of these novels were written and widely read demonstrates the growing consciousness of the suffering of the poor among the English middle-classes, suffering which implanted itself most vividly upon the imagination during the two decades following the passage of the first Reform Act. The disappearance of this literature after the death of Dickens, as well as the prosperity and stability of the middle years of Queen Victoria's reign, makes it plain that it was the economists rather than the novelists whose conclusions were valid. But the numerous reprints of these novels in the second half of the 19th century indicates that the novelists' conclusions continued to have influence.

Social propaganda literature continued to be written, of course. A stream of novels in a similar yet different tradition, largely concerned with the urban poverty in London, continued throughout the 19th century. This rather different tradition is founded on the Newgate novels, such as Bulwer Lytton's *Paul Clifford* (1830) and W. Harrison Ainsworth's *Jack Sheppard* (1839); on those novels of Dickens which dealt with the non-industrial poor; on George Reynolds' and collaborators' *Mysteries of London* (1846–50), Douglas Jerrold's *St. Giles and St. James* (1851), and Augustus Mayhew's *Paved With Gold* (1858); and on the vast array of later novelists, from James Greenwood and F. W. Robinson onwards, who tackled poverty in the East End of London, and in London to the south of the Thames, during the last quarter of the 19th century.[1] There are similarities between the novels on industrial poverty and on urban poverty: the description of poor living conditions; of the obstacles to escaping from misery and poverty; and the stress on violence (combined in the novels on urban poverty with the enticements to dishonesty and, later on, the monotony rather than poverty of living conditions). But, for the most part, the reader of the novels on non-industrial poverty is, quite properly, left to draw his own conclusions as to causes and forced to reflect on man's inhumanity to man.

Douglas Jerrold complained, in the Preface to the Collected Edition of *St. Giles and St. James,* that

'During the progress of the original publication of *St. Giles and St. James* certain critics would charge the writer with a cleaving desire to despoil the high for the profit of the low.'[2]

It was also complained of Jerrold that his account was bitter and wilfully exaggerated. Such complaints were to continue as other novels appeared, with some, but never full, justification. Thus comment upon Arthur Morrison's *Tales of Mean Streets* (1894)— that far worse examples of misery, poverty and depravity could be found in the East End of London—led to Morrison writing *A Child of the Jago* (1896), a fairly accurate portrayal of the very worst part of the East End.

---

[1] Some indication of the important nature of the difference between industrial poverty and urban poverty more generally is given by Charles Booth's recognition of poverty in London among 'the last relics of an older industrial system', and the better working conditions and regularity of employment in factories and larger workshops, a point often overlooked by social historians (cf. A. Fried and R. Elman, *Charles Booth's London*, Pelican Edn., 1971, pp. 68 and 167). The distinction is recognised by Gareth Stedman Jones, although he stresses London was a city 'virtually without a factory proletariat' (*Outcast London*, Oxford University Press, 1971, p. 337).

[2] Douglas Jerrold, *St. Giles and St. James*, Bradbury and Evans, 1851, p. iii.

But explicit attacks upon the competitive system in the novels of the 1880s and 1890s are extremely rare, the most notable attacks appearing in some of the novels of George Gissing and Sir Walter Besant. And it is interesting to note that where the competitive system and private enterprise are most frequently attacked as the cause of poverty, as in Sir Walter Besant's *All Sorts and Conditions of Men* (1882) and *Children of Gibeon* (1886), the novels are larded over with what one might term 'bourgeois sentimentality' rather than the harsh realities of working-class life. It is perhaps for this reason that Mr Alan Sillitoe has made the, at first sight surprising, remark upon Robert Tressell's moving novel, *The Ragged Trousered Philanthropists* (1914): 'This was the first good novel of English working-class life',[3] for there were a considerable number of good novels, set in a working-class context, published in the 1880s and 1890s by other novelists besides Arthur Morrison (the only person mentioned by Mr Sillitoe).

The 'continuing tradition' of the industrial novels of the 1840s and 1850s, therefore, comes down to us in a different, largely non-fictional, form. We see it in the writings of John Ruskin, especially in his four essays on economics: *Unto This Last* (1862); and in the writings of William Morris, including his Utopian novel *News From Nowhere* (1891), and Shaw. We see it in the novels and essays of D. H. Lawrence (for instance, in the essays 'Climbing Down Pisgah', written in 1924; and 'Nottingham and the Mining Country', written in 1929), and of George Orwell (especially in *The Road to Wigan Pier*, 1937). But, perhaps more significantly, we see it in popular works on economic and social history, in literary criticism, and in the introductions to recent editions of the 'Condition of England' novels themselves. The hostility to industrialisation and the industrial system which this continuing tradition represents is in harmony with the widely-held antipathy which exists today towards the bringer of unparalleled material wealth, and although the causal relationship cannot be judged with precision it may safely be taken as real.

Deriving from a largely misplaced hostility to the factory system in the early 19th century, the continuing tradition is in no small way accounted for by the blurring of the edges between fiction and non-fiction. An anonymous reviewer of Henry Mayhew's *London Labour and the London Poor* in 1862 wrote that the volumes were entitled

---

3 Alan Sillitoe's introduction to Robert Tressell, *The Ragged Trousered Philanthropists*, Panther Edition, 1965, p. 8.

'to a foremost rank in that peculiar literature which is now become so common, the literature not of common life only, but the commonest, oddest, and most out of the way.'

And P. J. Keating has commented on this review:

'It is not always possible, or sensible, to distinguish in this "peculiar literature" of urban life between fiction, non-fiction and semi-fiction.'[4]

There is a sense in which this comment is true. Thus Henry Mayhew's great non-fictional work has a good deal in common with the novel by his brother Augustus, *Paved With Gold*. But for the historian such a comment is of little practical value.

We see the limitations from the earliest 19th-century writings on industrialisation to modern times. It was of Carlyle, a major influence upon almost all these writings over the past century and a half, that G. K. Chesterton wrote: 'though his general honesty is unquestionable, he was by no means one of those who will give up a fancy under the shock of a fact'.[5] And we should not, therefore, be surprised to see that Arnold Toynbee, a key figure linking the 'Condition of England' novels with the literary tradition in the 20th century, believed that

'Of all those who assailed the new industrial world created by the "Wealth of Nations" and the steam engine, Carlyle was the greatest; and *Past and Present*, the book in which he flung out his denunciations, is the most tender and pathetic picture of the Past, the most unsparing indictment of the Present, that exists in modern English literature.'[6]

Carlyle's thinking was much embedded in the 'Condition of England' novels, and we have seen how erroneous that picture of the Past and indictment of the Present was, but it runs down through the literary tradition to the present time.

J. L. and Barbara Hammond were notable exponents of the method: the quotation of extreme cases, belief in a former Golden Age, repugnance at the industrial system expressed from a distance while surrounded by material comforts largely the product of the industrial system, but not directly earned within it. Towards the end of their lives, of course, the Hammonds conceded that the facts of history were against them, in spite of the contrary opinions they had ex-

[4] P. J. Keating, *The working classes in Victorian fiction*, Routledge and Kegan Paul, 1971, p. 36.
[5] G. K. Chesterton, *The Victorian Age in Literature*, Williams and Norgate (1919 edn., p. 53).
[6] Arnold Toynbee, *Toynbee's Industrial Revolution*, 1884 (1969 edn., David and Charles, p. 193).

pressed in their earlier and best-selling books. But their admission did little to change the influence their works have had on public opinion. Few historians have quoted the English novelists to such effect or with such frequency. It was the Hammonds who attempted to draw a parallel between Lord Shaftesbury, after a village on his estates had been found 'a disgrace to the owner of the land' in 1869, and mill-owners who spoke of financial difficulties and claimed that conditions had improved by the 1860s. The Hammonds commented (in 1923):

'the readers of Mrs. Trollope's factory novel, *Michael Armstrong*, however much they allow for such difficulties and such improvements, will feel that they do not qualify the terrible truth of the picture before them.'[7]

Such erroneous views have fortified those of the literary critics themselves. Sir Arthur Quiller-Couch in *Charles Dickens and Other Victorians* (1925) devoted much energy to the 'Victorian Background', invoking the support of the Hammonds by means of a full-page quotation from *Lord Shaftesbury* and a reference to *The Town Labourer*.[8] Michael Sadleir in *Trollope: a Commentary* (1927) also invoked the aid of the Hammonds in his treatment of Frances Trollope's *Michael Armstrong*. It is therefore not surprising that Sadleir incorrectly asserted of *Michael Armstrong*:

'the book has vigour and sincerity and—perhaps because conditions were so bad that exaggeration was almost impossible—the unabashed extremes of black and white are more convincing than in some other novels by the same hand.'[9]

The net result of all this error and confusion about the facts of economic history is demonstrated by this telling passage from Humphry House's *The Dickens World* (1942):

'Many people still read Dickens for his record and criticism of social abuses, as if he were a great historian or a great reformer . . . few English novelists have been treated with such respect by the professional historians themselves. He is often quoted as indicating the trend of opinion and taste, but also on matters of fact . . . because his words are often the best illustrations to be had. And as history filters down from original researchers and creative historians through the various strata of text books, references to Dickens become more frequent

---

[7] J. L. and Barbara Hammond, *Lord Shaftesbury*, Constable, 1923, p. 185. (The real setting of *Michael Armstrong* is 1803–1807.)

[8] Sir Arthur Quiller-Couch, *Charles Dickens and Other Victorians*, Cambridge University Press, 1925, pp. 173 and 190.

[9] Michael Sadleir, *Trollope: A Commentary*, Constable, 1927, p. 93. Trollope's most recent biographer, James Pope Hennessy, has similarly remarked upon Mrs Trollope's 'fiery sincerity' in *Michael Armstrong*. (*Anthony Trollope*, Jonathan Cape, 1971, p. 179.)

(one might add more careless), and proportionately of greater importance. The extreme is reached in the most popular History Text-Books for children between the ages of 11 and 14; the whole introductory chapter to the nineteenth century is given to Dickens. . .'[10]

The fact that only one of Dickens's novels is concerned with the industrial system is, as this essay has indicated, ignored. Instead, criticism of social conditions in non-industrial urban areas is improperly elided into criticism of the social and economic system generally, including industrialisation and the industrial system.

Contemporary criticism and teaching

Recent efforts to uphold the literary tradition, by literary critics and in the introductions to new editions of the 'Condition of England' novels, and by some ideologically-committed historians, have been indicated at length in the references to Part II, and in Part III, respectively. One of the most comprehensive and powerful attacks upon industrialisation and the industrial system has come from Mr Raymond Williams's *Culture and Society 1780–1950* (1958), a book which incorporates all the hostility of the literary tradition, and none of the economic evidence which would enable some approach to an objective assessment to be made.

Similarly biased treatment may be seen in Units 29–32 of the Open University's Arts Foundation Course, which deals with Industrialisation and Culture. *Industrialisation and Culture 1830–1914*, a book specially prepared for the Open University by three members of its staff, includes short extracts from some of the 'Condition of England' novels and in its general tenor is firmly in the literary tradition.[11] The Students' Text for Units 29 and 30 recommends Professor Hobsbawm's *Industry and Empire* in terms which would be deemed extravagant to the academic striving at impartiality:

'My first priority is a good introduction to the economic history of the period . . . : E. J. Hobsbawm's "Industry and Empire".'[12]

A similar observation may reasonably be made upon the Students' Text for Unit 31:

'Of all the books on the Recommended Reading list Raymond Williams'

---

[10] Humphry House, *The Dickens World* (2nd edn., 1942), Oxford University Press, p. 9.

[11] Christopher Harvie, Graham Martin and Aaron Scharf (eds.), *Industrialisation and Culture, 1830–1914*, Open University Set Book, 1970.

[12] The Open University (prepared by Christopher Harvie), *The Industrialisation Process, 1830–1914*, 1971, p. 7.

"Culture and Society" is invaluable as a study of the British literary tradition of social criticism from the French Revolution to the mid-twentieth century.'[13]

Such observations should not, of course, be taken as implying that either work is unimportant.

To the economist, the bias of the Open University's Arts Foundation Course is revealed in the list of 'pros and cons' of industrialisation in the Students' Text for Unit 31. Four items are suggested on the credit side, and seven items on the debit side. Although no weighting is given to the individual items, the debits include:

'*exploitation* both of the worker and the consumer by businessmen determined on maximising their profits and the possessors of unearned incomes through shares.'

'*wasteful competition and lack of planning* which resulted from "laissez-faire" and made the task of coping with industrial society's problems more difficult.'

and

'*loss of individual identity* in a society geared to a mass-market.'[14] (Italics in original.)

Each of these propositions is open to dispute, and each indicates fundamental misconceptions about the operations of a market economy. It is difficult to avoid the conclusion that it is misconceptions such as these from which the industrial system has always suffered, and that both truth and the industrial system would be better served if the following remarks of W. O. Aydelotte (1948) were more frequently recalled:

'While the novel with a thesis, even a social thesis, was nothing new, it was only in the 1840s that English literature began to deal on a major scale with the social problems raised by the industrial revolution . . . One would then expect them to be a mine of information for the social historian. Yet in effect they are not, for the factual information they provide about social conditions is highly suspect for the scholar's purposes; it is spotty, impressionistic, and inaccurate . . . It should be understood from the start that, for the facts about social conditions in this period, our other and more conventional sources are far more satisfactory; and the attempt to tell the social history of a period by quotations from its novels is a kind of dilettantism which the historian would do well to avoid.'[15]

There is, unhappily, reason to believe that failure to observe such cautionary words derives from the ideological commitment of writers

---

13 The Open University (prepared by Christopher Harvie and Graham Holderness), *The Debate on Industrialisation*, 1971, p. 4. 14 *Ibid.*, p. 11.

15 W. O. Aydelotte, 'The England of Marx and Mill as Reflected in Fiction', *The Journal of Economic History*, Supplement VIII, 1948, pp. 42–43. Ivan Melada has remarked that W. O. Aydelotte's advice 'is equally applicable to a literary study treating matters of social history' (in *The Captain of Industry in English Fiction, 1821–1871*, University of New Mexico Press, 1970, p. xi).

of all shades of political opinion, but especially from the Left. As Mrs Diana Spearman has remarked (1966):

'From the political aspect of Marxism one might think that the literature of one age, unless it was a literature of protest, could have no value or interest in another. Some Marxist critics have proceeded on the assumption that unless an author can somehow be twisted into an exponent of social wrongs, his work is worthless.'[16]

V. CONCLUSION

The heavily biased treatment of industrialisation and the industrial system in the 'Condition of England' novels of the 1840s and 1850s is not unique but it has proved highly influential. Yet these novels are generally not the best works of fiction of the novelists themselves and are widely considered to be poor literature. Nor are they sufficiently accurate or representative as economics to have been put to use in economic, social and literary history in the manner here indicated. They are not useless, but on grounds of scholarship their use should be much more carefully circumscribed than it has been. The most careless usage has been by ideologically-committed persons, particularly by those with commitments to Marxism, who have harnessed literature to plough their political furrows in the name of academic scholarship and literary criticism.

The 'Condition of England' novels are a major literary source for the antipathy which today exists against the industrial system and industrialists. Although German writers (Goethe, Novalis, Schiller) had influenced Coleridge and Carlyle, who in turn influenced the early Victorian novelists; and although Emile Zola's *L'Assommoir* and *Germinal* were to influence English 'Naturalist' writers of the late

---

[16] Diana Spearman, *The Novel and Society*, Routledge and Kegan Paul, 1966, p. 3. Mrs Spearman's conclusion from her study of 18th-century novels is also of interest, and has some similarity to the conclusion of this essay:

'The picture of eighteenth-century life drawn by Defoe, Richardson and Fielding does not, when considered as a whole, seem so accurate or so comprehensive as to deserve the name of "reflection" ' (p. 214).

Some Marxists would feel that the propaganda of the social novel has been waged against them, but without justification. Similarly, T. M. Wheeler, the Chartist author of *Sunshine and Shadow* (1849), complains in his dedication:

'The fiction department of literature has hitherto been neglected by the scribes of our body [the Chartists], and the opponents of our principles have been allowed to wield the power of imagination over the youth of our party.'

But the 'Condition of England' novelists were not opponents on principle, they merely recoiled from violent methods.

19th century, the attack on the industrial system is at this point peculiarly English in its origins. It is part of the cultivation of Culture, as opposed to Industrialism, which has divided society as surely as any actions by responsible industrialists anywhere. As Mr Raymond Williams has put it:

'We can now see that as a result of the changes in society at the time of the Industrial Revolution, cultivation could not be taken for granted as a process, but had to be stated as an absolute, an agreed centre for defence. Against mechanism, the amassing of fortunes and the proposition of utility as the source of value, it offered a different and superior social idea. It became, indeed, the court of appeal, by which a society construing its relationships in terms of the cash-nexus might be condemned.'[1]

Such cultivation falls into the error alleged of industrialisation, that it confuses a means with an end. In the last resort Culture and Industrialism are both means (by which self-fulfilment can be achieved). Neither is an end; and neither is mutually exclusive. When, as George Steiner has put it in his recent T. S. Eliot lectures, industrialisation 'provoked in the life of art and of intelligence certain specific, ultimately destructive ripostes',[2] industrialisation was questioned rather than the ripostes. A totally inadequate effort was made by those in the literary tradition to come to terms with the industrial system, and to improve it by positive criticism. But this takes us on beyond our subject. The important point here is that the attacks on industrialisation and the industrial system when claimed to be upon principle have been muddled and misconceived; when based upon practice they have been much exaggerated. For these errors the 'Condition of England' novels must bear some responsibility.

---

[1] Raymond Williams, *Culture and Society, 1780–1950*, Chatto and Windus, 1958, pp. 62–63.

[2] George Steiner, *In Bluebeard's Castle: Some Notes Towards the Re-definition of Culture*, Faber and Faber, 1971, p. 24.

Index of Authors